Monasteries

KNOW THE LANDSCAPE

Monasteries

Michael Aston

B.T. BATSFORD · LONDON

For James and Kathryn

First published 1993

Typeset by Goodfellow & Egan, Cambridge
and printed in Great Britain by
Butler and Tanner, Frome, Somerset
Published by B.T. Batsford Ltd
4 Fitzhardinge Street, London W1H 0AH

A CIP catalogue record for this book is
available from the British Library

ISBN 0 7134 6709 6

Contents

Illustrations

Acknowledgements

Writing a book like this involves the help of very many people, not only those who supplied ideas and information but others who assisted the research and writing.

For information, ideas and references to articles I am particularly grateful to my colleagues at Bristol University – Joseph Bettey and Michael Costen – together we form an island of sane monastic studies in a sea of adult education. I benefit greatly from the wide knowledge of my friend James Bond, who could have written a much better book on this subject. Others to whom I am indebted include Neil Becket, Ian Burrow, John Cloake, Glyn Coppack, Kate Douglas, Fred Hartley, Peter Hill, Joe Hillaby, Michael Hodder, Neil Holbrook, Mike Hughes, Carole Hutchison, Bill Klemperer, Jeremy Knight, Bernard Lane, Peter Liddle, Professor Philip Rahtz, David Robinson, Professor A.F. Shore, Paul Stamper and Chris Taylor. Ed Dennison in particular provided much useful material for the north-east of the country.

Many monastic sites are accessible to the public; I would like to thank the many custodians of the monuments in the care of the National Trust, English Heritage and Cadw (Welsh Historic Monuments) for taking the time to talk to me about their particular site. I am grateful to the Alnwick estate office for permission to visit sites in their care. I have benefited from the help provided by the staff of the Bristol University Library, particularly those in the Inter-Library Loan service who have obtained some very obscure material for me.

The 'enablers' are many. For general help I would like to thank Professor E.J. Thomas and Stewart Mossman. I have benefited from talking to the monks at Prinknash Abbey (Gloucestershire), especially Father Mark Hargreaves and the late Brother Hildebrand Flint, and to the Carthusian fathers at St Hugh's Charterhouse, Parkminster who I think would prefer to remain anonymous, and to Alec Grierson who introduced me to them. Thanks are also due to the monks of Downside Abbey where Father Philip Jebb, now prior, and the former prior, Daniel Rees, have made me welcome on a number of occasions, not just for their hospitality but in allowing me to use their superb library, an Aladdin's Cave for anyone interested in monasticism.

My colleague and friend Peter Hardy lent me his word processor at a critical moment when mine refused to work and I found James Bond's visualizer essential. My secretary Jane Geeson and office assistant Charlotte Buchan kept the office going while I was away writing. Carinne Allinson has assisted with editing as well as much critical discussion on the subject of monasticism generally.

For permission to use figures I am pleased to acknowledge:
The Warden and Fellows of All Souls College, Oxford: Fig. 64
Tim Allen and the Oxford Archaeological

Unit: Fig. 77
Joe Bettey: Figs 98, 101, 102, 103, 104
Birmingham University Field Archaeology
Unit, Peter Klein and Annette Roe: Fig. 51
James Bond: Figs 2, 5, 30, 31, 54, 93, 94
David Wilson and the Cambridge
University Committee for Air
Photography: Figs 2, 8, 11, 14, 17, 21, 43,
49, 52, 56, 60, 67, 79, 87, 88, 89, 90, 99
Canterbury Archaeological Trust: Fig. 20
Bob Carr: Fig. 23
Marjorie Chibnall and Oxford University
Press: Fig. 36, from *The English Lands of the
Abbey of Bec*
Glyn Coppack: Fig. 59
Michael Costen: Fig. 32
Rosemary Cramp, T. Middlemass and the
Bede Monastery Museum: Fig. 22
Bob Croft and Somerset County Council:
Fig. 57
Robin Daniels: Fig. 23
Wendy Davies: Fig. 12
E. Dennison and Humberside County
Council Sites and Monuments Record:
Fig. 42
English Heritage: Fig. 19
David Evans and the *Monmouthshire
Antiquary*: Fig. 66
Paula Gardiner: Figs 3, 6, 81, 82, 84
Fred Hartley: Fig. 68
David Hill and Blackwells: Fig. 29
Peter Hill, The Whithorn Trust and the
Whithorn Board of Management: Figs 9, 23,
24
Mike Hodder and Sandwell Metropolitan
Borough Council: Fig. 110
Richard Hodges: Fig. 78
Peter Huggins: Fig. 23
Heather James: Fig. 13
Terrence James: Fig. 62
Graham Keevil and the Oxford
Archaeological Unit: Fig. 30

Longmans: Fig. 2
John McDonnell: Fig. 47
Ordnance Survey, Crown Copyright: Fig. 2
Philip Rahtz: Fig. 23
John Rhodes and *Glevensis*: Fig. 70
Mark Corney, Chris Dunn, Paul Everson,
Graham Soffe, Chris Taylor and the Royal
Commission on the Historical Monuments
of England, Crown Copyright: Figs 69, 80,
105
Royal Commission on the Ancient and
Historical Monuments of Scotland, Crown
Copyright: Figs 10, 16
Royal Commission on the Ancient and
Historical Monuments of Wales, Crown
Copyright: Fig. 75
Thames and Hudson: Fig. 27
David Tomlinson and the Humberside
County Council Archaeology Unit: Fig. 23
David Williams and the University of Wales
Press: Fig. 92, from *Atlas of Cistercian Lands
in Wales*

I am grateful to the following for reading
and commenting on earlier drafts of the text
and for suggesting improvements and
additional examples – Joe Bettey, Father
Philip Jebb, James Bond, David Robinson
and Carinne Allinson who spent much of
our holiday on a French naturist beach going
through the text. Any mistakes, oddities and
eccentricities are inevitably my own.

As usual the editors and staff at Batsford
have been sympathetic and helpful. I am
grateful for the forbearance of Tony Seward
and Pauline Snelson.

My children, Kathryn and James, have
put up with visiting many abbeys and
priories over the years and so it is only right
that I should dedicate this book to them.

Lady Day 25 March 1993

Preface

The English countryside today bears witness to centuries of human activity and interference in numerous ways that can be interpreted by the informed observer using the skills of the archaeologist and the local historian. This new, wide-ranging series looks at the development of the landscape in Britain and examines the forces at work which have shaped its changing appearance from prehistoric times to the present day.

Each book takes a characteristic aspect of the landscape – such as the estates, monasteries, roads, canals and railways – traces its history and development, explains its function and studies its impact on the landscape throughout history. The subjects are popular and many have easily recognizable features that can still be visited and enjoyed, but some of the effects they have had on the landscape of today are subtle and unexpected and their influence has profoundly changed the look of the countryside around us.

For instance, castles and manor houses are still visible, but so too, to the trained eye, are their fishponds and kitchen gardens, long since demolished or destroyed above ground. What are the reasons behind barely discernible ditches and banks; why is an ancient track just where it is; why were certain villages deserted; less obviously, even why are some trees shaped the way they are? These are some of the intriguing questions discussed in this series.

The authors show how the techniques of landscape research can be used by anyone to enable them to recognize and decipher the signs of various periods of the human past in their own environment. They also guide the reader to some of the sources of documentary evidence and point out particular areas of research that can still be pursued, enabling the individual to make a real contribution.

The series builds up to present a new insight into familiar views and landscapes and brings out some of the hidden features of the British countryside.

Introduction

Monasteries are not a familiar part of the scene in Britain today and generally monks and nuns are a rare sight. In a largely non-religious or irreligious age there is little apparent need for armies of monks and nuns. But in earlier times the situation was very different. For a thousand years or so before the reign of Henry VIII (1509-47) and the Dissolution of the monasteries, monasteries were an important, dominant, and necessary part of society; indeed for most of that time they were thought to be essential. Over this long period it is likely that everyone would have had some contact with members of religious communities (that is monks, nuns, canons or friars), or would have had dealings with the lands and properties of monastic institutions.

Over the centuries, since the Dissolution in the 1530s, an elaborate folklore has built up about the former existence of abbeys and priories. Any stray piece of medieval architecture or fragment of medieval carving was in the past reckoned to be part of some long-lost monastery. Almost any building called 'abbey', 'priory' or 'grange' was thought to mark the site of a former monastery, and even lands or churches known to have been merely owned by medieval monasteries tended to be thought of as monastic sites. The most obvious and persistent form of this 'contrived monasticity' are the ubiquitous reports of tunnels, often recounted as folk memories and rarely, if ever, actually seen by the person recounting the story about them (Fig. 1). These tunnels are frequently credited with the most amazing, even fabulous, courses. They are said to run under rivers and hills for extraordinary distances, often, it is implied, linking male houses with nunneries and local churches. Much of this confusion is the result of careful building construction in earlier times and ignorance of monastic sites by lay people in later times.

This book has two main themes – how monastic institutions affected the landscapes in which they were built and over which they had jurisdiction, and how those landscapes in turn influenced the activities of the monasteries. The chapters will concentrate particularly on the sites chosen for monasteries; how they were laid out with especial reference to the land immediately adjacent – the precinct – and what lands were made available – the estates – to support the monastic community. Rather more attention will be paid to the rural landscape than that of towns; often the towns in which many sites are found were developed after the main monastic foundation. As a reflection of the availability of information rather more will be said of monasteries in the period after the Norman Conquest than before it.

There are many ways in which this topic could have been approached. I have chosen to deal with the relationship between monastic sites and their landscapes from a

1 *Hailes Abbey (Gloucestershire). The main drain running under the claustral buildings. The finding of such drains in post-medieval times led to persistent legends of 'tunnels' associated with monastic sites.*

chronological point of view. Thus the origins of monasticism and how it reached Britain, together with the influence, characteristics and extent of the Celtic church form one episode. In the seventh century, when the whole of England was converted to Christianity, monasticism was a fundamental tool and many of the oldest established sites belong to that period. Following the disruptions of the Viking raids, when monasticism was all but destroyed in this country, the great refoundations of the tenth century herald the major development of monasticism in the Middle Ages. The twelfth century in particular saw unparalleled expansion.

Much of interest for the early periods is lost or obscured; only in the Middle Ages can we really appreciate how monasteries operated in their contemporary landscapes. It is thus appropriate for this period to look in detail at the sites chosen for, the precincts around, and the estates belonging to, a selection of monastic houses. This has been done in two special chapters: one on precincts and one on estates, which concentrate on the Middle Ages rather than following the chronological theme. There was little development in the later Middle Ages, while the Dissolution of monastic institutions brought about another landscape development as large areas of land passed into secular hands and new estates and residences were created out of the old.

Henry VIII swept away many hundreds of monastic institutions in the decade 1530 to 1540 and monastic life ceased in England and Wales, and a little later in Scotland, for nearly three hundred years. It was revived in the early nineteenth century, though only a small number of houses exist today, so that there is still a limited monastic presence in the landscape. So what were these institutions that persisted for so long, many for over five hundred years? What did they do, how were they organized and what, if any, effect did they have on the people and landscape around them?

Many sites with monastic ruins and monastic buildings are cared for by English Heritage or the Scottish (Historic Scotland) and Welsh (Cadw) equivalents, as well as the National Trust and other bodies. These are open to the public, and visited by large numbers of people each year. At many there are guide books for sale and exhibitions and displays about the history of the site and it is not too difficult to find out something of the history of a monastery, and perhaps how it operated in its contemporary landscape. But as well as these sites there are many other monastic ruins which are not so obvious or accessible, or where only very scrappy

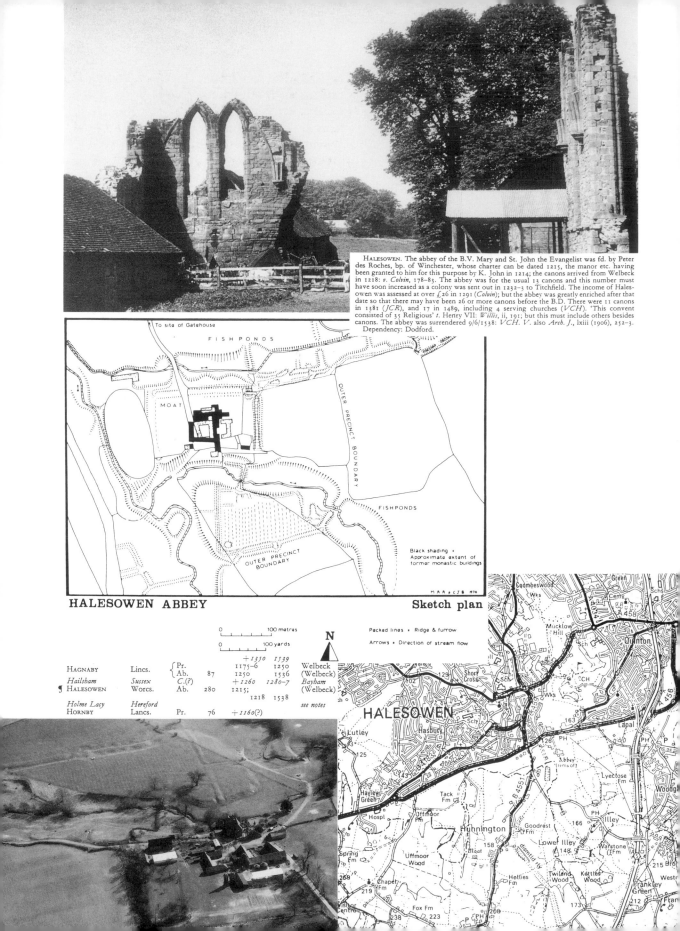

HALESOWEN. The abbey of the B.V. Mary and St. John the Evangelist was fd. by Peter des Roches, bp. of Winchester, whose charter can be dated 1215; the manor etc. having been granted to him for this purpose by K. John in 1214; the canons arrived from Welbeck in 1218: v. Colvin, 178–83. The abbey was for the usual 13 canons and this number must have soon increased as a colony was sent out in 1232–3 to Titchfield. The income of Halesowen was assessed at over £26 in 1291 (Colvin); but the abbey was greatly enriched after that date so that there may have been 26 or more canons before the B.D. There were 11 canons in 1381 (JCR), and 17 in 1489, including 4 serving churches (VCH). 'This convent consisted of 35 Religious' t. Henry VII: Willis, ii, 191; but this must include others besides canons. The abbey was surrendered 9/6/1538: VCH. V. also Arch. J., lxiii (1906), 252–3. Dependency: Dodford.

HALESOWEN ABBEY

Sketch plan

FISH PONDS

MOAT

To site of Gatehouse

OUTER PRECINCT BOUNDARY

FISHPONDS

OUTER PRECINCT BOUNDARY

Black shading = Approximate extent of former monastic buildings

0   100 metres
0   100 yards

Packed lines = Ridge & furrow
Arrows = Direction of stream flow

N

HAGNABY	Lincs.	{ Pr.		+1350	1539	
		{ Ab.	87	1175–6	1250	Welbeck (Welbeck)
Hailsham	Sussex	C.(?)		1250	1536	Bayham (Welbeck)
¶ HALESOWEN	Worcs.	Ab.	280	+1260	1280–7	
				1215;		
Holme Lacy	Hereford			1218	1538	see notes
HORNBY	Lancs.	Pr.	76	+1160(?)		

HALESOWEN

remains are left. How do we find out about these places, when they were founded, how they were organized and whether there is anything left of their buildings which can still be visited?

There are now some very good sources which we can look at to get us started. In most cases the Ordnance Survey maps (1:50,000 scale) show in gothic script the sites of monasteries, along with other medieval sites such as castles and moats. Readers will perhaps be familiar with 'Abbey' or 'Priory' and 'remains of' or 'site of' labels on the maps. On modern Ordnance Survey maps such notes can be trusted but the same cannot be said for many earlier maps.

As a result of the 'folklore' described above, a number of attempts have been made to identify all the genuine early monastic sites, not only in this country but also abroad, and for each monastic order in Europe. For England and Wales R. Neville Hadcock, for the Ordnance Survey, and David Knowles, a Benedictine monk, have produced a gazetteer of all documented sites and those with clear architectural and archaeological remains. The result – *Medieval Religious Houses: England and Wales* – is the basis for any study of monastic sites. There are companion volumes for Scotland and Ireland. For England, Wales and Scotland there are also the complementary

maps of *Monastic Britain*, North and South sheets, issued by the Ordnance Survey. A similar map is available for Ireland. For earlier periods the Ordnance Survey maps of *Britain before the Norman Conquest* and *Dark Age Britain* have useful gazetteers of pre-Conquest monasteries, while David Hill's *An Atlas of Anglo-Saxon England* has much useful material as well.

For most counties there is often a useful and accessible survey of monasteries and their history, with some account of their lands and possessions, in the first or second volumes of the series of the *Victoria County Histories*. Many of these were written a long time ago but there is still much useful information in them and they are usually easily available in public libraries.

It is not too difficult, therefore, to find out something about a local monastic site. From the above sources the name, the order and a few details of when the house was founded, can be discovered, as well as when it was dissolved and the briefest of histories.

What cannot be found in these initial sources is why the monastery was founded, how it fared in the Middle Ages and on what its economy was based. We might also want to know what the difference was between the various 'orders' – Benedictine, Cistercian, Dominican and so on – and what was meant by the terms 'monk', 'canon' and 'friar'. Further, we might want to find out how such people, and so many of them at times, were supported in such elaborate buildings over such long periods. How were they fed, clothed and housed, for example? Above all, perhaps, we might question what the effect was of so many monasteries, with so many monks, nuns, friars and others living in them, on the rest of the population and the countryside and towns around them. It is the purpose of this book to answer some of these questions and perhaps indicate to readers how research could be initiated on their own local monasteries.

2   *Halesowen Abbey (Worcestershire). Basic information about a monastery. Included here is the extract from the current 1:50,000 Ordnance Survey map centred on 'Abbey' in gothic writing and 'rem[ain]s of' in brackets; extracts from Knowles and Hadcock 1971; a view of the scrappy remains as they were in 1964; an air photograph looking south taken in 1968 from the Cambridge collection; and a sketch of the earthworks. The latter shows that beyond the claustral buildings the site is very extensive with moats, precinct banks and fishponds.*

1 Monasteries in the landscape

There is a vast literature on monastic houses, orders, architecture and individual histories, but there are far fewer books that look at the role of monasteries as social and economic centres or see them as specialized institutions operating within a contemporary landscape. Following on from the work and approach of William Hoskins and with the growth of interest in landscape archaeology generally, this book tries to adopt a different point of view and is an attempt to show monasteries as economic institutions coping with the difficulties and opportunities presented by the landscapes in which they were built.

Monasteries are interesting sites to look at from this point of view, as they provide a great contrast to other topics which have been studied in the landscape, such as rural settlements or field systems. In general, a clearer idea of the role of many monasteries in the landscape is available, because of the abundant surviving documentary evidence, than for these other aspects. For the period after the Norman Conquest the dates of foundation and dissolution of a monastery are often known, as well as something of the numbers and status of people involved in the establishment and the running of it. Also the high investment in the infrastructure at many sites and on the estates belonging to them, with the construction of elaborate buildings and the engineering of major landscape projects, has frequently resulted in the survival of more physical evidence than could be expected from sites associated with the activities of peasant communities. It is

3 *Cleeve Abbey (Somerset). An example of a well preserved monastic site. It was founded between 1186 and 1191 by William de Roumare II, the grandson of William de Roumare who founded Revesby Abbey (Lincolnshire) in 1143, its mother house (see Fig. 43). The river in the valley was moved to the far side to create space for the buildings seen here. All the land around belonged to the abbey and was worked from a series of granges.*

thus possible to see the impact of the establishment and later development of a monastery on a landscape rather more clearly, and to understand the processes involved rather better, than it is to explain, for example, the origin, development and demise of a medieval rural settlement. In some cases we can learn something of what the site and landscape were like before the monastery was built, and sometimes the reasons why it was built and by whom can be determined. We can also find out how it operated during its existence, with the construction of buildings and the exploitation of its estates. In many examples alterations following the dissolution of the monastic community and the change of use of the site to a secular estate are all discernible. Little, if any, of this is possible with other aspects of the medieval landscape.

This book sets out to examine the ways monasteries were founded, how their sites were chosen and what modifications were made during the life of the monastery. The decisions taken in the Middle Ages to establish and support a monastic community have in many cases had considerable influence upon later landscapes. The lands and estates that belonged to monastic institutions will be looked at, in particular where they were situated, how they were acquired, what was there already and what was done under monastic ownership.

Siting a monastery

Monasteries at all periods were rather special places and this is reflected in their layout and operation. By the Middle Ages elaborate buildings were erected to accommodate the religious personnel, and particular sites were chosen on which to erect these buildings so that life could be adequately sustained. At their foundation monastic communities were given land and they frequently

purchased much more. These estates were exploited to support the monks and nuns back at the monasteries. It is thus possible to see monasteries in the Middle Ages as the focal places of very elaborate social and economic systems. In order to support the religious in them, who were essentially non- or un-productive, the landscape had to be managed and manipulated to provide a substantial surplus.

The ways in which sites were selected for monasteries or lands acquired and managed in the Middle Ages are not fully understood. For the pre-Conquest period these aspects are a particular problem, as will be seen in later chapters. It would be useful to know, for example, if there was something special about when, why and where monasteries were founded and if there was something unusual about which particular sites were chosen. It is necessary to investigate the way monasteries acquired, organized and exploited their lands and to compare this with the history of lay estates to see if it was different. Were there in fact any distinguishing features about monastic estates which would have made them obvious to people in the Middle Ages and which might have left distinctive traces in the landscape today, so that we can say when we are in a 'monastic landscape'? Often monastic lands seem to have been characterized by distinctive husbandry, with a greater degree of investment in more permanent buildings and other structures. The distinctive and elaborate architectural treatment of buildings such as the numerous great barns is noticeable. The chances of investigating and answering these questions are greater for the later periods, since the historical, archaeological and architectural evidence is better preserved than that for pre-Conquest sites (see, for instance, Figs 73 and 74).

It should be borne in mind that this discussion is dealing with a long period of time, roughly a thousand years, from around 500 to 1500. Inevitably over that time there would have been very great changes which would have included not only different types of monasteries being founded at various times, but also the changing aspirations of their founders. Monasteries as institutions evolved through the Middle Ages and their role in society altered accordingly. At any one time there were different types of institutions in existence with a variety of roles – from contemplative communities to social foundations dealing with the sick and elderly. The great variety of monastic institutions and the element of change are two very important aspects which need to be taken into consideration all through this book.

Founding a monastery

The foundation of monasticism and monasteries will be studied in some detail in the early chapters. There is a great deal of information about when and by whom some monasteries were founded, although inevitably the information is better for the period after the Norman Conquest. Less often, however, are we told why a particular monastery was founded. Was there something special about the times when so many monasteries were founded, especially the seventh, tenth and twelfth and thirteenth centuries? It is perhaps easier to explain why fewer were founded in the eighth, ninth, fourteenth and fifteenth centuries and why there was a revival of interest in the nineteenth century.

Looking particularly at the twelfth and thirteenth centuries, one question that can be asked is: what were the motives of the founders and patrons of monasteries? After all, they were giving up land and privileges and perhaps introducing a foreign element into the vicinity of their own holdings. It would be interesting to know what, if

anything, they expected to get out of it; why found a monastery? We need to ask what the needs and aspirations of the founders were and what the descendants thought of their inheritance being given away. The founders were presumably interested in the piety and devotions of the religious communities, regarding them as a sort of insurance policy, both in having them living nearby as well as using their churches as family mausolea, with prayers and masses in perpetuity for the dead. Perhaps the motives were more mercenary. A patron may have acquired a certain status with a newly-founded monastery, as with a castle, deer park, fishponds and so on, and this status may well have varied with the cost of foundation and the particular order of monks or nuns settled on the land.

Having decided to found a monastic house, how was the actual foundation undertaken? It would be useful to know how far in advance the site was selected and the endowment worked out (see Fig. 42 and p. 77). It might be expected that building work was undertaken before the community arrived on the site. There would also be the difficult matter of recruitment of religious personnel. Religious life would have had to be very buoyant indeed for successive founders to be able to continue to take out a dozen or more religious at a time to found new monasteries. Continual recruitment and training of novices would need to have been very vigorous and the quality of the personnel very high for the large number of sites which were established at some periods to have been sustained.

Once these preliminaries were sorted out, the lands and estates to be given over to the new house had to be decided upon. Why were certain lands chosen and not others? Perhaps the founder attempted a balance – to give enough land, but not too much, and only to give land perhaps of a certain quality rather than the best or even the better quality land. It is difficult to guess the cost to the patron of the land lost in the foundation of a new monastery. Clearly with the foundation of so many houses, particularly in the twelfth and thirteenth centuries, the costs were seen to be worthwhile, but it would be useful to know if patrons had any misgivings, and how far these went, when founding a monastery. Balancing the saving of their souls, and those of their ancestors and descendants, against the loss of dynastic property, rights and privileges cannot always have been easy. How much moral, religious and even intellectual pressure would have been applied in some cases by local bishops or the heads of already established houses, before a family decided to found and endow a new monastery on its lands and give away part of its inheritance?

The landscape before monasteries

England was already an anciently settled country by the twelfth century when the great period of monastic colonization and settlement got under way (Fig. 4). Most land, especially in southern England, was already farmed and the landscape was thickly dotted with farmsteads and villages. Even those areas which were once thought of as empty at this time, such as the forests and wastes and the low-lying fen areas, were utilized and many of them were populated as well. In wooded areas many people were required to manage and exploit the woodlands to produce the timber needed in such prodigious quantities in the Middle Ages.

4 *Witham Priory (Somerset). Even though this charterhouse, founded around 1179 by Henry II, was built in the extensive wooded Royal Forest of Selwood, there were around 150 peasants who were living here and working the land who had to be relocated. The earthworks on the site include the gardens of post-medieval mansions.*

Thus, lands given to monasteries in the twelfth and thirteenth centuries were in many cases already exploited by other people. Even if no one was living in the area it would be used by people at some time. All land belonged to someone, especially by the twelfth century, so that the idea of pioneer monks moving into unknown and undeveloped primeval lands in this country in the early Middle Ages is a romantic but untenable myth.

As a preliminary then, it is necessary to know what was going on in the lands given to the monasteries before they acquired them, and what if anything was there. Only with such questions answered will it be possible to gauge the changes that took place after monastic acquisition. What in fact was the monastic contribution to a particular landscape's development?

Changes in land use or intensity, new engineering works or heavy investment of time, money, and technological skills should be looked for in these new monastic landscapes. Two extremes, at least, are possible. On the one hand, land acquisition may have meant little change to the landscape if the monastery was not directly involved in its exploitation, choosing merely to take rents from it; on the other hand there was frequently direct involvement of the monastery in the running of the new estate with close attention paid to its full exploitation. In such cases, the landscape became a direct reflection of the individual decisions taken by abbots and other monastic officials. The latter situation is best seen in the colonizing activities of the new orders of the post-Conquest period with their emphasis on manual labour and the use of lay brothers to exploit their estates directly.

These two extremes of estate exploitation are a reflection of whether the land was worked directly by the monastery ('in demesne'), or was let out – and of course circumstances changed as time went on. The question must be – did monastic land look different to land belonging to other landowners in the Middle Ages or not, and were any differences so obvious that they can still be distinguished in the landscape today?

The requirements of a monastery

Similar questions can be asked of the actual site chosen on which to build the monastic house. The site and the finished buildings had to fulfil a number of requirements if the community was to be adequately supported in the monastery, and for it to survive and continue the religious devotions and activities for which the house had been founded. These requirements and the way they were satisfied can be viewed as a system which had to be established when the monastery was set up.

By the eleventh century, if not before, it is clear that a good water supply was regarded as an essential basic requirement of most new monastic foundations (Fig. 5). Two supplies were needed: one for drinking water, preferably from a spring; and one for cleansing and drainage, which could come from a river or stream. Sites often seem to have been chosen with this as the paramount determining factor; the availability of springs and streams not only influenced where the house would be placed within its estates, but was also reflected in the exact orientation of the buildings on a particular site. While water for drinking could have been obtained from rivers, streams or wells (or even off the roof), invariably elaborate and costly conduits were built to ensure a good, clean, constant and adequate flow.

Drainage of kitchens and latrines was given considerable attention by the engineers in most monasteries. Usually this involved the construction of a leat of water from a stream or river, taken off above the monastery and led along the contour in such

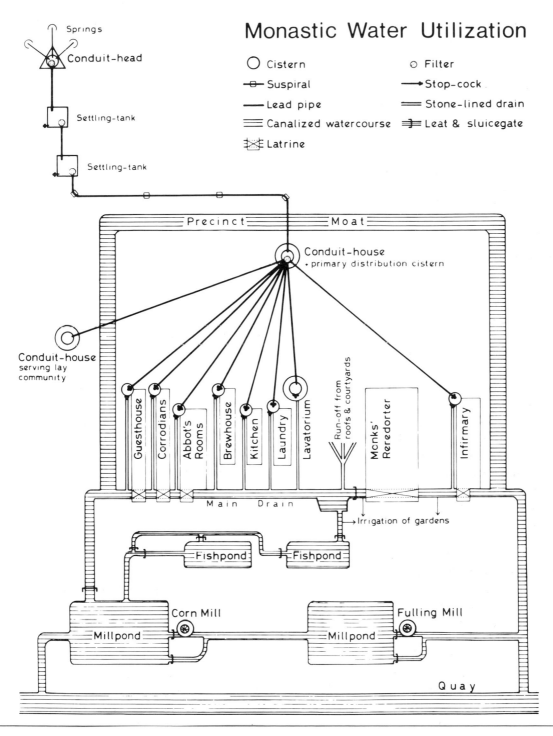

5 *Monastic water utilization. This diagram shows the two sources of water required in a monastery; the clean water from a spring is led to various offices while a stream or river can supply the mill and fishponds and flush out the drains.*

a way as to flush out the drains before flowing back into the stream or river. It is the finding of these well-built stone drains in later times which produced many of the 'tunnel' stories (see Fig. 1). The provision of sluices and hatches was usually needed to control the flow of water and its level through the drains. Frequently such systems were also used to drive mills and feed fishponds alongside the monastic buildings. Considerable technological and engineering expertise was called for in the construction of such systems, taxing to the full the skills of surveyors and engineers, which were clearly readily available in the early Middle Ages.

Food could be brought in either from an estate with granges supplying the monastery directly – without any middlemen – or by purchasing supplies from the local markets, or of course from a combination of both. For much of the time income derived from lands leased out to laymen would have provided the finance to make purchases. Whether directly produced or purchased, the food brought in would have to be stored before being consumed and this storage would need to be adequate if an unacceptable level of spoilage was to be avoided. This meant proper buildings with the necessary investment of time, materials and skill to build them and keep them in good order. The processing of the foodstuffs before consumption also required specialized equipment and buildings – such as mills, powered by either wind or water, for grinding cereals for flour (see Figs. 85 and 86).

Beyond the basic requirements of a place to sleep and a roof over their heads, there was usually little attempt made to provide a comfortable environment for the monks and nuns in medieval monasteries. Though the dormitory or separate rooms ('cells') could range from very small and spartan to quite well appointed with a fair degree of warmth and privacy.

It could be argued that all of the above points were just as applicable to other sections of medieval society, particularly at the higher levels, but there were other aspects of monastic life which were obviously peculiar to monasticism. These included the provision of religious space in the form of a large church, an organizational or committee room area – the chapter house, and space for study, the compilation of records, the copying of manuscripts and the storing and protection of archives. As with lay estates the provision of such specialized buildings required adequate investment in skills, building materials, the technology to put them up and keep them standing, and, where appropriate, the execution of ostentation and ornamentation in the decoration of such buildings. Foundations would need to be established, with rafts of timber or pebbles. Stone would have to be brought in, either from the quarries on the monastery's lands or from elsewhere. With the quantities required in building and maintenance at the larger houses, a good, plentiful and local supply would clearly be a major asset and might even be a contributory factor in the siting of a monastery. The same was probably true in terms of supplies of timber for roof construction among other things, although it can be shown from documents that timber was moved over large distances in the Middle Ages. It was also an advantage to have other building commodities such as roofing materials and lime for mortar close to hand or readily available.

Following construction, continual maintenance had to be considered, so that repairs to stonework, replacement of timber frames and roofs, re-roofing in lead, clay or stone tiles or wooden shingles could be quickly carried out. Buildings housing masons, tilers, leadworkers and so on were needed next to the greater complexes of monastic buildings, while in some cases tile and pottery kilns might be provided as well

6 *Tintern Abbey (Gwent, Wales). View over the Wye valley with the site of the Cistercian monastery. This was founded in 1131 under the patronage of Walter fitz Richard (de Clare) but was substantially enlarged in the thirteenth century with the church being completely rebuilt under the influence of the Bigod family from nearby Chepstow castle.*

as facilities for glass and window repairs.

What emerges very strongly from these considerations, which largely relate to the building of monasteries in the early Middle Ages, is that a sympathetic patron making suitable provision of a good site and an adequate endowment of estates could ensure the successful foundation of a monastery in the landscape – and hence successful economic exploitation of its lands. Without the interest of the founder in the establishment of the house and the continuing involvement of the patrons of the monastery in the welfare of the community within it, many would have failed. Some suffered economically when the interest or the fortunes of the patronal family waned. It is therefore important in any examination of monasteries in the landscape, to ascertain the influence and role of the lay patrons in the fortunes and exploits of the house (Fig. 6).

2 The earliest monasteries

Monasticism began in the late third century in Egypt, with Paul the Theban and St Antony retreating into the desert and living as hermits. Many others joined them so that eventually whole religious villages of monks and nuns were organized into communities. The dual aspects of monasticism – hermits (the eremitic life) and communities (the coenobitic life) – were there from the beginning.

Antony (251–356) retreated into the isolation of the desert on the east bank of the Nile around 285 and by 305 he had a number of followers, all living an eremitic lifestyle. By about 400 there were probably five thousand hermits living in the deserts of north (Lower) Egypt in the Mount Nitria and Wadi Natron areas.

In about 320 Pachomius (286–346) founded the first true monastery with communal work, prayer, meals and services and absolute obedience to him as leader, or *Apa* (*Abt* – father). This was in south (Upper) Egypt at Tabernisi, opposite Dendera on the right bank of the Nile. He was a Copt, that is a native Egyptian rather than a Greek, and had been a soldier; the latter may account for the 'rule' he developed to run his communities in their communal life ('*koinos bios*' – hence coenobitism). By his death in 346 there were nine large monasteries and two nunneries in Upper Egypt. A little later Schenoute of Atripe (?–466) developed an even stricter and more military rule at his White Monastery in Sohag. There were thus two centres in Egypt in the fourth century and the two themes of hermits and communities were both represented.

The Desert Fathers

By the fourth century it had become a common practice for holy men and groups to retreat to the deserts of Egypt, Palestine and Syria seeking solitude, shunning the mundane (and tempting) aspects of the world and engaging in lengthy prayer and meditation sessions in order to get into closer communion with God. The deserts, with their loneliness, isolation, quiet and few resources, were seen to be ideal places for spiritual fulfilment. In such places, men living very ascetic lives, needing few possessions and doing very little physically, established reputations as 'holy men'. These 'Desert Fathers' had enormous influence on the development of monasticism in the West in later times, providing the ideal aimed at by successive waves of monastic reformers over the centuries. They lived in caves and on hilltops, in groups of ramshackle buildings or the ruins of temples, tombs and buildings of former cultures, both Egyptian and Roman. They needed little in the way of food or material goods, being dressed simply and spending many days fasting or living on bread and water. The only essential item required for such an existence was a large area of empty land – the 'desert'.

During the fourth century these ideas of hermits and religious communities of both men and women spread widely, not only through the Middle East in Egypt, Syria and areas of the later Byzantine empire, but in Greece and Italy and as far as western Gaul and other parts of the western Roman empire. Significant stages can be seen, along with the important religious personages involved. With St Basil the Great of Caesarea (*c*.330–79), eastern monasticism took a coherent form with detailed rules of how monastic life should be conducted, and monasteries assumed the social roles of hospitals, orphanages, schools and charitable centres. Under St Basil the roots of Orthodox monasticism began, such as can still be seen at Mount Athos and Meteora in Greece.

In Italy such ideas were rooted at Rome by the middle of the fourth century, while at Milan, Ambrose and his sister Marcellina had established monastic villages on their rural estate. It was from here that St Augustine of Hippo (354–430) learnt monasticism and it was thus spread to North Africa. Augustine's 'rule' was used in the Middle Ages in the West as one of the major planks in the organization of houses of canons and other groups.

Monasteries in the West

The introduction of the monastic idea into the West can be traced to the late fourth and early fifth centuries and it can be seen in the far west, in Ireland, by the early fifth century. At Tours, in the Loire valley in west central Gaul, St Martin (316–97) had organized a monastic community at Ligugé, near Poitiers, by 360–70, only some forty to fifty years after Pachomius in Lower Egypt. The monastery on the island of Lérins, now St Honoratus off Cannes on the south coast of France, which was to have so much

influence in the West, was founded around 400–10.

What did these early monasteries look like? While the detail may not be precise, the basic outlines of the Egyptian sites are clear. They are best described as 'monastic villages', with each monk or nun living in a little house or cell. In the centre of the settlement there would be one or more churches and communal buildings, such as the dining hall, store buildings, mill and guest-houses. Usually the whole was enclosed by a wall. Beyond, in the surrounding 'desert', there would be isolated hermitages in caves or on hilltops. Thus the description of St Martin's monastery at Tours by Sulpicius Severus in his *Life of St Martin*, around 400 tells how 'the ensemble gave more the impression of a village or settlement than of a monastery', with huts against the wall and, in the centre, St Martin's cell and those of some of the brethren, together with several small, dim churches and the dining hall. Other cells were situated in caves in the limestone cliffs on the side of the valley and there was a wall around the whole site. A later monastery was built on the site, now Marmoutier in the eastern suburbs of Tours, together with a modern nunnery, but the limestone cliffs with their troglodytic dwellings still give something of the atmosphere of the early site.

At Lérins, St Honoratus (?–429) established a similar site with the sea as the 'desert'. The layout there was similar to that at Tours and elsewhere, with numerous detached hermitages with chapels scattered across the island beyond the main monastery – 'Here the whole range of the desert experience seemed to be institutionalized: there was a central coenobium under an abbot and a cluster of satellite hermitages where the elders, who had been trained in the community, could venture out to the solitary struggle of the desert.' Later on some Irish monasteries and those in

Scotland, Wales and Cornwall took the same form.

The two lifestyles established in monasteries at this time dominated ascetic existence all over Europe for over a thousand years. The quest for some sort of 'desert' to provide isolation, the rejection of the outside world, the lack of interest in all but the barest of essentials in food and clothing, are all early aspects which influenced later monks in their choice of sites in the landscape and their impact upon it.

In Italy, St Benedict of Nursia (480–553) wrote a 'rule' or set of guidelines for his followers to help them lead a well-regulated monastic life. This was not the first or the only 'rule' to be compiled, as already noted, but following its adoption by the whole of the Western church in 816, it became the most important. By the year 1000 it provided the basis by which many hundreds of monks and nuns conducted their lives and was to remain of paramount significance for the development of monasticism through to the present day.

7   *Glastonbury Tor (Somerset). Philip Rahtz has recently suggested that the enigmatic remains excavated on the top of the Tor in the 1960s (around the tower of the demolished church of St Michael seen here) may represent a hermitage or early monastery dating from perhaps the later fifth or early sixth century.*

Celtic monasteries

When did the idea of monasticism first arrive in the British Isles and how did it develop? These are, in fact, very difficult questions to answer, partly because of the problem of recognizing early monasteries from their often scanty archaeological remains and also because references to them in documents are often either lacking or unclear and inadequate.

At present it is not possible to say for certain if there were monasteries in Britain before the end of the Roman period, around 400, but it seems unlikely. However, with the existence of sites like Tours in Gaul in the mid-fourth century on the one hand, and the earliest monasteries in Ireland in the mid-fifth century on the other, it must remain at least a possibility. At present the

suggestion by Charles Thomas that monasteries were probably first developed in Britain in the last quarter of the fifth century (475–500) seems to be the most plausible, with the idea of monasticism spreading from Gaul to Cornwall and Wales.

The sites most likely to have been chosen at that time would have been the offshore islands and the more remote areas in the marshlands. On this basis, the site at Glastonbury in the Somerset Levels (Fig. 7) seems at least a possibility for an early monastery, although at present adequate archaeological evidence is lacking. It is an intriguing possibility that perhaps the origins of the great medieval abbey do indeed go back as far as the fifth century.

Ireland

We can be more certain as far as the British Isles in general are concerned, because the evidence from Ireland shows that monasticism was established there by the late fifth century. In 431 Prosper (a native of Aquitaine but actually in Rome at the time) reported, 'Palladius consecrated as first Bishop by Pope Celestine is sent to the Irish believing in Christ [*ad Scottos in Christo credentes*]'. He died within the year and was succeeded by Patrick (385–461). Sites such as Armagh and Downpatrick were established by St Patrick, who had been at Auxerre and possibly Lérins in Gaul, and others followed under St Columba (521–97), St Finnian (*c*.495–579), St Brendan (484–*c*.580) and St Columbanus (530–615). In the far west the rugged coast with numerous islands, peninsulas and windswept countryside provided many sites for isolated monasteries and hermitages (Fig. 8). Many of these can still be seen; they consist of walled enclosures with cells for the monks, oratories and chapels, cemeteries and crosses, together with small gardens where a few vegetables and crops could be grown.

Scotland

From Ireland monks went out as both missionaries and bishops to the surrounding lands. Whithorn in Galloway, Scotland, probably began in this way in the fifth century (Fig. 9), although claims have been made for an even earlier origin. There St Ninian (367–432) built a church, later called *Candida Casa* by Bede, dedicated to St Martin of Tours. Excavations since 1984 have revealed a complex sequence of occupation on the site. In the fifth century the 'settlement comprises a number of rectangular timber buildings linked by a network of paths and yards'. Because of the rather high-class finds, the excavator, Peter

8 *Skellig Michael (Co. Kerry, Ireland). This air photograph shows the cells, chapels and gardens of this remote island hermitage site off the south-west coast of Ireland.*

9 *Whithorn (Galloway, Scotland). Reconstruction of the site as it may have appeared about 500; the large basilica church is conjectural. This should be compared with Fig. 24.*

Hill, interprets the site as a traders' settlement of between 550 and 700 rather than the cells of a monastic establishment.

There were also burials in coffins of split logs and the whole site seems to have been surrounded by a boundary consisting of a ditch and wall.

In the area around Whithorn there are numerous other sites associated with St Ninian. These include St Ninian's Cave at Prysgill, with a probable hermitage of the seventh century; an enclosure half a mile to the south of Whithorn, with a chapel and stone associated with St Peter the Apostle and probably of the seventh century; and the Isle of Whithorn with the later medieval chapel of St Ninian's Kirk just off the coast. A little distance away in Wigtown Bay is also Ardwall Island, where Charles Thomas excavated a chapel and a cemetery in an enclosure dating from the fifth to seventh century at least. The whole complex of sites is 20km (12 miles) across and, like the original desert monasteries and those of Gaul, seems to have comprised a central monastery with a series of surrounding hermitages.

The most famous Scottish monastery is Iona, but there were others at Old Melrose, Kingarth (Bute), Hoddon (Dumfriesshire), Birsay (Orkney), Govan and Kintyre. At Iona (see Figs 16 and 17) the monks lived in small cells of wood and earth, with a rather larger cell set aside for the abbot. The whole site was surrounded by a bank and ditch which still exists in part as an earthwork.

Other less well-known, but well-preserved sites exist on remote islands off the west coast of Scotland. On Tiree the site at St Patrick's Chapel, Ceann a'Mhara, preserves structures of probable monastic origin, such as a drystone enclosure wall, a group of cells and hut platforms and a small, later medieval chapel close to the shore on the remotest part of the island. It could be described as a 'communal hermitage' or an 'eremitic monastery' and it compares well with such sites as Church Island, Illauntannig and Reask in Co. Kerry, Ireland. There are others on Mull, including

Treshish (Kilmoluag) on the west shore and the caves at Carsaig and Scoor on the south coast, the latter with crosses carved on the walls probably indicating the caves were used by hermits, and at Cill Earnadail (Keils) on Jura. One of the most evocative and impressive sites, however, is that on the small island of Eileach an Naoimh (the name means 'little island of the priests'), in the Garvellachs off the coast of Jura (Figs 10 and 11). It must have been founded by a hermit like Columba's friend Cormac, sent 'to find a desert place in the ocean'; it consists of an enclosure, a double beehive cell, three cross-inscribed grave markers, a circular 'special grave' and two chapels – one of the eleventh to twelfth century – all above a narrow landing place in the rocks of the seashore.

Monasteries in Wales and the West

There is a great deal of folklore and legend associated with Christianity in Wales and Cornwall, but there is no doubt that there were important early monastic settlements in both areas. For Wales, the laws of Hywel Dda – codified in the tenth century but probably referring back to around 700 – distinguish mother churches (always with a head or abbot ('abab'), at least one priest and other canons) from other churches. There seems also to have been a distinction between the great foundations of the sixth and seventh centuries, which must include St David's and Llantwit Major (see Figs 13 and 14), and the smaller, less significant but nevertheless monastic sites, each called a 'clas'. There were also communal

10 *and* 11   *Eileach an Naoimh (Jura, Scotland). Plan and near vertical air photograph (looking south-west). This hermitage site consists of a chapel, cells, burial grounds and enclosures above the landing place.*

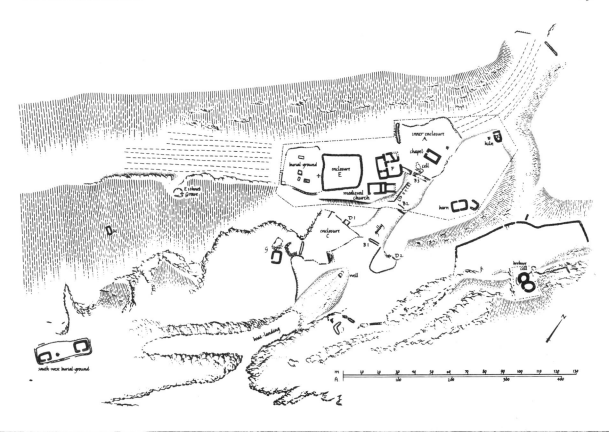

hermitages such as those at Beddgelert and on the island of Bardsey. Elsewhere there were a host of other churches, often indicated by the term 'llan' or enclosure, which were not always monastic in origin but whose names indicate an association with a local saint who may have been the founder or a patron.

North Wales

In North Wales a case can be made out for a number of early monasteries including many on offshore islands. Examples include Bardsey off the Lleyn peninsula (Gwynedd); Penmon on Anglesey together with the site on the island of Priestholm (or Puffin Island – Ynys Seiriol) associated with St Seiriol; Caer Gybi on Holy Island off the coast of Anglesey, associated with St Cybi living in the abandoned late Roman stone-walled fort there; Bangor and Clynnog Fawr (Gwynedd); and St Tudwal's Island off its south coast. Of these, Enlli or Bardsey was said to be the oldest religious house in Wales, and was known as the 'Welsh Rome', because of the long and risky journey to get to it and because of the holiness and purity of the place. It was the burial place of saints Dubricius (Dyfrig), whose relics were removed from the cemetery by Urban, first Norman bishop of Llandaff, in 1120, and Deiniol who was buried there in 584. There was a close relationship with a site at Aberdaron on the mainland. Beddgelert, the later priory of the Valley of St Mary of Snowdonia, was said to be the second oldest site.

At both Bardsey and Beddgelert, Gerald of Wales in 1188 says of the inhabitants:

they were devoted to serving God, living in a holy and common bond, having nothing private, in the manner of the Apostles. They were bound to no particular order of monks or canons but were celibates or culdees, that is, worshippers of God, given alike to continence and to abstinence, chiefly outstanding for their works of charity and hospitality.

Not only is it interesting to see 'Celtic' monasticism surviving so late, but we also know that each of these and other sites had compact blocks of land around them making up their estates at this time.

It is also noticeable that many of these monasteries were double complexes of monasteries and hermitages. This can be seen at Penmon, on Anglesey, where the hermitage of St Seiriol consisted of a cell with a holy well between a cliff and a marsh; this was later replaced a little way away by a larger establishment as the original site was cramped and could not be expanded. Nearby was the island of Priestholm, there the monastery included a small church of later date, with several phases of cells along the north side of an enclosure.

A similar relationship probably existed between Bardsey and Aberdaron. At some time the main monastery or coenobium may have existed on the mainland, with hermitages on the islands, as has already been described elsewhere; at other times the island would have provided the main site, particularly in periods of uncertainty, when a degree of defence or isolation was required.

South Wales

In south Wales there is rather more information, particularly for the south-east of the country, in what is now Gwent (Fig. 12). From the abundant documentary evidence, mainly from the Llandaff charters, Wendy Davies has been able to detect over fifty probable monasteries in the area, with eleven further west and a lot less over the rest of Wales – perhaps no more than 35 altogether outside the south-east. There may have been monasteries at Welsh Bicknor and

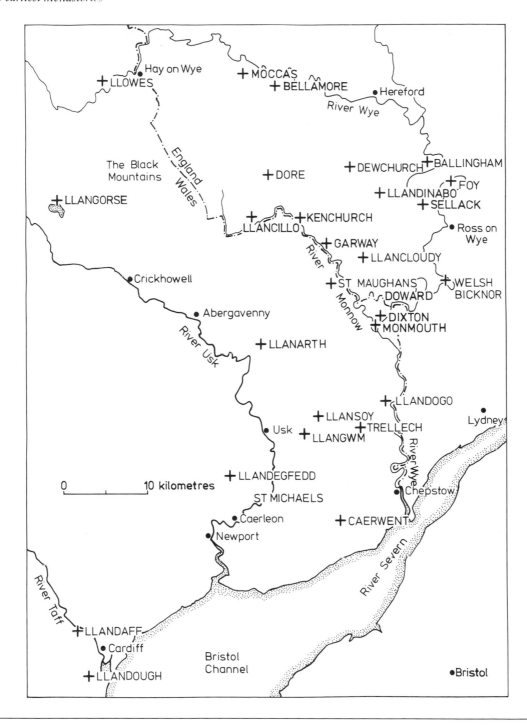

12 *Early monasteries in south-east Wales and the Wye valley. Most of these date from the late sixth and early seventh centuries although there are no traces of structures of that date at these places today. A further forty or so places in this region were described as 'ecclesiae' at this time and probably had small religious communities associated with them.*

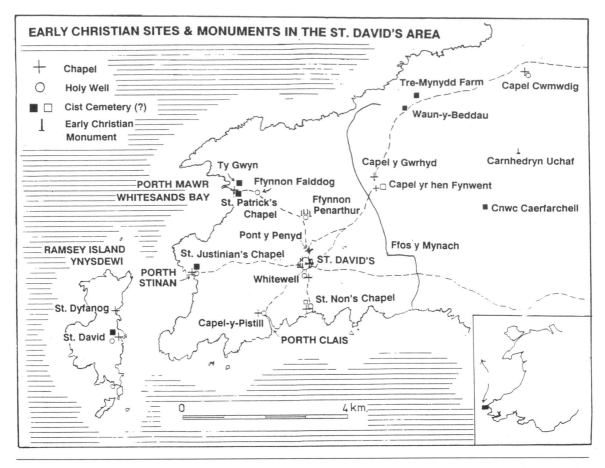

EARLY CHRISTIAN SITES & MONUMENTS IN THE ST. DAVID'S AREA

13 *St David's (Pembrokeshire – Dyfed, Wales). Map of the early Christian sites in the St David's peninsula.*

Llandinabo by the late sixth century, while Bellimoor and Garway, both in Ercyng, were founded in 610 and 615 respectively by King Gwyrfoddw. Most were, however, of the late sixth century, with the expansion of monasticism mainly in the late sixth and early seventh centuries. The larger foundations were at Llancarfan, Llanbadarn, Llantwit and St David's. It has been suggested by E.G. Bowen that many of these were great federated communities up to 90km (50 to 60 miles) across, indicated today by common church dedications to such saints as Teilo and Cadog in the south and Beuno in the north.

At St David's (Fig. 13) there was a bishopric at Mynyw in the eighth century

and a monastery of Rosina Vallis represented by the present religious complex at St David's, where there has been continuity of community if not of actual site. All around there are chapels and cemeteries and the peninsula is demarcated by a linear earthwork, the Ffos y Mynach, to the east. There were many associated hermitages, not only at the numerous chapels but also on Ramsey Island – Ynys Dewi or St David's Island.

Llantwit Major (Fig. 14), which used to be called Llanilltud Fawr, may be a very early site associated with an important Roman villa. Illtud (450–535) is regarded as the founder in the sixth century, when there was a school where Samson (of Dol) (*c*.490–

14 *Llantwit Major (Glamorgan, South Wales). The site of the fifth- and sixth-century and later monastery was probably under and around the church in the centre of the air photograph. In the foreground is the site of the Tewkesbury Abbey grange of the Middle Ages (see Fig. 75).*

?565), Gildas (*c.*500–*c.*570) and possibly Dewi (David) (?–*c.*601) were educated. This is confirmed in the '*Life*' of St Samson compiled shortly after, in the seventh century. It was a major centre in the ninth century, when a '*Life*' of St Paul Aurelian refers to '*Iltuti monasterium*', while a twelfth-century '*Life*' of St Illtud describes the settlement in the Hodnant valley with its little dwellings, cemetery and oratory all surrounded by a stone wall and ditch. The monastery was almost certainly at the present church of Llantwit Major, which has a rather unusual plan and form. There is a fine collection of early memorial stones here, including a tenth-century cross mentioning '*Samsoni apati*' – a later 'Abbot Samson'. Llantwit at this time was the royal

burial place for the kings of this part of Glamorgan.

At Llancarfan, the former Lann Gharban (Gabran), also known as Nantcarfan, mentioned in a ninth- to tenth-century '*Life*' of the Irish St Finnian, there is a large churchyard in a valley by a stream. Llangyfelach near Swansea, where the '*monasterium Langemelach*' mentioned in a twelfth-century '*Life*' of St David may have stood (one of twelve said to have been founded by David himself), has three memorial stones in the church and the large rounded churchyard may reflect the monastic enclosure.

There were eremitic monasteries and hermitages off the south Wales' coast as well. Examples include Caldey off Dyfed, Barry

15   *St Buryan (West Penwith, Cornwall). The site of an early monastery is now covered by the medieval church and graveyard within the circular churchyard.*

Island off Glamorgan and both Steep Holm and Flat Holm in the Bristol Channel, while one that has been excavated can be seen on the island of Burry Holms off the north-west coast of Gower. A chapel, with enclosure and memorial stones, probably of a hermitage, can also be seen on Lundy island.

While little can be seen in detail of what these monasteries looked like in the pre-Conquest period, as so often they are covered by later churches and churchyards, the general plan seems to have consisted of an enclosure marked by a bank and ditch, within which stood separate cells for the individual monks. There was one or sometimes several oratories and churches, the principal one containing the shrine of the founder. There was a cemetery adjoining where there would have been crosses and memorial stones to the dead. There would have been a guest-house, a scriptorium, a library and a school, especially in the larger establishments. Also there must have been barns and other domestic and farm buildings nearby. Crosses would have been positioned around the enclosure.

Sites selected might be conditioned by pre-existing earthworks or enclosures, as with the Roman fort at Holyhead, but there seems to have been a definite preference for sheltered valleys near small streams, not far from but not actually on the coast. On Anglesey and in Gwynedd where the field evidence survives well, the monasteries seem to have been sited near to, but not in, contemporary settlements of round houses and this may also be the case elsewhere.

Cornwall

In Cornwall a recent study by Lynette Olson has looked very critically at the evidence for early monasteries. Those sites of reasonable certainty include St Buryan in West Penwith (Fig. 15), St Keverne near The Lizard, Probus, Crantock, Padstow, St Kew and Perranzabuloe. The latter, the site in the sand dunes near Perranporth, is associated with St Piran; there is a small early oratory now preserved under a concrete shell in the sand dunes, together with a later church and a stone cross. Interestingly, this list does not include Tintagel island, always said to be the classic example of a Celtic monastery, which has recently been discussed by Charles Thomas and is now seen as a high-status royal centre, perhaps associated with King Mark. All of these Cornish sites were isolated, although the only site actually on an island is that at Looe. There is no clear evidence for a monastery on the Isles of Scilly, although there was a series of hermitages, on St Helens and Tean for example. It is possible that the central monastery was on Tresco where there is an early inscribed memorial stone at the site of the medieval priory. Several of the sites about which there is some doubt were later settled with medieval monasteries and incorporated into towns – Bodmin and St Stephen's by Launceston for example. At many of these Cornish monastic sites there are circular enclosed churchyards, chapels and oratories, inscribed memorial stones and holy wells.

When Augustine came to Britain in 597 to re-establish the Roman church, he was coming to a country that was Christian in some areas and where there was already a considerable number of monasteries. This was not true of the more Romanized southern and eastern parts of the country, but it was true of Wales and the west of England and it was particularly true of Ireland, which had never been part of the Roman empire.

As the Roman form of monasticism gained ground and one by one the areas of the Celtic church agreed to adopt Roman forms of (for example) the tonsure and the calculation of Easter, the Celtic church lost its influence. At the Synod of Whitby in 663 the Northumbrian church agreed to adopt the Roman customs. The church in southern Ireland had already submitted in 625–38 and that in northern Ireland did so by the end of the seventh century. Iona adopted Roman rites in 716 and the church in Strathclyde in the early eighth century. Cornwall and Devon submitted in about 705, but for Wales the matter was not settled until 768 under a Welsh monk called Elfodd, a full century and a half after the Synod of Whitby and nearly two hundred years after Augustine's mission. But for several hundred years Celtic monasticism was of great significance in the West and, as we have seen, aspects of it survived into the twelfth century. It is also arguable that its influence, via Iona and the foundation of Lindisfarne in Northumbria, was much greater than was that of the Roman church, through Canterbury and Augustine, in the eventual conversion of England to Christianity.

Apart from the little historical information that exists for these sites, almost nothing can be said about the founders of these monasteries and the interest of local patrons; neither is anything known of the lands that were attached to them or what farming was carried out. The number of sites involved, their layout of buildings and lands and their influence on their surroundings all remain as topics to be investigated.

3 Anglo-Saxon monasteries before the Vikings

In the seventh century Britain was converted to Christianity. There were already Christians before this and paganism persisted later in some areas, but most of the conversion took place in the period 597 to 686. This was achieved by missionaries who were invariably monks and came from existing monasteries. Further monasteries were established and these then also acted as missionary bases; some were later developed into cathedrals, with some monks becoming bishops.

Elsewhere many independent monasteries were established. The process was carried out on the one hand from Canterbury under the influence of Rome by Augustine, his monks and their successors, and on the other by the well–developed and organized Northumbrian church. Many monasteries, which were in later centuries to become important and famous, were established at this time.

Development continued into the eighth and ninth centuries but it was then destroyed by the raiding of the Vikings; monasticism was virtually extinguished in Britain. Archaeology is only just beginning to look seriously at these sites, despite important earlier work by Rosemary Cramp and others, and it is now possible to say a little about the sites on which the monasteries of the seventh and eighth centuries were built and how monastic complexes fitted into their contemporary landscapes.

Northumbria

The story begins with the establishment of Iona or Hy, off the west coast of Scotland beyond the Isle of Mull (Figs 16 and 17), in 563 by St Columba. A description of the site shows that the monks lived in cells built of wood and earth with a rather larger cell for the abbot. There were several small churches with detached towers and the whole complex was surrounded by a wall. Something of this arrangement is still discernible at the site today, where a medieval and modern abbey have since been constructed.

Lindisfarne, or Holy Island, in Northumberland was founded from Iona in 635 by St Aidan, a great Irish Celtic monk. The exiled King Oswald of Northumbria returned and this was the catalyst needed to bring the Iona monks to Northumbria. This event marked the beginning of remarkable monastic development in Northumbria, the influence of which spread south over much of England and eventually beyond, to the continent of Europe. Lindisfarne was near the royal palace at Bamburgh, and the abbots of the monastery were intended to be the bishops of the new see of Bernicia. Its most famous monk was Cuthbert (c.634–87) and it is from his time at Lindisfarne that something can still be seen of the arrangements of the monastery.

Both Iona and Lindisfarne are famous early monastic centres and both became

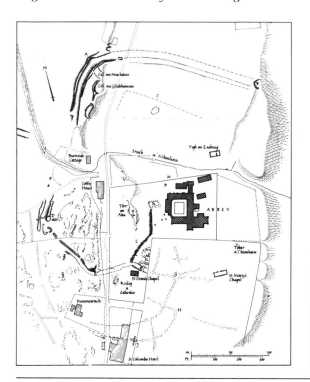

16 *and* **17** *Iona (Scotland). Plan and vertical air photograph showing the later abbey within the earlier monastic enclosure defined by banks and ditches.*

great centres of learning and influence in the seventh and eighth centuries. At both, the communities were physically isolated, living on predominantly uninhabited islands. At Lindisfarne (Fig. 18) the seventh-century site is assumed to be under or near the later medieval Benedictine priory which is on the south-west corner of Lindisfarne island. If so, it would have been sheltered below and behind a great ridge of volcanic rock to the south, the Heugh, which lies between it and the sea. Alternatively it may have been on the Heugh itself, where there are earthworks. There are beaches nearby to the west and east and the land rises very slightly to the north. This early monastery probably also followed the Irish arrangements, with small cells irregularly grouped around one or more churches, probably all surrounded by a bank and ditch. The churches may have

been in line, as at other early sites, in which case the present St Cuthbert's church and the ruins of the medieval priory church may reflect this alignment. There would have been other related buildings nearby and some evidence of these can be gleaned from later sources.

In the seventh century St Cuthbert was based at Holy Island and a number of sites are associated with him in the vicinity. Just off Lindisfarne, to the south-west and facing the later priory, is the small islet called St Cuthbert's Island; it can be reached at low tide by scrambling across the boulder-strewn beach. On this there are the foundations of an enclosure with a small chapel and house still remaining in the thick tussocky grass. As if Lindisfarne, cut off by rising tides twice a day, was not remote enough, St Cuthbert probably spent some

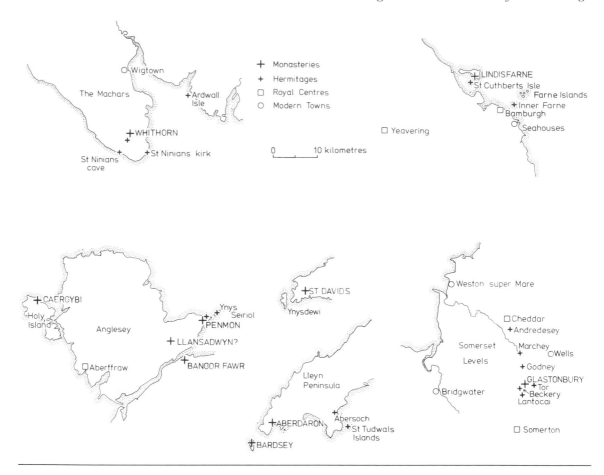

18   *Plans of Whithorn; Lindisfarne (Holy Island); Anglesey; St David's and the Lleyn peninsula in Wales; and Glastonbury. Early monastic landscapes with royal centres, monasteries and surrounding hermitages.*

time at this further retreat off the main island.

Even more remote was another hermitage 11km (7 miles) to the south, on the island of Inner Farne in the Farne Islands group, where Cuthbert is known to have lived and where he eventually died (Fig. 19). Reconstructions of what this site might have looked like in the seventh century show one or two cells with a church set within a circular enclosure with small garden plots nearby. A fine painting of 1856 in the pre-Raphaelite tradition by William Bell-Scott shows the visit of King Egfrid and Bishop Trumwine to persuade Cuthbert to leave Inner Farne to be made bishop in 684.

Cuthbert is shown gardening in his onion patch within a walled enclosure just above the beach. Coquet Island off the Northumberland coast near Amble was another island hermitage site, famous from as early as 684; few other islands were available for hermitages off this part of the English coast.

From Lindisfarne, monasteries were established all over the north-east by monks who were both missionaries and bishops. Eata became abbot of Melrose, Cedd (?–664) became abbot of Lastingham in Yorkshire and eventually established monasteries at West Tilbury and Bradwell-on-Sea in Essex. Chad (?–672), his brother, established the see of Lichfield in Mercia and, with King Wulfhere of Mercia, the monastery of Barrow-on-Humber when he was bishop (669–72). Benedict Biscop (*c*.628–89) who had been at Lérins in 666, founded St Peter's at Monkwearmouth in 674 and St Paul's at Jarrow in 682 (see Fig. 22). Wilfrid (634–709) established both Hexham and Ripon, as well as carrying out missions to Friesland and Sussex. He introduced the rule of St Benedict to Northumbria and was the leading figure at the Synod of Whitby.

Women were also involved in this movement. St Hilda (621–80) founded a monastery at 'Streanaeshalch' (later called Whitby) in 657 for monks and nuns, and reorganized another double monastery at 'Heruteu', later Hartlepool. A number of these double houses were established in the seventh century and there were nunneries as well, such as the famous house at Coldingham.

Kent

In 597 Augustine arrived with his band of monks to convert the heathen English to Christianity. Between 597 and 604 on the orders of Pope Gregory the Great, he established bishoprics and cathedrals at Canterbury (597) and Rochester (604) for the people of Kent, and London (601) for the East Saxons. Initially only one monastery was established, St Peter and St Paul, later St Augustine's, outside the city wall to the east of Canterbury (Fig. 20), which was the royal centre for the people of Kent under the

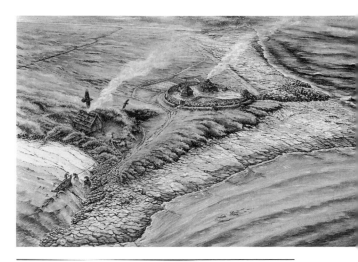

19 *A reconstruction of Cuthbert's hermitage on Inner Farne as it may have appeared in the late seventh century. Drawn by Peter Dunn.*

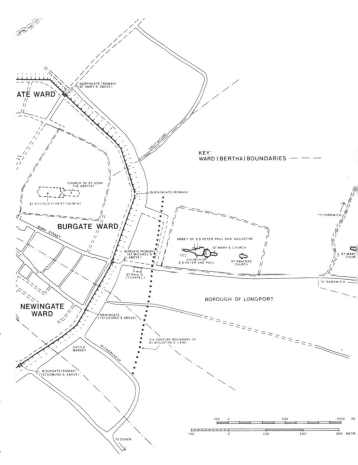

20 *St Augustine's Abbey, Canterbury (Kent). Plan of the east side of the city as it might have been in 1050 with the abbey of Sts Peter and Paul founded by Augustine with the probable seventh-century boundary of its land together with other early churches in the vicinity.*

pagan king Aethelberht. The foundations of the seventh-century church can be seen at this site, lying in line with other early churches – St Mary's and St Pancras. A little later a house for women was established at Lyminge and in 669 a house for men at Reculver, and before long there was a series of monasteries established in Kent, at Thanet, in Sheppey and elsewhere. The origins of these sites are reflected in the plans of the churches that have been excavated which are all based on the basilican, that is Roman, arrangements of nave, side chapels, narthex and apsidal east end.

Pope Gregory granted to Augustine 'authority over the British churches', so that it was assumed that the differences in the computation of Easter, the tonsure and the rites of baptism in the Celtic churches would be ruled on by Rome; as already noted, this proved to be a protracted process. In fact it is impossible to separate out the differing influences of the Latin, Celtic and Northumbrian churches in subsequent developments – as Stenton says: 'The strands of Irish and continental influence were interwoven in every kingdom and at every stage of the process by which England became Christian', a process which lasted from the foundation of Iona in 563 and the arrival of Augustine in Kent in 597 to the conversion of the people of the Isle of Wight in 686.

Monasteries and the Christian mission to the English

The monasteries established across England in the seventh century were part of the process of bringing Christianity to a pagan country – many were established as missionary centres, a role not easy to reconcile with the wishes of many of the monks for detachment from the world. Nevertheless, it is clear that while a site for a monastery might have been chosen for its

isolation, the role of the monastery was often to provide a missionary base and the monks in it were expected to operate in the surrounding area. Something of the process can be seen with the grant of land to the late seventh-century monastic foundation of Breedon-on-the-Hill (Leicestershire) (Fig. 21), an isolated hilltop site reminiscent of the hermitage sites selected elsewhere. The grant was made in view of 'the growing and multiplying of the number of Christians in the island of Britain . . . so that a monastery and oratory of monks serving God should be founded . . . and also a priest of honest life and good reputation instituted, who should bring the grace of baptism and the teaching of the gospel doctrine to the people committed to his care'. The site is still impressive and there are fine sculptural features from the pre-Conquest period.

Contemporary records, particularly the *Anglo-Saxon Chronicle*, enable the process of the conversion to Christianity to be seen reasonably clearly, together with the development of cathedral centres, the relationships of monasteries with the Anglo-Saxon kings and their kingdoms, and the importance of monasteries in the social, cultural and economic life of the country. It is, however, very difficult to assess the exact number of monasteries that were established during this period or how many were in existence at any particular point in time. It is also not at all clear how many were true monasteries; it seems likely, from what Bede tells us, that some at least were the equivalent of modern 'tax dodges', with families living together as Christians but not under a rule or under the authority of an abbot or living the strict life that might be expected of monastic communities.

The problem of identification is exacerbated by the later changing fortunes of many of the sites established during this period. Some of the most famous became the centres of the new bishoprics and of extensive dioceses. These include the sites at

Lindisfarne, Hexham, Lichfield, Worcester, Leicester, Dorchester-on-Thames and Sherborne, though they were developed at different dates. Others formed the basis of the later tenth-century refoundations, including the most famous of the late Saxon monasteries – Bath, Gloucester, Abingdon, Pershore, Peterborough and Malmesbury. Some were clearly important in their day but did not survive as later monasteries. Examples of the latter include Nursling (Hampshire), Hanbury and Fladbury (Worcestershire) and Breedon-on-the-Hill (Leicestershire) (see Fig. 21). Yet others seem to have been failures almost from the start, such as the 'tax dodge' sites mentioned above. Often all that is known of many of these sites is their approximate date of foundation, a brief outline of their history and sometimes a few details of which saints, monks or patrons were associated with

them. Invariably little is known about their buildings, layout or economic life, often the exact site is not certain, while subsequent changes to the local topography, which might lead to an appreciation of why a particular site was chosen, have rarely been investigated.

A good example of such a site is Castor, near Peterborough. In an area of extensive prehistoric and even more intense Roman activity, a monastery was established some time in the 660s. It was a nunnery founded by St Kyneburgha (or Cyneburg), third daughter of Penda, the king of Mercia, and her sister Kyneswitha (or Cynesfryde); their sister was Paeda who founded Peterborough. The monastery was established among the ruins of Roman buildings which can still be seen nearby in the village today. It survived until the 870s but was eclipsed by Peterborough, where its

21   *Breedon-on-the-Hill (Leicestershire). Air photograph of the seventh-century monastic site and the later church inside the earlier hillfort. Much of the hilltop has been quarried away since this picture was taken in 1949.*

relics were taken in the eleventh century. The present church is a large impressive Romanesque structure dated 1124, but of the exact location and detailed plan of the monastery nothing is known.

Archaeological evidence

Numerous other monasteries were founded around the same time but there is little, if any, evidence surviving to identify even the exact site of many of them and what their surroundings looked like. Only in a few places is there sufficient archaeological evidence to see any details of a site. Structural evidence dating to the seventh century exists still at Hexham, Ripon and Repton in the form of impressive crypts which can still be visited.

Of all the sites which have been examined belonging to this period, the monastery at Jarrow has received the most attention (Fig. 22), with extensive excavations being carried out adjacent to the surviving early church, under the direction of Rosemary

22   *A model of part of the monastery at Jarrow (Northumberland) based on the excavations carried out by Rosemary Cramp. It gives the best impression available at the moment of the central part of the precinct of a Northumbrian monastery with its churches in line, domestic halls, workshops, wooden cells, cemetery and gardens.*

Cramp. These have enabled us not only to see the plan of the early monastic buildings but also to appreciate the site chosen in relation to the locality. The layout of the buildings bears little relation to the plans of later monasteries: there is no cloister but there were two churches in line, now linked to form the present parish church. The domestic accommodation lay parallel and to the south. Gardens lay on the south-facing slope leading down to a creek off the river Tyne. There have been considerable alterations to the landscape around Jarrow and it is now difficult to appreciate (following land-fill operations) that the site originally chosen was a peninsula pointing eastwards, with the river Tyne on the north and the river Don on the south and east; the land within shelves gently to the south. Most probably a precinct was defined by a bank and ditch on this peninsula.

Recently, archaeological research has located a number of previously little-known or unsuspected sites from this period (Fig. 23). At Nazeingbury (Essex) a Middle Saxon cemetery was found associated with two probable timber-built churches. Radiocarbon dating from two of the skeletons produced dates centring on 670 and 830. Analysis of the burials by Glenys Putnam showed this to be a very different cemetery to what might be expected of a village community, since the majority were old women. 'It is most likely that the core of the community was female, and well nourished. The small proportion of men present all show signs of hard work, and may be assumed to be the labourers of a community burying its dead here.' She concludes 'it is a fair assumption that we are dealing with a religious community . . .' consisting of nuns, a few men (priests? or workers) and children; the site seems to be undocumented.

Another undocumented monastic site, which might be the sort of 'tax-dodge' monastery complained of by Bede, has been claimed for the site found at Flixborough (Humberside) (see Fig. 23). The collection of buildings located there could be a secular site were it not for the existence of a probable church and a metal plaque with what is claimed to be a list of names of religious personnel. Reconstructions suggest a family monastery with a church and living quarters. It was located on a west-facing ridge, overlooking the river Trent, north of Scunthorpe.

At Brixworth (Northamptonshire), the Saxon church site has been the subject of extensive archaeological research, including detailed analysis of the stones used in its construction. The conclusion is worth quoting in full as it shows how useful such research can be, in this case suggesting that the earlier monastic connection was not with the famous Saxon monastery at Peterborough but with a site at Leicester:

The surprising absence of Barnack stone from the church fabric may indicate that the Peterborough connection has perhaps been overstressed in the past. The abundance of Leicester (and possible Towcester) stone in the initial phase of the building may be the result of direct royal patronage, and if this is so it could mean that Brixworth's connection with the secular authority was of more importance than its monastic affiliation. Thus the petrological study may illuminate even the institutional history of the monastic foundation at Brixworth.

It is suggested furthermore that the stonework in the west end of the church indicates that a large Roman building was dismantled and reused in the construction of this Saxon monastery church.

Archaeological work has been undertaken at some of the other famous northern monasteries. Following the foundation of Lindisfarne other monasteries were built all over Northumbria. Peninsulas or headlands were frequently chosen as the sites for these and the buildings seem often to have been laid out in rectilinear plans orientated east–

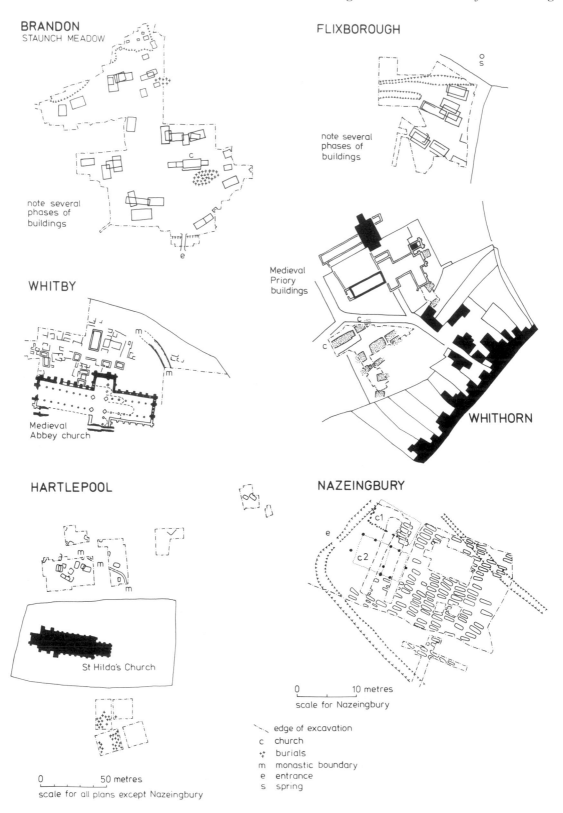

west alongside one or more churches. The most completely excavated is Jarrow, but there has been work in the past at Whitby as well. There, a number of stone structures were found in the excavations of the 1920s. The plan has now been re-examined by Philip Rahtz, who has shown that there were rooms, complexes of buildings, burials and a series of wells. The area excavated was in the northern part of the precinct with cells and workshops and was probably bounded by a stone wall. The site on this bleak and exposed headland overlooking the North Sea was later built over by the medieval abbey.

Recent excavations at Whithorn and Hartlepool (see Fig. 23) have given us rather more extensive plans. Whithorn, with its possible earlier origins (see p. 27), has produced abundant evidence for the eighth and early ninth centuries (Fig. 24). In the area to the south-west of the later priory there were a number of timber buildings, halls and so on, lying alongside a path which led to a stone-built church and a burial chapel or mausoleum. At Hartlepool, work has revealed plans of 18 timber buildings of mid-seventh- to late eighth-century date, forming part of the monastic complex and suggesting the typical dispersed plan already encountered elsewhere. The buildings seem to have been on the edge of the main monastic complex, which probably lay to the south near St Hilda's church, and may have been used for accommodation and craft working. A series of post-holes probably

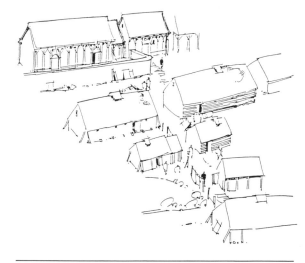

24 *Whithorn (Galloway, Scotland). Reconstruction of the Northumbrian church and monastic settlement around 750. This should be compared with Fig. 9.*

indicates the position of the boundary fence – if so, the monastery was on the top of the peninsula later occupied by the medieval town.

A rare glimpse of the way the monastery operated in its landscape can be gleaned from the environmental evidence from the site: '. . . the community was largely self-supporting in food. Flocks of sheep and herds of cattle were driven into the settlement from outlying estates and butchered. In addition a variety of fruits, and no doubt cereals, were available, as were coastal species of fish'. It is remarkable that the monasteries excavated so far for this period bear a close resemblance to contemporary lay settlements such as Cowdery's Down and Catholme; the only distinction seems to be the quality of finds or the documentary evidence.

As well as the archaeological view of the seventh-century monasteries, a later manuscript from Abingdon gives a description of the monastery there as it was around 675 and compares it to the layout as it existed in the later Saxon period.

23 *Plans of the Anglo-Saxon monasteries at Staunch Meadow, Brandon (Norfolk); Flixborough (Humberside); Whitby (Yorkshire); Whithorn (Galloway, Scotland); Hartlepool (Cleveland); and Nazeingbury (Essex). The sites at Brandon and Flixborough may be secular rather than religious communities.*

How the first Monastery at Abingdon was built. The monastery of Abingdon which was built by Heane the first abbot in that place was as follows: It was 120 feet in length, and was apsidal both at the west end and the east end. The foundations of this monastery were in the place where the monks' cellar is now situated, and the altar stood where the washing place now is. Within the circuit of this monastery there were 12 dwellings, and the same number of chapels, and in the dwellings there were 12 monks eating and drinking and sleeping; they did not have a cloister as they have now, but there were surrounding high walls which were for them an inclosure . . . They had a parlour next to the gate . . . On Sundays and the principal festivals they met together, and celebrated mass in the church, and ate together.

The description suggests that the whole complex bore a remarkable resemblance to the Egyptian 'laura' sites of the fourth century, with individual hermit monks living within an enclosure.

Church organization

Frequently in early monasteries the abbot was also the bishop of a diocese, however ill-defined or embryonic in layout. This has been discussed for south Scotland and northern England by Charles Thomas and for early Wales by Wendy Davies. The early church in the fourth, fifth and sixth centuries in Europe was organized according to bishops and dioceses which related to Roman towns and provinces, and clearly this worked well in the highly urbanized provinces of the Roman Empire. It was, however, much more difficult to develop in the post-Roman centuries in Britain where urban life had completely collapsed and equally, if not more so, in those areas such as Ireland, Wales, Scotland and the south-west of England where there had been little or no Roman civil government and urban

development had been minimal. In these areas monasteries were founded at the central places of tribal territories and served as cathedrals, the abbots acted as the bishops for the diocese which was coterminous with the tribal area, and the monks acted as the missionaries for the conversion of the populace. In such circumstances the monasteries were frequently large and were described as 'cities'; in reality they performed some of the functions of towns while acting as missionary centres for mainly rural landscapes.

The conversion of the people in a region tended to follow that of its leader, with further monasteries acting as missionary centres (but not cathedrals) being established in the area. Thus Dorchester-on-Thames was the mission centre for part of Wessex, with Birinus, one of the monks accompanying Augustine, the first bishop and head of the religious house established there, while Worcester was the cathedral for the Hwicce and Hereford for the Magonsaete, both sub-groups of Mercia. In this period, therefore, it is necessary to look not only at the foundation of monasteries, but also at the progress of diocesan development, with the selection of bishops' seats and the elevation of some churches to become cathedrals; often the monastery was synonymous with the cathedral, as was frequently also the case in the Middle Ages.

The initial intention of Gregory and Augustine seems to have been to establish two metropolitans at London (in fact Canterbury; see Fig. 20) and York, each with bishops in twelve dioceses, but this plan was a long time in being achieved. Only in 735 was York elevated to an archbishopric and not until 737, with the creation of the see of Leicester, was the twelfth bishopric established – all in the southern part of the country.

Northumbria and the North

The influence of Canterbury and the Roman model can be seen in Northumbria in the mission of Paulinus, who was one of Augustine's group, when he baptized King Edwin in York in 627. Edwin had married Aethelberga, daughter of the recently converted king of Kent, Aethelberht, and a special wooden church, St Peter's (forerunner of the Minster), had been built for Paulinus. Conversion of the people in the kingdom took place at Yeavering, where the royal palace stood, with mass baptism in the river Glen, as well as at Catterick and near Leeds. In 627 Paulinus also undertook the conversion of the kingdom of Lindsey, building a church at Lincoln and baptizing people in the river Trent at Littleborough. It is noticeable that these missions had no involvement with the existing Celtic monks and monasteries in the area, and that the conversions were organized in a very different, largely non-monastic, way from those based on missionary monasteries in the Celtic areas. In East Anglia a similar situation can be seen, with Felix establishing his see at 'Dommoc' (which might be Dunwich, Old Felixstowe or the old Roman shore fort of Walton Castle) on continental lines, while in the 630s the Irishman Fursa was given the old Roman shore fort of Burgh Castle (*Cnobheresburh*) for a monastery. Within the East Saxon area, based on London, Cedd similarly established a monastery on Northumbrian lines in the Roman shore fort of *Ythancester* at Bradwell in the 650s.

The Midlands

In 653 the Northumbrian church, with no contact from Canterbury, began the conversion of the Mercians in the Midlands. In 654 a vast see was created covering Mercia, Middle Anglia and Lindsey. The Middle Angles had begun to be converted under Irish influences but there is no Celtic influence in the early history of Medeshamstede, or Peterborough, the greatest monastery of the region, founded in 655–6. Ceadda (St Chad) was send to Mercia and established a see at Lichfield, close to the old Roman centre at Wall (*Letocetum*) in 669. In 677 a separate diocese for Lindsey was created out of Lichfield, at a place called Sidnacester and, although it is not certain where this was, the old Roman fort and settlement at Horncastle seems a likely candidate.

Wessex and the South

Birinus (?–650) established a church on the Roman model in north Wessex in 635, based in the old Roman town of Dorchester-on-Thames, and baptized King Cynegils there. In 660 Winchester was chosen as the centre of the see, Birinus' relics were moved there in about 690, and the older centre at Dorchester was abandoned for a time. It was not until 705 that Aldhelm, abbot of the monastery at Malmesbury, established Sherborne as another diocesan centre for 'Wessex beyond Selwood' with himself as bishop. Aldhelm was a significant figure in the development of the Church in the west. He was educated at the monastery at Malmesbury and founded others at Frome and Bradford-on-Avon.

Sussex remained heathen long after the other kingdoms had been converted, although there were Irish monks at Bosham; it was eventually converted by the exiled Wilfrid from Northumbria from the centre of a new diocese at Selsey, a site now destroyed by the sea. With the conversion of the people of the Isle of Wight in about 686 all of England was Christian, at least nominally.

In 669 Theodore of Tarsus arrived in Britain to be Archbishop of Canterbury and to continue the work begun by Augustine.

He was accompanied by Hadrian and Benedict Biscop, and although he was already old by this time and had more in common with eastern Christianity than that in the west, he undertook a visitation of his province. He found that only at London, Ripon (Wilfrid) and York (Chad) were there bishops, while at Rochester, in Wessex, Mercia and East Anglia the sees were vacant. By 672 he had made great progress and there were bishops in all the established dioceses – Canterbury, Rochester, London, Dunwich (later divided with the creation of North Elmham for Norfolk), Winchester and York. By 680 further dioceses had been created out of Lichfield – Worcester for the Hwicce and Hereford for the Magonsaete. Also Leicester was made a bishop's seat for the Middle Angles although this did not become permanent until 737. By the time Theodore died in 690 he had been twenty years in Britain and the Church was in a better state than when he arrived. He had managed to achieve the sort of organization of the English Church that Augustine had always intended but not been able to accomplish.

Under Theodore a great council was held in Hertford in 672 at which it was decided, among other matters, that 'monks were forbidden to leave their monasteries without their abbot's licence and bishops were forbidden to trouble monasteries or take away their possessions'. This of course can be taken to imply that such practices had been going on, but this legislation also shows that monasteries were now numerous enough to warrant regulation and that some general rules were being applied to places with disparate origins. Wilfrid, who died in 709, is generally credited with introducing the Rule of St Benedict to the British Isles and even though this did not gain official acceptance until much later (probably after the Synod of Aachen in 817), it shows again that standardization was coming in by the end of the seventh century.

Monasteries

What then was the progress of monastic plantation in these newly Christianized kingdoms? Although unlike elsewhere, England had not been converted solely by monks from monasteries but by missionaries setting up cathedrals in new dioceses, by the time the Viking raids began many dozens of monasteries had been established.

A number of seventh-century monasteries were deliberately sited on islands in rivers and marshes; they were not as remote as the islands in the sea selected by earlier monks but something of the isolation they afforded was clearly still needed. Glastonbury is perhaps the best example since, while it may have been founded earlier, the earliest structures found in excavations date to this period. Some of the other sites associated with it, such as Godney, Marchey and Beckery, also seem to date from this time and are on islands in the marsh.

The Fens of eastern England have a whole group of monasteries founded at this time (Fig. 25), either on the edge of the fens or on the numerous islands – Peterborough, formerly Medeshamstede (655), Ely (673), Crowland (716) and Thorney (675). The Fens were then a vast undrained morass described by Felix, an eighth-century monk, as 'a fen of immense size . . . there are immense marshes, now a black pool of water, now foul running streams, and also many islands, and reeds, and hillocks, and thickets, and with manifold windings wide and long . . .'. Ely was founded in 673, and we are told by Bede that it was an island surrounded by marsh and water and that it obtained its name – 'the eel district' – from the large numbers of eels found there. But the most evocative site is Crowland, founded in 716 by St Guthlac. It was described as a place of horror and solitude inhabited by devils and therefore ideal as a place to retreat to. Felix reports:

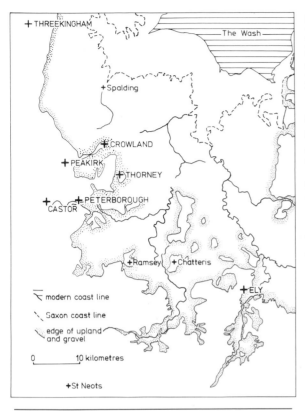

25 *Anglo-Saxon monasteries in the Fenland of eastern England. The large crosses and names in capital letters are the seventh-century foundations; the others are later Saxon monasteries.*

Guthlac . . . inquired of the inhabitants of the land where he might find himself a dwelling place in the wilderness. There was a man named Tatwine, who said he knew an island especially obscure, which oft-times many men had attempted to inhabit, but no man could do it on account of manifold horrors and fears, and the loneliness of the wild wilderness.

Another important group of sites was founded in the seventh century in the valleys of the rivers Avon and Severn. The most famous were the abbeys of Gloucester (679), Evesham (701), Pershore (689) and Worcester (680) but there were others at Deerhurst (715), Tewkesbury (715), Fladbury, Stratford and Beckford. Some of these were sited with regard to earlier Roman centres, others at the centres of Saxon estates. All were on gravel terraces or peninsulas above the flood-waters of the rivers.

In the Thames valley Westminster Abbey seems to have been founded in the early seventh century, and it was certainly in existence by 785. Its earlier name was Thorney, a reference to the island site selected on the west bank of the Thames where the river Tyburn joins it. A charter, probably a forgery, records the grant of lands in Hertfordshire to St Peter and the needy people of God in Thorney 'in the awful place which is called Westminster'. The island, roughly half a mile square, eventually developed into the precinct of one of the most important Benedictine abbeys in the country. On a similar riverside site was Chertsey Abbey (Surrey). Bede tells us this was founded on *Ceroti Insula*, the island of Cerotus, a gravel island in the Thames valley surrounded by marsh in earlier times and still occasionally outlined in times of flood. In 666 Chertsey and its sister abbey of Barking were founded by Erkenwald, later bishop of London, under King Egbert. Later on, extensive lands were granted by Frithuwold, sub-regulus of Wulfhere of Mercia, much of which formed the later hundred of Godley.

Most of these sites exist now in well-managed urban and rural surroundings, a tribute to the labour of generations of monks and their workers draining and enclosing land and developing markets and towns. The original sites were selected by recluses to get away from the world – the wild, untamed condition of the surrounding landscapes in the seventh and eighth centuries was ideal for this. As the hermitages developed into monasteries it proved impossible to provide all the food and other commodities for larger communities of monks from the original small or restricted island sites. Improving the productivity of the landscape around was achieved by drainage and enclosure of the marsh and clearance of woodland. In the twelfth and thirteenth centuries in particular, enormous effort was put into this reclamation but frequently, with the larger and wealthier monasteries, the process of reclamation and agricultural improvement must have begun earlier. As time went on, the changing ideals and circumstances of the monks, from hermits to communities, are reflected in the development of the landscape from a wilderness to fully managed, productive countryside.

Early monastic precincts, estates and economy

It is as difficult to define the sites and the estates of these monasteries as it was for the earlier ones. The role of founders and patrons is also largely unknown. While it is clear that communities such as Iona, Lindisfarne and Jarrow had the support of the local rulers, and they were therefore able to prosper and develop, it is not certain how such monasteries actually organized their lands to produce all the supplies they would have needed. By the seventh century in the south many monasteries were already being granted estates with extensive tracts of land. The charters show that Glastonbury Abbey, for example, was given lands at Meare, Pennard, Brent, Doulting, Sowy and elsewhere in Somerset in the seventh and eighth centuries. Presumably much of their sustenance was increasingly derived from the careful management of such estates, but there is little detailed information about this and only a patchy view of the contemporary landscape.

Considering the large numbers of monasteries that were established in the seventh and eighth centuries, very little is known about them with regard to their

plans, the layout of their precincts and the extent of their estates. For only a handful is there even a partial plan, such as those already discussed, and only for Jarrow is there a more or less complete outline. Even with the destruction caused by overlying tenth-century and medieval buildings, it is remarkable how little is known of these early sites.

A model for Celtic, Northumbrian and Saxon monasteries

It is possible, however, to say something in general terms about these early monasteries, where they were sited and how they related to their surrounding landscapes. Using the models of Egypt and Gaul, we can suggest what the arrangements were likely to have been in a pre-seventh-century 'Celtic' monastic community (see Fig. 18). It would clearly have had a central coenobium, the main 'mother' monastery, the 'clas' of later Welsh sources. This would have had one or more small churches, surrounded by cells for the monks, built of wood or stone and either circular or square in plan. There would have been a burial ground with memorials to the dead and a number of monumental crosses. The cells would have had gardens and there would have been workshops where a variety of crafts could be carried on, including metalworking. There would probably have been a guest-house and there may have been a dining hall and kitchen in the larger establishments. The whole complex would have been defined by a barrier, if not the sea or cliffs then certainly a bank and ditch and in some cases probably a substantial wall. There seems to have been no clearly defined plan to such a settlement, unlike that which was to emerge in later times. These monasteries may well have been sited in relation to the high-status residence of some important ruler, at this time usually a local king, although an isolated island, hill-top or peninsula, or an island surrounded by marshes, were preferred for the actual monastic site.

All around the monastery at varying distances there would have been hermitages, where single or small groups of hermits could pursue a more rigorous life. These might be sited on islands, hill-tops or in marshes, as long as they were relatively more remote than the monastery. At these sites there would be small enclosures with chapels and cells, gardens and perhaps burials. In this hypothetical monastic landscape there would also have been independent hermitages, as well as other churches in their own enclosures (the 'lans' and 'llans' of Cornwall and Wales).

Such monasteries served as missionary centres and, although often isolated and invariably in a landscape that was totally non-urban, they were expected frequently to be the diocesan centres and their abbots doubled also as bishops. The places that have been discussed, such as Tours, Lérins, Whithorn and Lindisfarne, conform to this model quite well. Other places such as St David's in west Wales, Glastonbury (Somerset) and perhaps Llantwit Major in south Wales probably do also. Such complexes are the landscape manifestation of John Cassian's (c. 360–435) description of the aims of the monks – aspirants proceeding from the 'praiseworthy exercises of the community to the lofty burdens of the anchoritic life'.

Something similar can be suggested for the later monasteries although there seems to be little evidence at most of those sites for surrounding hermitages. From both the surviving description and from the limited archaeological work that has been undertaken so far, the sort of buildings to be found in such sites can be suggested – several churches, living cells and workshops, some communal buildings. Some of these seventh- and eighth-century sites seem to

have been very regular in layout, with rows of buildings aligned east–west parallel with the church(es). The whole complex was enclosed with a wall, fence or similar. The evidence suggests that the 'Celtic', seventh- and eighth-century sites were far less regular in the disposition of their buildings around the precincts than were sites based on a central cloister that were developed in the tenth century and later.

Complexes of monasteries and hermitages do not seem to have existed in later landscapes, although the same ideals were catered for in a different form. In the Middle Ages, the Durham Cathedral priory estates showed something of the same central and peripheral arrangement. As well as the main monastery at Durham there were the dependent priories of Farne, Finchale, Jarrow, Lindisfarne, Lytham, Monkwearmouth, Tynemouth and Warkworth, all looking to the church where Cuthbert and Bede were buried.

The end of the early monasteries

Viking raids on England began in 787. In 793/4 the monastery at Lindisfarne was sacked by Vikings and by 870 monastic life north of the Humber had been extinguished by the great Danish invasion. The Fenland monasteries were destroyed at the same time. In the half century between 830 and 880 the monasteries in Wessex and south Mercia were destroyed, the few that survived at all being reduced to houses of clerks who looked after the records and ran the schools. By the time of Alfred (849–99) it was said that organized monasticism had collapsed in Britain; it had to be refounded anew fifty years later in the great tenth-century reformation.

However, before all this destruction of the ninth century overtook the monasteries they had become numerous, wealthy and influential institutions playing a significant part in the religious, social and economic activities of contemporary society. It is very difficult in many cases to be sure of either the exact foundation date of many of them or the date they ceased to operate as organized communities. In virtually all cases we know nothing of what they looked like in the seventh and eighth centuries; we assume they were on the same sites as the better known later monasteries, minsters and churches and it is only on this basis that anything can be said about the sites chosen.

Any dealings with lay people are only recorded in relation to the highest levels of contemporary society, invariably kings, queens and bishops. Next to nothing is known of the economy of such sites, what lands they possessed and how their estates were run. From the analogy with sites in Europe, it is probable that by the eighth and ninth centuries monasteries had become, in many cases, centres of agriculture, links in a chain of defence, hosts to a peripatetic royal court, schools, chanceries, centres of research and writing, and missionary bases – in many respects the 'central places' of the non-urban society from the fifth to the tenth century and beyond.

In most respects our lack of knowledge of these sites is reflected by a lack of information about similar aspects in the rest of Anglo-Saxon society. The documents, such as they are, do not help us to see these monasteries operating in their landscapes; it will be up to archaeology and the related natural sciences to put them in their proper context.

4 Saxon and Norman monasteries

Alfred defeated the Danish king Guthrum at the battle of Edington in 878; while this did not mark the end of the Viking threat to Britain, it did herald the faint glimmer of a new dawn for monasteries in this country. Alfred had used Athelney, an island in the Somerset marshes, as a base and it was on the eastern end of this island that, sometime around 888, he founded a monastery as a thank-offering (Fig. 26). At the same time he ordered the construction of a monastery at Shaftesbury for women; this was built sometime between 880 and 893 and his own daughter, Aethelgifu, was to be the abbess.

Asser, Alfred's biographer, tells us of the founding of these monasteries and of the problems experienced. He says that Alfred

ordered two monasteries to be constructed. One of these was for monks and was located at a place called Athelney . . . In this monastery he gathered monks of various nationalities from every quarter, and assembled them there. The reason is that, at first, he had no noble or free-born man of his own race who would of his own accord undertake the monastic life . . . not surprisingly, since for many years past the desire for the monastic life had been totally lacking in that entire race (and in a good many other peoples as well!), even though quite a number of monasteries which had been built in that area still remain but do not maintain the rule of monastic life in any consistent way.

Alfred ordered the monastery for nuns at

Shaftesbury to be built outside the east gate of the fortified burh, or town, there.

It is clear from this that monastic life was at a low ebb in Wessex and elsewhere by the late ninth century as a result of the constant and intensive disruptions of the Viking raiders. A few monasteries still existed but they amounted to little more than houses for clerks with no monastic regime, discipline

---

26 *Athelney (Somerset). Air photograph from the east showing the raised area of the former island (right) with the site of the monastery founded by Alfred marked by the monument to the right of the farm in the foreground.*

or organization. Not for the first time, revival of the monastic ideal needed to be imported from elsewhere.

Shaftesbury became the most wealthy and important nunnery in the country in the Middle Ages; it was built next to a commercial centre of population on a prominent fortified hill-top on the edge of the chalk downs, where the land falls to the west to the claylands of the former Forest of Selwood and the Blackmore Vale. The monastery must always have been prominent on its hill-top site. Athelney, by contrast, was built right on the edge of the floodable land in the Somerset Levels. William of Malmesbury who visited it in the twelfth century has left us this description:

Athelney is not an island of the sea, but it is so inaccessible on account of bogs and the inundation of the lakes, that it cannot be got to but in a boat . . . the firm land, which is only two acres in breadth contains a little monastery and dwellings for monks . . . Accordingly [Alfred] erected a church, moderate indeed as to size but as to method of construction singular and novel: for four piers, driven into the ground, support the whole fabric, four circular chancels being drawn round it.

Athelney was never as important as Shaftesbury; it was always overshadowed by the more powerful Glastonbury nearby.

What did these monasteries look like in detail? There are no contemporary descriptions and so far no archaeological research has been carried out on the sites to give a detailed picture. It is likely, however, that these two sites were rather differently planned to all those that had gone before. The description by William of Malmesbury above implies that the church of Athelney was rather like the cruciform churches on the continent of Europe and that there were cells around for the monks to live in. A fully developed claustral plan is not implied in William's description but something more like the later medieval sites may nevertheless

have been built. In 816 and 817 synods were held at Aachen, now in northern Germany, at which not only were various monastic reforms carried out in the Carolingian empire, including the universal acceptance of the rule of St Benedict, but also the development of a monastic plan outline, which included a cloister with buildings around it with the religious living, eating and sleeping in common accommodation.

The monastery of St Gall

These ideas were incorporated into the plan for a hypothetical or ideal monastery, now known as the St Gall plan (Fig. 27) after the monastery in Switzerland where the plan is kept. This plan, showing 'all the buildings required for the life and work of an exemplary Carolingian monastery', was probably drawn by Haito, Bishop of Basle (803–23), in the scriptorium of the monastery of Reichenau, of which he was also abbot, at the request of Abbot Gozbert of St Gall (816–36). He intended to reconstruct the monastery there, replacing a 'Celtic' arrangement of buildings with new ones following the latest fashion and arrangements. The plan was to be the guide; it dates to about 820 and demonstrates what was required in a monastery at that time.

The plan shows a cloister with the church (only one church) on the north side; there are ranges for the dormitory, refectory and so on around this cloister, with other ancillary buildings beyond. The whole complex of buildings is surrounded by a precinct enclosed by a wall. Within this there are complexes of farm, estate and industrial buildings as well as gardens, orchards, vineyards and cemeteries, together with accommodation for guests, novices and workers. Although no water supply system or drainage scheme are shown, the layout of the buildings would make the provision of an adequate supply

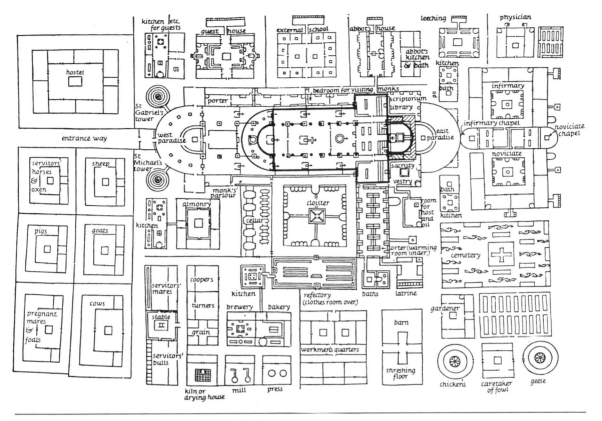

27   *Hypothetical plan of an early ninth-century monastery, St Gall, Switzerland. This plan, redrawn from the original, shows the ranges of buildings thought to be necessary within a monastic precinct at that date. Note the church with the cloister and the surrounding domestic buildings.*

entirely feasible, particularly if the monastery was sited on the north side of a stream or river with the supply of water being brought in from either the east or the west.

When Alfred founded Athelney and Shaftesbury in the late ninth century, and brought in foreign monks and nuns to run the establishments, it would seem highly likely that he would have laid out the new sites using the style which had developed over the previous century on the continent. The same is probably true for the monasteries founded or redeveloped by Dunstan, Oswald and Aethelwold in the mid-tenth century in Wessex and beyond. We can therefore perhaps assume that these

royal foundations incorporated a monastic plan of a cloister with communal buildings around, and that they represented a clear break in tradition from the layout and organization of the monasteries of the pre-Viking era. Developments in the layout of monastic buildings and precincts in the late ninth and tenth centuries provide the models for much that is to follow in later centuries.

The foundation of Cluny

The developments that were to shape monasticism in medieval western Europe originated in Burgundy, Flanders and Lorraine at the beginning of the tenth

the exceptionally able management of its first abbots (Odo 927–42, Majolus 954–94, Odilo 994–1049, Hugh 1049–1109 and Peter the Venerable 1122–56), each of whom ruled for a long period, Cluny prospered, becoming increasingly more powerful, influential and wealthy. Many pre-existing monasteries in France were refounded and other new sites developed. All of these were in some way dependent on Cluny itself and while the concept of a separate 'order' of Cluniac houses did not exist in the tenth and eleventh centuries, Cluny clearly acted as the main 'mother house'. It grew immensely wealthy and by the late eleventh century the monastic church was rebuilt for the third time, on a truly gigantic scale, together with extensive and palatial claustral and guest accommodation. The remains are still remarkable today, while the degree of artistic ostentation displayed in the surviving eleventh- and twelfth-century architectural fragments cannot fail to impress. Unlike much that had gone before, Cluny was laid out on a level lowland site, with carefully planned buildings, and although it was in a rural setting, the first monks do not seem to have been so concerned to achieve the isolation of earlier monasteries. It became a very worldly institution involved in all the high affairs of church and state in western Europe.

Cheddar, Edmund and Dunstan, and the tenth-century monastic reform

Cluny did not have a direct effect on the few monasteries in England in the early tenth century. However, with the re-establishment of monastic life at Glastonbury under Dunstan in 940 we can see the beginning of six hundred years of continuous monastic development, some of which was initially affected by Cluny's daughter house at Fleury, now Saint Benoît sur Loire.

28 *Cluny Abbey (Burgundy, France). This is only one small part, the larger of the two south transepts, that survives of the once vast late eleventh-century abbey which dominated the Church and monasticism in the eleventh and twelfth centuries.*

century, while those of most significance to Britain began in Somerset in the mid-tenth century.

The monastery at Cluny was founded in Burgundy in 909 (Fig. 28). The foundation was made by William of Aquitaine with the blessing of Berno, the abbot of Beaume in the diocese of Besançon. In order to avoid corruption, only too evident in other monasteries of the time, the new abbey was to be independent of all lay control and of the local bishops; it was to be under the direct authority of the Pope. The papacy was, however, weak at this time and so the effect was that Cluny operated as a completely independent institution. Under

The story has been told many times of how monastic life returned to Glastonbury. King Edmund was hunting at Cheddar when his hounds fell over Cheddar Cliff into the Gorge chasing a deer. Just as he was about to follow he relented of his previous harsh treatment of Dunstan, his horse reared up and he was miraculously saved. He returned to the royal palace at Cheddar nearby and granted the site at Glastonbury to Dunstan to carry out the reform of the clergy there and to restore the full monastic regime and the Rule of St Benedict. Clearly there were still buildings at the monastery and the place seems to have been a centre of teaching and scholarship. Excavations over the last half century have provided some indication of the development of the claustral buildings and of the precinct but as they are largely unpublished the details are not at all clear. There was, however, a cloister to the south of the earlier churches and Dunstan developed a larger church to the east of these. This group of buildings and the early cemetery were enclosed within a large ditch and probably also a bank. There may also have been a lay settlement to the west.

Glastonbury under royal patronage collected notable recruits, some of whom had been abroad where they had been influenced by the spirit of reform of Cluny via the site at Fleury; in their turn they colonized old and new monastic sites in southern, central and eastern England. Dunstan is credited with the refoundation of Malmesbury and Bath before he went on to become Archbishop of Canterbury. The prime personalities were Aethelwold, who refounded Abingdon in 954 and made foundations at Ely, Peterborough and Thorney, and Oswald who founded Westbury-on-Trym, near Bristol, and later Ramsey in the Fens and introduced monks into the cathedral at Worcester.

As a result of all this activity, around thirty monasteries were set up in southern England in the three decades following the re-establishment of Glastonbury. These included many of the most famous of the medieval Benedictine monasteries; from Glastonbury were derived not only Abingdon, Malmesbury and Bath, but also, in Wessex, Athelney, as well as Muchelney in Somerset, Cranborne, Horton and Milton in Dorset, and Exeter, Tavistock and Buckfast in Devon. Elsewhere Westminster and Canterbury (both Christchurch and St Augustine's) were refounded. From Abingdon the Midland sites of Pershore, Evesham, Eynsham, Coventry and Burton-on-Trent, the Wessex sites of Abbotsbury, Cerne and Winchester (Old and New Minsters) were founded and refounded, while in the Fens the important group of Ely, Peterborough, St Neots, Crowland, Thorney and Peakirk were all developed. Outliers included Stow in Lincolnshire, St Benet of Hulme in Norfolk and Bury St Edmunds. From Westbury-on-Trym and Ramsey were developed Gloucester, Winchcombe, Deerhurst and St Albans.

There was, however, no familial connection in practice between these monasteries; each was an independent abbey interpreting the rule of St Benedict as it saw fit and there was certainly no concept of an English Benedictine 'order' at this time. With the object of regulating these communities, a great council was held at Winchester under King Edgar in 973 to draw up what was called the 'monastic agreement of monks and nuns of the English nation', now usually known as the '*Regularis Concordia*'. This among other matters established that the Rule of St Benedict would be the only rule to be used in the monasteries. From this time English monasteries experienced their great flowering of artistic and scholastic achievement.

Houses derived from or influenced by –   Glastonbury +   Abingdon ●   Ramsey and Westbury ○

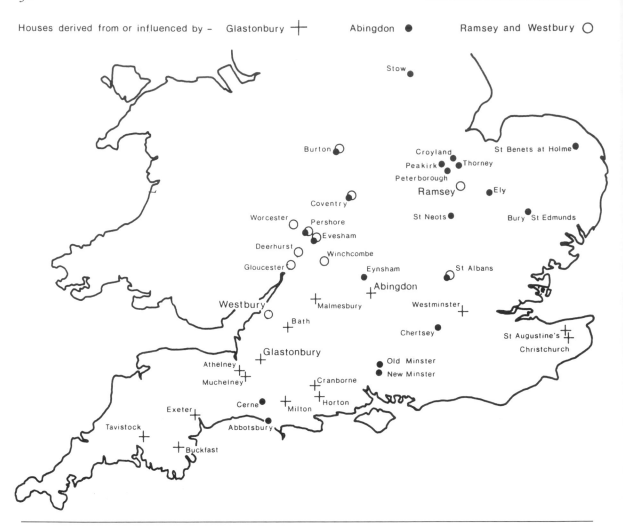

29   *Monasteries founded and refounded as a result of the tenth-century monastic reform based on Glastonbury, Abingdon and Ramsey. With a few additions (such as the nunneries in Wessex) this is the complement of monasteries in England at the time of the Norman Conquest in 1066.*

Tenth-century monasteries

What is known of the sites, buildings, precincts and estates of these tenth-century foundations and refoundations? Many of the sites had been occupied before and were now being redeveloped with new buildings and structures; we assume, though from little information, that the later structures were on the same site as the earlier monasteries and that there was a sequence of

30   *Eynsham Abbey (Oxfordshire). Recent excavations by Graham Keevil and the Oxford Archaeological Unit have revealed fragments of a mid- to late Saxon minster and several domestic buildings of the late Saxon abbey founded in 1005, as well as considerable remains of the medieval abbey's domestic buildings. These excavations can be seen in the context of the extent of the later medieval precincts as worked out by James Bond.*

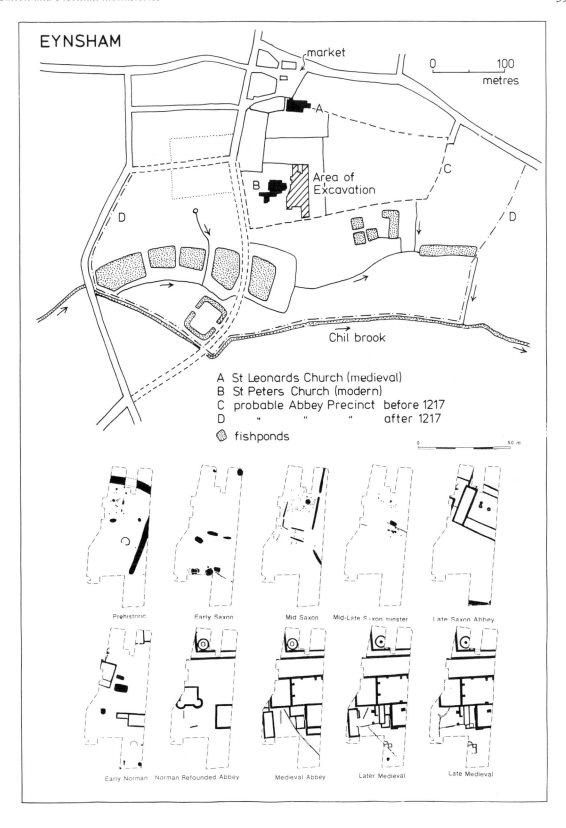

EYNSHAM

market

0   100
metres

A

C

B

Area of
Excavation

D   D

Chil brook

A St Leonards Church (medieval)
B St Peters Church (modern)
C probable Abbey Precinct before 1217
D   "   "   "   after 1217
fishponds

0   50 m

Prehistoric   Early Saxon   Mid Saxon   Mid-Late Saxon minster   Late Saxon Abbey

Early Norman   Norman Refounded Abbey   Medieval Abbey   Later Medieval   Late Medieval use of the same site. Of the new foundations, many sites seem to have been selected on level or gently sloping ground so that the buildings could be laid out to a regulated plan with an adequate water supply provided through the buildings. Tavistock (Devon), founded 975–80, was built on the north side of the river Tavy, while in the same county Buckfast, founded 1018, was built on level land on the west side of the river Dart. Cranborne, founded about 980 in Dorset, was sited in a valley on the south side of the river Crane; in the same county Milton (*c*.933–64) was built in a valley bottom to the west of the Milbourne stream, Horton (*c*.970 and *c*.1050) on an

east-facing slope at the springs of a stream and Abbotsbury (1044) on a flat terrace between two streams, just back from the coast. Other foundations at this time include Ramsey (*c*.969), St Neots (formerly Eynesbury, *c*.974), Burton-on-Trent (1002–4) and Eynsham (1005) (Fig. 30), as well as three of the great Wessex nunneries Romsey (*c*.907 and 967), Amesbury (*c*.979) and Wherwell (*c*.986).

Documentary evidence from this time gives the first indications of that great interest in water management which was to develop into such a characteristic of monastic siting in the twelfth century. James Bond has shown at Abingdon (Fig. 31) that

31 *Abingdon Abbey (Oxfordshire). Map of the site of the abbey showing Aethelwold's mill leat of about 960, together with other watercourses.*

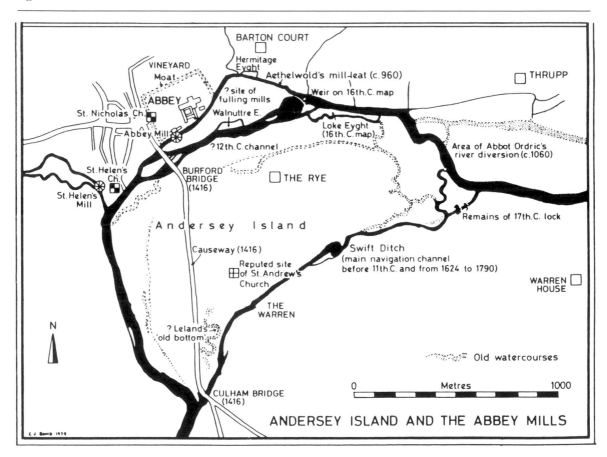

Abbot Aethelwold diverted part of the Thames into a leat for a new mill and had a drainage channel dug from the reredorter (latrines) in about 960. This work involved over a kilometre of ditch digging. Later, in 1060, Abbot Ordric engineered a diversion for part of the river Thames.

Archaeology has so far provided only fleeting glimpses of these late Saxon monasteries. Glastonbury has already been mentioned and at Winchester the extensive series of excavations by Martin Biddle has shown the development of two monasteries, the Old and New Minsters, within the Roman and late Saxon planned city. The claustral buildings of the Old Minster probably lay to the south of the monastic church, which has been excavated, under the west end of the present cathedral, while the New Minster, the site of which was carved out of the holdings of the Old, had its buildings to east and west of the church. To the east was the Nunnaminster. The whole complex was on a cramped site within the property boundaries of the Saxon city. Other work has been done at Abingdon, Eynsham, Romsey and Sherborne. Jarrow has been extensively examined, but this is arguably a special case, as has St Oswald's, Gloucester, where Carolyn Heighway and Richard Bryant have completely excavated the church. But it is probably a fair assessment to say that at no site founded or refounded at this period has the plan of a complete monastery and its precinct been revealed so far.

Monastic estates

Research into the estates which supported these monasteries is now under way. Recently Michael Costen has examined the land belonging to Glastonbury Abbey in the tenth century at the time of Dunstan (Fig. 32). Perhaps contrary to expectations, he has been able to show that only a relatively small part of the eventual endowment had been acquired by about 1000, with the principal estates being centred on Shapwick, Brent and the land around the abbey itself. Very large areas of land were then acquired in the early eleventh century and the rough area of these can be mapped from information in Domesday Book (1086) (Fig. 33). In fact it seems to have been the deliberate policy of some abbots at this time to buy and acquire estates and build up the assets of their monasteries as quickly as possible.

At Ely the *Anglo-Saxon Chronicle* shows that Aethelwold 'bought many villages from the king and made it rich'; he acquired great manors such as Northwold and Stoke as well as small properties of five and seven acres. 'In fact, the later history of the lands of the church of Ely is almost exclusively the history of the assets garnered, with astonishing rapidity, in the two or three generations after 970.' Patrons were already important in the fortunes of monasteries by this date. Brihtnoth, ealdorman of Essex, along with his wife, daughter, son, daughter's daughters, son-in-law and grandson, three generations in all, all gave land; 'a score or more [manors] can be traced back to gifts by this single family'.

During this time a compact estate was built up on the Isle of Ely and in Cambridgeshire and north-west Suffolk. Aethelwine performed the same function as patron to Ramsey Abbey. Many more examples could be given, so that by 1086, using the data from Domesday Book we can see the great extent and immense wealth of the holdings of these late Saxon monasteries. It has been estimated by David Knowles that almost a sixth of the actual revenue of England was in the hands of monastic owners at that date, representing an astonishing area of land and value of property acquired by monasteries in a little over a hundred years.

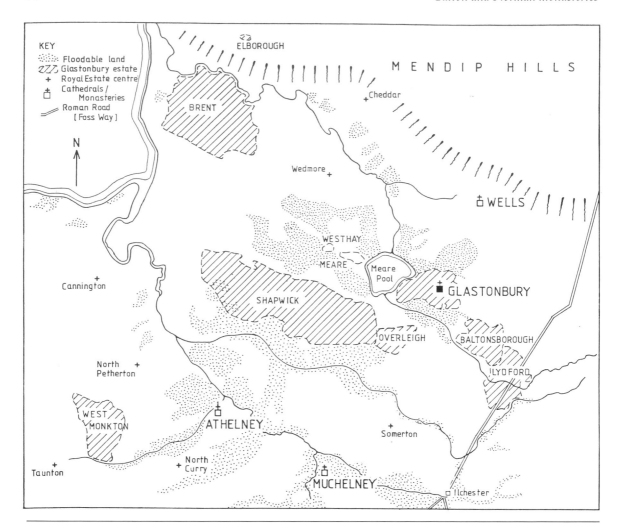

32   *The tenth-century estates of Glastonbury Abbey (Somerset).*

The Norman Conquest and after

These monastic foundations and refoundations of the tenth and eleventh centuries, numbering about sixty in 1066, were to form the basis from which the huge expansion took place from the time of the Norman Conquest onwards. There were probably no more than about a thousand monks and nuns in these houses at the time that William the Conqueror arrived. He, and his contemporaries, rebuilt all of them in the new Norman style, probably on slightly different sites and alignments (partly so that they were orientated more correctly on an east-west alignment and partly so that the old buildings could continue in use until the new ones were ready), as has been shown from the excavations at the cathedrals of Winchester, Exeter and Wells. This building campaign was probably structurally quite unnecessary, as there is no evidence that these buildings were in a dilapidated condition, but it did serve to stamp the mark of the new regime on the country.

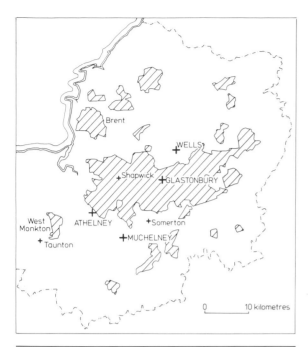

33 *The estates of Glastonbury Abbey at the time of Domesday Book (1086) in Somerset.*

Such was the thoroughness of the Norman builders that, although there is much to see of Romanesque monastic buildings at the sites of these old Saxon abbeys, there is virtually nothing upstanding and little known of pre-Conquest structures, and particularly domestic ranges, at most sites. This means that it is usually impossible to say with any certainty exactly what the pre-Conquest layout was of any particular monastery. The situation is much the same as for the seventh-century foundations already discussed – later rebuilding has totally removed or obscured earlier structures and so little modern archaeological research has been done that we are almost totally ignorant of what tenth-century monasteries looked like. It is impossible to be sure that the layout of later precincts in any way reflects the late Saxon arrangements but it is assumed, perhaps reasonably, that the site of the medieval claustral building is a reflection of the central

parts of the earlier monastery in most cases. With regard to the estates, there is more information if the charters and documents have survived as is sometimes the case, since monasteries were bureaucratic land owners with efficient archives in which records were copied and stored.

Domesday Book and eleventh-century monastic estates

It is with the compilation of Domesday Book in 1086 on the orders of William the Conqueror that, almost for the first time, a clear view of the lands that were held both by the great Benedictine monasteries of this country, and by abbeys in Normandy can be obtained. A certain amount can be gained from Anglo-Saxon land charters, particularly of the tenth century, but the data in Domesday Book are so comprehensive that a much more complete picture can be built up.

It would take a much larger book than this to detail the information contained in Domesday Book about the estates belonging to only a selection of the larger monasteries listed in it. David Knowles has shown that Glastonbury was the richest house with an income of £828, while the median value of the recorded houses is around £100; some of the smaller monasteries, Buckfast, Athelney and Horton for example, had incomes of only around £10. The group of houses in Wessex was the richest, while those in the Midlands were somewhat poorer. The houses in the Fens were also rich, with Ely second only to Glastonbury with an income of £768. Bury (St Edmunds) with £639 and Ramsey with £358 were among the dozen richest.

The disposition of the estates of these monasteries clearly affected their wealth. Those with compact blocks of land, which were both easier to control and to exploit, tended to be the richest – such as Canterbury Cathedral Priory with all its lands in Kent and most between the city and Thanet – whereas those with scattered estates tended to be relatively poorer. Westminster was such a case, with no demesne estate close to the monastery and lands spread over fifteen counties. In this respect it was the precursor to the sort of estate distribution typical of monasteries founded later and stands in great contrast to the compact estates of other monasteries built up so wisely by late Saxon abbots in the previous century.

New Norman monasteries

In the first generation after the Norman Conquest few new monasteries were established. It is as if the Normans were not sure whether they were going to be able to hold the country and were therefore not prepared to invest too much in it. They had

recently refounded at least twenty-five monasteries in Normandy and much of their energy was devoted to making these secure. The Norman barons felt their primary responsibility, therefore, towards their recently-founded monastic houses in their own homeland. There were exceptions of course – notably Battle Abbey founded in 1067, as the result of a vow by William, on the site of the battle and with its high altar on the spot where Harold fell – and others founded before 1100 at Selby (1069–70), Chester (1092–3), Shrewsbury (1083–6) (Fig. 34), Binham (1093), Belvoir (1076–88), Eynsham (refounded 1094–5), Wallingford (1087–9) and Exeter St Nicholas (1087). It is noticeable how many of these were sited in urban centres alongside new castles. Indeed there is a very close relationship in the twelfth and thirteenth centuries between castles, the fortified houses of the wealthiest section of society, and monasteries which become their spiritual support.

34 *Shrewsbury Abbey (Shropshire). One of the new Norman foundations, it was begun by Earl Roger de Montgomery some time between 1083 and 1086 and colonized by monks from Sées in Normandy.*

The other major innovation in this early Norman period was the plantation of Cluniac priories in Britain. Land was granted to Cluny in Burgundy for the foundation of monasteries in England but they were often settled from its dependencies, such as La Charité sur Loire. By 1100 the following had been built – Lewes (1077), Bermondsey (1089), Castle Acre (1089), Montacute (*c.*1078), Much Wenlock (1080–1) and Pontefract (*c.*1090). These were founded by royalty or members of the major baronial families; they were also built frequently in the shadow of major castles and sometimes next to towns. Although some, Lewes and Bermondsey for example, became important and well-respected houses, many of the others were inadequately endowed and had too few monks in them to perform satisfactorily as monasteries. David Knowles comments 'the growth was quite haphazard, depending entirely on the accident of gifts of land, and it was the Cluniac practice to occupy an estate with half a dozen monks or less, who had no stable existence or the power of receiving recruits . . . The sporadic and gradual evolution of the group in England, its isolation from public, national life, and the insignificance of the majority of its houses, prevented it from exerting any noticeable influence, as a group, upon English monastic history.' He says they were a 'loosely knit aggregation of mediocre and half-alien houses, with many of the disadvantages of dependence and few of the advantages of centralisation, a source of weakness rather than of strength to the monastic body, as future centuries were to show.'

Alien priories and cells

Many of the earliest Norman foundations were small Benedictine priories founded from, and dependent on, monasteries back

35 *Chepstow (Gwent, Wales). Founded as an alien priory by 1071 and dependent on Cormeilles near Rouen in Normandy.*

in Normandy or on the new Norman abbeys built soon after the Conquest; others depended on the existing English houses. Some of the new priories were sited in old established towns, while others were built in newly planted and planned towns, founded in the eleventh and early twelfth centuries, particularly in Wales and on the Welsh border. In many cases they were located adjacent to the new Norman castles, planted at the same time and part of the 'package' of new features introduced by the Normans. Others such as Cogges, Minster Lovell and Wilmington were in quite rural situations. Examples of those priories which were dependent on foreign abbeys include:

Abergavenny (1087-1100 – St Vincent, Le Mans), Blyth (1088 – Holy Trinity, Rouen), Chepstow (1071 – Cormeilles) (Fig. 35), Eye

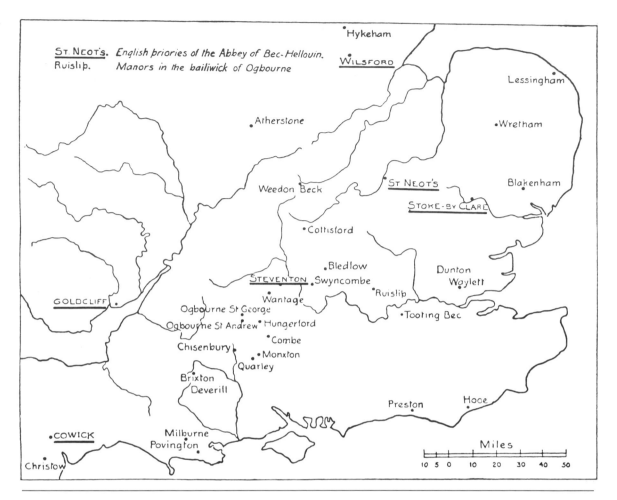

ST. NEOT's. *English priories of the Abbey of Bec-Hellouin.*
Ruislip. *Manors in the bailiwick of Ogbourne*

36 *Alien priories in England belonging to the great abbey of Bec in Normandy and manors all over southern England attached to the abbey's bailiwick of Ogbourne in Wiltshire.*

(c. 1080 – Bernay), Folkestone (1095 – Lonlay), Monmouth (1086 – St Florent, Saumur), Pembroke (1098 – St Martin, Sées), St Neots (1081 – Bec Hellouin), Spalding (1074 – St Nicholas, Angers), Tickford (1100 – Marmoutier) and Tutbury (1080 – St Pierre sur Dives).

Those dependent on English abbeys include:

Brecon (1110 – Battle), Cardiff (by 1106 – Tewkesbury), Cardigan (1110 – Chertsey), Carmarthen (1110 – Battle), Ewenny (1141 – Gloucester), Ewyas Harold (1100 – Gloucester),

Kidwelly (1114 – Sherborne) and Morville (1138 – Shrewsbury).

Rather than found new independent abbeys, the first generation of Norman owners preferred to grant their English estates to monasteries on the other side of the Channel, in Normandy and elsewhere. In their turn these monasteries often sent two or three monks to supervise the running of the estates. They would live together in what was no more than a manor house, often adjacent to the church and with a farm attached. Such establishments – alien cells – could never have been run as proper monastic institutions and must have been seen by local people at the time as merely exploitation by foreign monks. As David Knowles says, 'their appearance must be pronounced one of the most unfortunate by-products of the Conquest in England; . . . they served no religious purpose whatever, and were a source of weakness to the house that owned them.'

Dozens of sites are known but usually there is little to be seen, and there is little significance in the sites originally selected. At some, however, there are 'alien' features: the fine church at Stogursey (Somerset), for example, with its elaborate plan and highly ornate Romanesque carvings looks more like a French church than anything in the contemporary locality. It belonged to Lonlay (now Lonlay L'Abbaye on the borders of Normandy and Maine). On a larger scale the lands of the famous abbey of Bec in Normandy were scattered all across southern England (Fig. 36); some estates have familiar names such as Tooting Bec and Weedon Bec. These dispersed lands were administered from the central estate at Ogbourne St George, near Marlborough (Wiltshire). There are no traces of the alien cell but presumably something like a medieval estate office with warehouses must have existed near the church and the manor.

By 1100 there were around seventy monasteries for men and twelve for women in England and Wales, with eight to ten new houses of canons. In the nearly twenty years of Stephen's reign (1135-53) 120 more houses were founded; by 1175 thirty to forty more houses had been added. Most of these belonged to the newer orders of monks and canons. As in other parts of western Europe, a return to a more ascetic lifestyle closer to the tenets of the Rule of St Benedict proved more attractive to those wishing to enter a monastery and, perhaps more importantly, to those wishing to divert part of their family's inheritance to the founding of a monastic house.

5 The new orders

Around 1105 St Bernard of Tiron and a group of monks from the Benedictine abbey of St Cyprien de Poitiers founded a new monastery in the forest of Savigny, a wild and wooded area on the borders of Normandy and Maine in France; in 1109 they moved to Tiron near Chartres. At St Dogmaels in Dyfed a daughter-house of Tiron was established in 1113–15 by Robert fitz Martin, Lord of Camain, around the earlier church of Llandudoch. In 1124 Stephen, Count of Boulogne and Mortain and later king of England, founded a monastery at Tulketh in the Ribble valley (now the western suburbs of Preston, Lancashire) for monks from Savigny Abbey, another reformed house established in 1112 by St Vitalis also in the forest of Savigny. In 1127 the Tulketh community moved to a better site in the remote vale of Bekanesgill and the great abbey of Furness began.

In the following year the first Cistercian monastery was established at Waverley (Surrey) by William Gifford, bishop of Winchester, but colonized by monks from L'Aumône (le Petit-Cîteaux), north of Blois in France. The abbeys of Tintern, Rievaulx and Fountains began soon afterwards. In time there would be over seventy Cistercian monasteries in England, Wales and Scotland and they were only one part of a mass movement of 'new orders' which originated in France but spread all over Europe in the twelfth century.

In western Europe in the tenth and eleventh centuries religious feelings were changing and the foundations just described reflect this. There was widespread dissatisfaction with the existing situation in Benedictine and Cluniac monasteries, together with a yearning to return to the ideals of the 'desert fathers'. The relatively comfortable life in the average Benedictine monastery, with its well-fed, well-housed religious community, fully involved in elaborate liturgy at the monastery and equally integrated into the feudal agrarian system on their estates, was increasingly seen by some to be anathema to the monastic ideal and strict observance of the Rule of St Benedict; a return to the 'desert' was seen to be essential by many. It was difficult to find the sandy and stony wastes of the deserts of Egypt, Palestine and Syria in northern Europe and so the isolation provided by mountains, forests, marshes and wastes was sought out as a suitable alternative.

The beginnings of this movement can be detected in northern Italy with the foundation of the monasteries at Camaldoli in 1015 (by St Romuald of Ravenna, c.950–1027) and Vallombrosa in 1039 (by St John Gualbert of Florence, c.990–1073). At each of these the founders tried to emulate the lives of the early hermits in the desert, in the case of Camaldoli with each monk living in his own cell separated from the others by gardens and open space. A completely new group of illiterate monks – the lay brothers – was also recruited to provide the manual

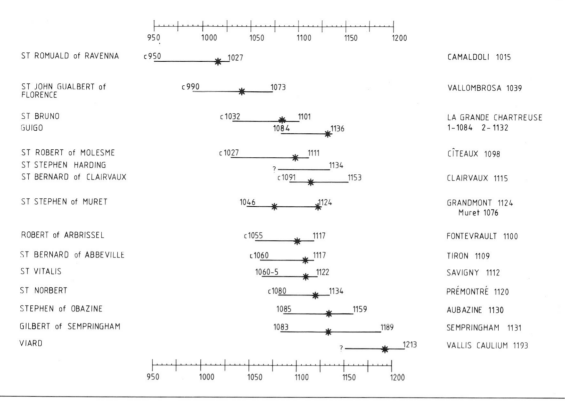

37 *The New Orders developed in the twelfth century, their founders and the 'mother' houses.*

labour for the monastery, not only so that the rest of the monks could be physically separate from the world but also so that they need not be tenurially linked with lay communities. Manual work for all the monks was reaffirmed and officials were appointed to act as intermediaries with the outside world.

The Carthusians

The idea of hermits living together in a monastery was most successfully developed in western Europe with the establishment of La Grande Chartreuse in the French Alps by St Bruno (*c.*1032–1101) in 1084 (Fig. 38). Following considerable wanderings by Bruno and his companions in the forests and marshes of eastern France, Bishop Hugh of Grenoble suggested that the inhospitable and inaccessible limestone massif of the Chartreuse, north of the city, might provide the sort of isolation from the world that they were looking for. There, they built a chapel next to a spring and established their cells and a church. Some way below this was established a lower house, or 'correrie', for their lay brothers. The scenery here is still magnificent, with almost sheer limestone cliffs surrounding the steep valley with limited areas of pasture but extensive tracts of pine forest. It must have seemed a remote and desolate wilderness to these early monks and its solitude and peacefulness are still impressive.

There does not seem to have been any intention on the part of Bruno to establish an

38　*La Grande Chartreuse in the French Alps near Grenoble. This is the mother house of the Carthusians. The small houses or 'cells' for each monk can be seen on the left together with the church and communal buildings to the right.*

'order' or any other similar monasteries; indeed he was called away to Italy by the pope shortly after La Grande Chartreuse was founded. It was not until the time of the fifth prior, Guigues (1083–1136), that a group of further houses was founded in the alpine area, and the ideas of the earliest houses were drawn up into some sort of rule – the '*Coutumes de Chartreuse*'; with this, the distinctive character of this group of monasteries came to be recognized as a special and separate order. By that time the original chartreuse had been destroyed in an avalanche (1132) and the present monastery begun on a lower site by Guigues.

At La Grande Chartreuse, and the other early sites, the layout of Carthusian monasteries was established and this has remained basically the same for nine hundred years; generally remote, isolated, upland sites were sought out in the early centuries. The early (pre-1132) site at La Grande Chartreuse was described by two visitors and it is clear that already a large

cloister surrounded by cells and gardens with small communal buildings of church, chapter house and refectory had emerged as the distinctive Carthusian plan. Water from the spring was conducted around the cells in a channel. Each cell had a small garden in which vegetables could be grown and, as well as this manual work, each monk was expected to have a trade which would be of use to the monastery as a whole and which could be carried out in a workshop under his cell. Below the main monastery for the monks or fathers, the lower house for the lay brothers had the farm buildings and guest accommodation. From here the upland pastures were worked and the firewood for fuel collected.

The Carthusians arrived in Britain in the 1170s. As part of the penance of Henry II for the murder of Thomas Becket in 1170, Witham (Somerset) was established as the first charterhouse (a corruption of 'chartreuse'). It was sited in the Royal Forest of Selwood but there was nevertheless a large lay population on the land selected and a number of difficulties had to be overcome before the community could be established. It was only with the arrival of the able and energetic Hugh of Avalon, later Bishop of Lincoln, that a successful foundation could be made. The house was endowed with land in the Forest, on which a number of granges, or outlying farms, were eventually established; an extensive tract of land on the top of the Mendips became a sheep ranch at Charterhouse on Mendip. The lower house for the lay brothers was about a mile from the main monastery up the valley of the river Frome at Witham Friary, a name which refers to the brothers (frères) and which has nothing to do with any later friars.

It is noticeable that a royal patron was involved in bringing this order to England, as with the Savigny group at Furness, while one of the most important bishops (Winchester) introduced the Cistercians. It is also remarkable that, even in the twelfth century in a large forested area like Selwood, the isolation sought by such monks had to be created by the eviction and resettlement of lay people, indicating perhaps that the landscape even in wooded areas was already fully utilized by that date, an observation that will also be made in connection with the foundation of many Cistercian houses.

The second Carthusian house, originally established on the Cotswolds at Hatherop in 1222 by William Longspée, illegitimate son of Henry II, was moved by his widow Ela, Countess of Salisbury, into the seclusion of her park at Hinton near Bath in the period 1227–32 (Fig. 39). Again, it is noticeable how the patron was from the highest level in contemporary society and that this interest was vital in the establishment of the house. The isolation required was only achieved in this case by the use of the private hunting preserve of the family at Hinton. The lower house was built, again about a mile away, at the small hamlet of Friary.

No other Carthusian monasteries were

---

39 *Hinton Charterhouse, near Bath (Avon). A plan of 1785 shows the site of the charterhouse, founded in a medieval park, together with the 'correrie' or lower house for the lay brothers a mile away at Friary. Inserted is the plan of the charterhouse with the cells and cloister as recovered from excavation.*

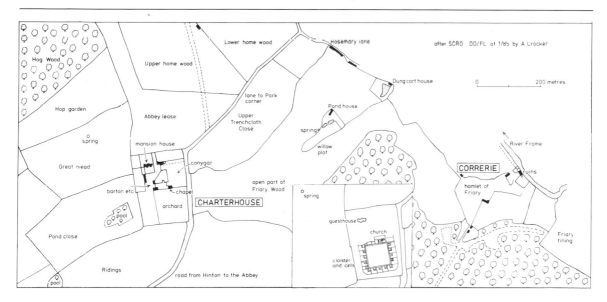

established for over a hundred years. Then Beauvale (Nottinghamshire) was built in 1343, again in a park, by Nicholas Cantilupe, a local lord. There may have been a 'correrie' here as well but this is not certain. Many of the later houses of the order, however, were built in suburban situations, such as Perth, Coventry, Hull and London, and all had their lay brothers' and servants' accommodation around separate courts adjacent to the main cloister. The plans of these later houses are best exemplified by Mount Grace in Yorkshire.

An even more austere group than the Carthusians was that of the Grandmontines, founded by St Stephen of Muret (1046–1124) at Muret near Limoges in 1076 and moved in 1124 to Grandmont nearby. While the Carthusians lived singly in cells and led a very isolated existence they were nevertheless well fed, well clothed and well housed. The Grandmontines lived as hermits, communally in a miniature claustral monastery, but in abject poverty. Again lay brothers looked after the daily affairs of the monastery. There were only ever three of their houses in Britain. The first was founded in about 1204 at Grosmont (Yorkshire) though there is now no trace of it. At Alberbury (Shropshire) there are substantial remains of a Grandmontine priory which began as an Augustinian house for canons (see Figs. 64 and 65). Earthworks, air photographs and an early map enable us to reconstruct the site there.

It is at Craswall (Herefordshire) (Fig. 40), however, that the best impression can be gained of one of these small, poverty-stricken monasteries. There, in a deep valley of the Black Mountains above Hay-on-Wye, are the substantial remains of the small priory founded about 1225 by Walter de Lacy, one of the powerful lords of the Welsh Marches. To visit this isolated house in deep snow in February gives a very good impression of the sort of life that was sought out by these new monks of the early Middle Ages.

The Cistercians

If the Carthusians and the Grandmontines were the most severe of the new orders and the earliest to develop, it was another group which was to have the greatest impact both in Britain and Europe in the twelfth century – the Cistercians. Robert of Molesme (c. 1027–1111) had been a Benedictine abbot but finding the life not austere enough he retreated with some followers into the forests and marshes of Burgundy. Here in 1098 was founded Cîteaux, a community which followed the Rule of St Benedict more strictly than the contemporary Benedictine and Cluniac houses. Manual labour was reinstated as an important part of the monks' day and lay brothers were taken on to work the estates and outlying land. An Englishman, Stephen Harding from Sherborne Abbey in Dorset, was among the early group of monks at Cîteaux and it was he who compiled the 'rule' for what became the Cistercian order when he wrote the 'Carta Caritatis', the 'charter of charity'.

Again, it does not seem to have been the intention of Robert to found a new order, merely to live in isolation from the world and follow the Rule of St Benedict more closely. It was not until the early twelfth century, and particularly after the arrival of Bernard of Fontaines, later of Clairvaux (1091–1153) in 1113, that a number of 'daughter' houses were established and a separate order began to develop. During the first half of the twelfth century, up to the time of Bernard's death in 1153 and before the unsuccessful attempt by the order in 1154 to prevent further foundations, over 330 monasteries had been founded all over Europe.

Under Bernard's influence a rigorous and austere regime was established and this was sustained very largely by the institution of an annual General Chapter meeting held at Cîteaux of all the abbots of all the houses; other orders later adopted the same idea.

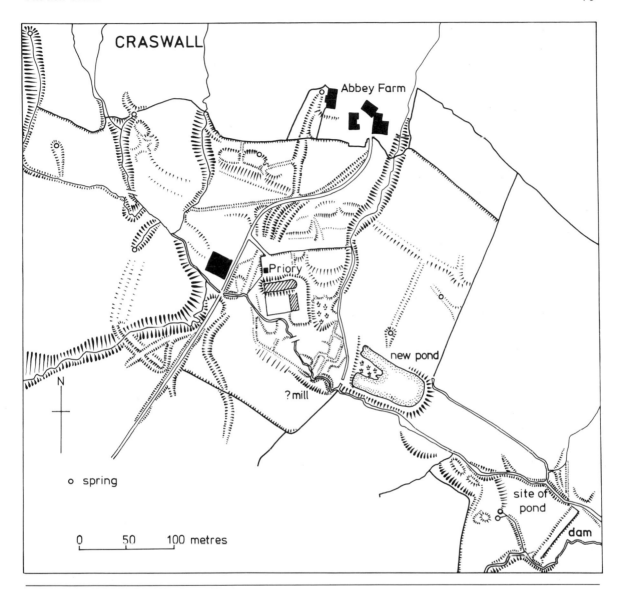

40 *Craswall Priory (Herefordshire). Plan of the earthworks around the surviving medieval buildings of the small Grandmontine priory founded in the early thirteenth century.*

There was to be none of the finery in architecture, fittings, services, clothing and diet enjoyed by the Benedictine and Cluniac monasteries and even the plans of the buildings and layout of the precincts were to be subject to standardized regulation. Bernard made the position of the Cistercians clear in his famous letter of 1125 to Abbot William of St Thierry:

I marvel how monks could grow accustomed to such intemperance in eating and drinking, clothing and bedding, riding abroad and building, that, wheresoever these things are wrought most busily and with most pleasure and expense, there Religion is thought to be best kept. For behold! spare living is taken for covetousness, sobriety for austerity, silence for melancholy; while, on the other hand, men rebaptize laxity as 'discretion', waste as 'liberality', garrulousness as 'affability', giggling as 'jollity', effeminacy in clothing and bedding as 'neatness'. Who, in those first days when the monastic Order began, would have believed that monks would ever come to such sloth? . . . But these are small things; I will pass on to matters greater in themselves, yet seeming smaller because they are more usual. I say naught of the vast height of your churches, their immoderate length, their superfluous breadth, the costly polishings, the curious carvings and paintings which attract the worshipper's gaze and hinder his attention . . .

The church is resplendent in her walls, beggarly in her poor; she clothes her stones in gold, and leaves her sons naked; the rich man's eye is fed at the expense of the indigent. . . . In short, so many and so marvellous are the varieties of divers shapes on every hand, that we are more tempted to read in the marble than in our books, and to spend the whole day in wondering at these things rather than in meditating the law of God. For God's sake, if men are not ashamed of these follies, why at least do they not shrink from the expense?

With armies of lay brothers and the accent on manual labour, isolated Cistercian monasteries could begin to tame their surroundings, clearing woodland and scrub, draining marshes and building canals, mills and fishponds. Even though such activities by Cistercians may have been over-emphasized by researchers in the past, and such landscape changes were in any case widespread by the twelfth century, it was nevertheless a major aspect of early Cistercian monasteries to modify dramatically the landscape in which they were built.

   Much has been written about the impact of the Cistercian settlement on Britain. Following the establishment of Waverley in 1128 the next houses to be founded were Tintern (1131) (see Fig. 6), Fountains (1132)

(see Fig. 58) and Rievaulx (1132) (see Figs. 46 and 58), three of the most magnificiently preserved abbeys to be seen anywhere in Europe. Tintern was founded direct from L'Aumône by Walter fitz Richard de Clare and was endowed with lands in Gwent and beyond. Rievaulx was founded directly from Clairvaux by Walter Espec and held lands in much of upland Yorkshire. Fountains, mirroring the development of many houses of the new orders, was founded by disaffected monks from the Benedictine abbey of St Mary's, York who applied directly to St Bernard to become part of the Cistercian order. It, too, had extensive lands in upland Yorkshire.

   The year 1147 was an '*annus mirabilis*' for the Cistercians in which a large number of new monasteries were founded. In Britain this included:

Abbey Dore (Herefordshire; from Morimond in France) (see Fig. 104); Barnoldswick in the Pennines which later moved to Kirkstall outside Leeds (Yorkshire) (see Fig. 58); Biddlesden (Buckinghamshire); Bruern (Oxfordshire); Bytham (Lincolnshire) which later moved to Vaudey; Margam in Glamorgan; Roche (Yorkshire); and Sawtry (Cambridgeshire) (Fig. 87).

In the same year all the monasteries that had been attached to Savigny joined the Cistercian order. In Britain this mean that the following abbeys were henceforth part of the Cistercian group:

Basingwerk (1132), Buckfast (1136), Byland, after several moves, Calder (1142), Coggeshall (1140), Combermere (1133), Furness (1127) the most important of the group, Neath (1130), Quarr (1132), Stratford (1135), and Swineshead (1135).

Altogether by the time of Bernard's death in 1153 there were something like 43 Cistercian monasteries in England, six in Wales and four in Scotland. What does this explosion of Cistercian monasticism tell us about the

landscape at the time and what was the effect of so many new monasteries being founded in such a short period?

Firstly there were already groups of hermits living in the wilder parts of Britain in the early twelfth century and this may have been the case for a hundred years before; it would seem that the same feelings that had given rise to the new orders were evident in Britain too. At Revesby (Lincolnshire) (see Fig. 43) for example, 'the actual choice of location may have been influenced by the fact that . . . it was at that time (1143) a hermitage, and it may have been hoped that the occupants of the site would join the Cistercian community'. Elsewhere the Cistercian monasteries of Kirkstead and Kirkstall and the Augustinian houses of Bicknacre, Bridlington, Bushmead, Calwich, Charley, Felley, Healaugh, Llanthony (see Fig. 66), Nostell, Poughley and Ulverscroft (see Fig. 68) were also established on the sites of hermitages.

At other sites the account of the foundation often describes, rather fancifully,

41 *Cistercian lay brothers felling a tree and splitting wood in the early twelfth century.*

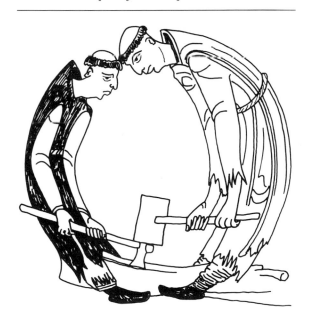

how the first monks lived in hovels under branches and cliffs, living on berries and braving the rigours of the winter weather until the monastic buildings could be built. In most cases this must indicate the desire of the original religious (or more likely their later chroniclers) to appear to be like the 'desert fathers' in the poverty of their material state in contrast to their spiritual wealth and reflects the 'horrible places' 'far from human habitation' referring to deserts in the Bible. At Fountains, for example, we are told that the place settled was 'uninhabited for all the centuries back, thick set with thorns, and fit rather to be the lair of wild beasts than the home of human beings'.

Founders and patrons

It is quite clear now that there were close connections between the founders of the earliest Cistercian houses. There seems to have been something of a fashion for founding abbeys among the greatest families, with some of them equally active in the foundation of houses of the other new orders. The crown, in the reigns of Stephen (1135–54), Henry II (1154–89), John (1199–1216) and Henry III (1216–72), together with their retainers and officials, was involved in the foundation of many sites.

The same is true in Wales where the Welsh princes were active in the establishment of Cistercian houses. This was part of a general pattern in which the foundation of monasteries was an important aspect of dynastic development. As Susan Wood shows, 'out of 425 monastic houses (excluding cathedral priories) whose patrons have been found for a substantial part of the thirteenth century, 106 were of royal patronage, including most of the greatest'; at least 27 houses had bishops as patrons, 89 earls or their widows and 203 houses were in the advowson of 148 barons and country gentlemen.

It has already been noted that Stephen introduced monks to Tulketh, and he was also responsible for founding Coggeshall (Essex; 1140) and Red Moor (Staffordshire; 1135). In 1136 he had given the abandoned abbey site at Buckfast (Devon) to found a new monastery. Bordesley (Worcestershire) was founded in 1136 on land given by Queen Matilda, daughter of Henry I. Stanley (Wiltshire) was founded first at Loxwell by Empress Matilda and her chamberlain Drogo (1151) and then later moved by her son Henry II to the site near Calne (1154). Henry II also allowed the monks of Red Moor to move to a new site at Stoneleigh (Warwickshire; 1155). John founded Beaulieu (Hampshire) in 1204. His first son, Henry III, established Netley (Hampshire) in 1239 and his second son Richard, Earl of Cornwall, founded Hailes (Gloucestershire) in 1246. Holmcultram (Cumberland) was started in 1150 by Henry, son of King David I of Scotland and Vale Royal (Cheshire) was moved from Darnhall by Edward I in 1281.

Even more remarkable are the connections between the major baronial families of the time. The founders of these early Cistercian monasteries all shared the fact that they were frequent visitors to the royal court. As a place where members of the higher ranks of the clergy and of the lay baronage could meet, the court was an important forum for the exchange of ideas.

Walter Espec, for example, not only founded Rievaulx (1132) but also Warden Abbey (1136). He had previously founded Kirkham, an Augustinian priory (1122). Several members of the Beaumont family founded Cistercian monasteries. Robert 'le Bossu' founded Garendon (Leicestershire; 1133), his twin brother Waleran founding Bordesley, as a daughter-house of Garendon, in Worcestershire in 1138 when he became Earl of Leicester. The steward of Robert 'le Bossu', Ernald de Bosco, founded Biddlesden from Garendon in 1147.

The earliest Cistercian abbey sites

Many of the sites given to the early
Cistercians were on poor quality land and
the founders, in fact, were giving little
away. That the Cistercians would have
preferred better quality land is shown by the
foundation of Meaux Abbey (Yorkshire)
(Fig. 42 and see also Fig. 83). This was
founded in 1151 by William, Count of
Aumale and Earl of York, a powerful
northern magnate who had already founded
Vaudey Abbey (1149). He had made a vow
to go on a pilgrimage but his age and obesity
meant that this was impossible and so
Adam, a builder monk of Fountains
involved in the construction of Vaudey,
suggested that the foundation of another
abbey would be a suitable compensation.
The fourteenth-century chronicle of Meaux
Abbey gives an unusually vivid description
of the selection of the site for the monastery.
Adam and the earl made a tour of the earl's
estates with the purpose of selecting a site:
Adam had evidently been given a free hand
for he chose the spot which Aumale had
recently purchased for a deer park. Adam
would not hear of choosing another piece of
land despite the earl's pleas. In the end
Aumale gave in and granted lands for the
support of the community as well as
temporary accommodation for the monks.

Many of the sites granted were in or near
Royal Forests or other tracts of woodland
but in many cases this land was not
untamed, wild woodland but already in use
by groups of peasants. In a number of cases,
and it may be more than are documented,
the monks were not averse to evicting
peasants to create the solitude they desired
and as Robin Donkin remarks, they 'quickly
acquired an unenviable reputation as
depopulators'. There are authenticated cases
at Old Byland (Yorkshire), depopulated and
later refounded as a planned village with a
green, and at Meaux. At Barnoldswick, the
original site of Kirkstall Abbey, the

42 *Meaux Abbey (Humberside). Air photograph
from the north of the earthworks of the Cistercian
abbey founded by William, Count of Aumale, on the
advice of Adam, a monk, in 1151 on a site intended for
a deer park. The site of the church and other robbed out
claustral buildings can be seen in the centre surrounded
by extensive areas of earthworks.*

inhabitants of East and West Marton,
Bracewell and Stock were evicted and the
church of Barnoldswick pulled down.
Elsewhere there was depopulation of
Musden by Croxden Abbey, Rushton by
Hulton Abbey, Yanley by Combermere,
Sellergarth by Furness and at Pipewell
(Northamptonshire), Rufford
(Nottinghamshire – in Sherwood Forest),
and Combe and Stoneleigh (Warwickshire –
in the Forest of Arden). In Wales,
Langewydd was depopulated by Margam
Abbey, the church was demolished and the
site converted into a grange. At Revesby
(Fig. 43) the villages of Revesbia, Thoresbi
and Schictlesbia were depopulated; the Earl
of Lincoln, the founder of the abbey, offered
the villagers fresh land or their freedom –
seven accepted the former but 31 the latter.

It is easy to overemphasize the
depopulating activities of the early
Cistercians. In some cases it is clear that
people were moved to new settlements, as at
Old Byland, while elsewhere peasants
would have been needed to supplement the

43 *Revesby Abbey (Lincolnshire). Air photograph of the earthworks of the abbey site. A village was removed and peasants relocated when this monastery was founded in 1143.*

work of lay brothers at the granges. When Rufford Abbey was founded, the settlements of Rufford, Cratley and Winkerfield were destroyed but the new village of Wellow came into existence. When the community that had been at Red Moor, and which was to go to Stoneleigh, settled briefly at Cryfield the inhabitants were moved to Hurst.

Nevertheless, what is clear is that it was difficult to find empty unused spaces in the twelfth century, especially in southern England, even in the wooded areas. The land may have been poorer in quality in some areas but someone was usually trying to extract a living from it before the monks arrived. This was not the case over much of Europe and may have been less true in Wales and the North, where colonization by Cistercians could result in the trans-formation of the landscape. Nevertheless, even in Yorkshire many of the granges and farms established by Cistercians were either former villages which had been deserted or depopulated, or villages which had been downgraded to farms.

Site moves

Another aspect of interest connected with these early Cistercian monasteries is the number of times they moved sites. This occurred in other orders as well but not on such a prodigious scale. Robin Donkin has identified thirty or more communities which moved for one reason or another. Sometimes these were minor, rather like Clairvaux Abbey in Burgundy moving a little down the valley, but elsewhere the moves were drastic – Byland Abbey had formerly been at Calder, Hood, Old Byland and Stocking before finally settling. Numerous reasons are possible for the moves, including a better water supply (Kingswood, Bindon, Beaulieu, Strata Florida), unsatisfactory climatic conditions (Kirkstall, Salley, Jervaulx, Croxden, Stoneleigh), restricted original site (Loxwell to Stanley) and flooding of original site (Louth Park, Thame, Whalley, Furness, Vaudey).

Changes in the landscape

The combination of the Cistercians' preference for isolated areas so that they could be 'the world forgetting, by the world forgot' and their attention to manual labour, means that landscapes in which they settled could be radically transformed over a few decades. The employment of large numbers of lay brothers and labourers based on the granges, a system they invented, meant that the Cistercians had the means for transforming landscapes quite dramatically. They not only had a large, highly motivated, directly employed, labour force but wherever possible they tried to distance themselves from peasant farming and the common field system. This was not always possible but where land could be worked directly from a grange, great efficiency of organization and production could be

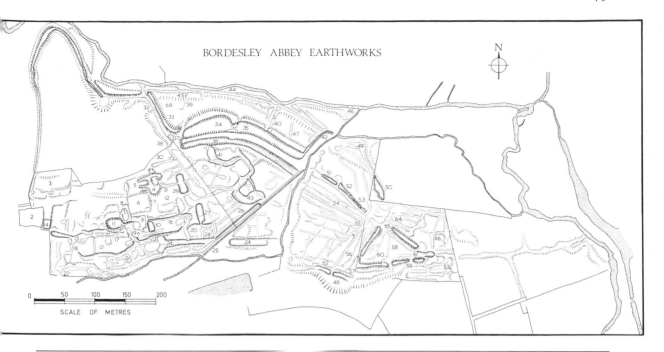

44 *Bordesley Abbey (Worcestershire). Plan of the earthworks. The site of the church and the claustral buildings can be seen to the left (west) (4–9), while further east can be seen fishponds (34–6), water meadows (54), a mill pond (58) and mill site (61).*

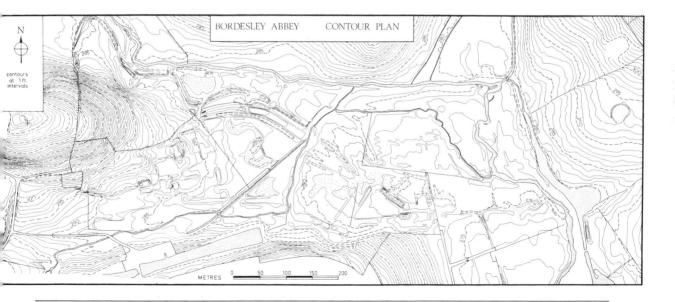

45 *Bordesley Abbey (Worcestershire). Plan of the contours. This shows the former course of the river Arrow (stippled) together with the new, straighter, course to the north on the valley side; this is carried across the side valley on an embankment.*

achieved. Knowledge of engineering skills in building and water control, together with the means to use it, resulted in major landscape changes.

At Bordesley Abbey (Worcestershire) (Figs 44 and 45), for example, the valley of the river Arrow was transformed some time in the twelfth century. Earthworks and detailed contour maps show that the river formerly meandered across the meadows below the abbey site. At some time the river was shifted, not only into a straighter course but also into an embanked channel on the valley side. The drained valley bottom was utilized for the construction of a mill with its pond (excavated by Grenville Astill), together with fishponds and a system of waterleats. None of this appears to be documented but the evidence is clear on the ground.

A well-documented scheme can be seen at Rievaulx (Yorkshire) (Fig. 46). There the abbey was founded on a narrow terrace on the east side of the river Rye above Helmsley. Canals were constructed to north and south of the abbey and the course of the river Rye diverted in several places. This elaborate engineering scheme may have been carried out to bring in stone during the long building campaign in the twelfth century. Alternatively it may reflect leat construction to a number of mills associated with a series of grants and exchanges of land, one with the neighbouring abbey of Byland, which enabled Rievaulx to acquire land on the west side of the valley, redirect the river in several places and thereby extend the precinct westwards.

Not far away, the drainage pattern around Byland Abbey (Fig. 47) was dramatically changed in an elaborate scheme carried out in collaboration with the neighbouring Augustinian priory of Newburgh. The Holbeck stream was diverted from its eastward-flowing course to feed the precinct of the abbey. To the south of the abbey two of the headwater streams of the Thorpe

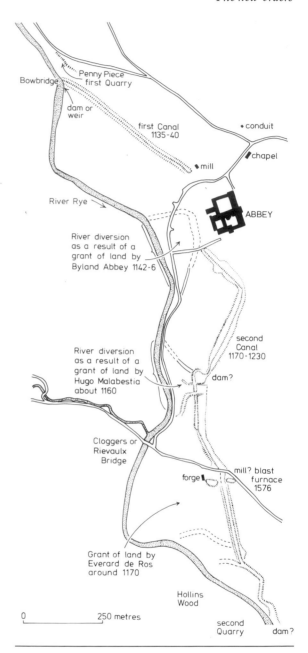

46 *Rievaulx Abbey (Yorkshire). Map of the Rye valley showing the canals built and the river diversions carried out by the monks in the twelfth century (largely after Weatherill's research).*

Beck, which also flowed eastwards, were diverted into a stream and a long canal, called Long Beck, running south-

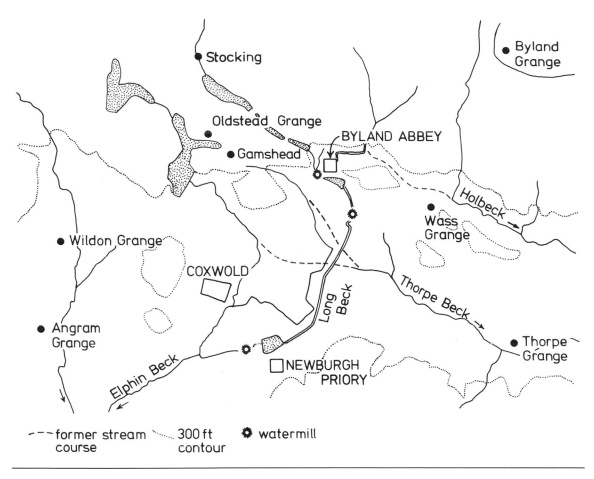

47 *Byland Abbey (Yorkshire). Plan of the water scheme engineered by Byland Abbey and Newburgh Priory whereby numerous streams were diverted and a new canal, the Long Beck, was created to drain the area and drive mills (largely after John McDonnell).*

westwards. Water from the precinct which had been used to drive two mills fed into this and the resulting flow fed a pond and a mill at Newburgh Priory. The scheme turned the whole local drainage pattern round from east flowing to south-west flowing, drained several square miles between the two monasteries and canalized some 3 to 4km (2 miles) of streams.

Many more examples could be cited since almost every Cistercian foundation demonstrates something of the same skills and similar impact on the landscape. More is known about the effect of the Cistercians on

the landscape because so much research has been carried out on their schemes, but it should not be forgotten that monasteries of other orders were involved in the same sort of activities.

The military orders

The Knights Templar and the Knights Hospitaller (see Fig. 71) were groups of fighting monks formed to protect the holy places in Palestine and the pilgrims making the long journey from western Europe to

visit them. The Templars were established
in 1118 in Jerusalem and in 1128 they
adopted a rule similar to the Cistercians,
written with St Bernard's help. They came
to Britain in 1128 when the London Temple
was established as their main house. The
order was suppressed by the pope in 1312
and most of the lands and preceptories were
passed to the Hospitallers. These began with
the establishment of the Hospital of St John
in Jerusalem in the early twelfth century,
while later they provided armed escorts to
protect pilgrims journeying to the Holy
Land. They were introduced into England in
about 1144 with the first house being
established at Clerkenwell outside the walls
of London.

Their establishments, preceptories and
commanderies, were similar to
contemporary manor houses and served as
collecting centres for the goods and revenues
produced by the estates which had been
granted to the knights. Their impact on their
local landscapes was slight in most cases, the
land being worked by peasants to produce
rents and goods for sale, and little remains of
their buildings. For the Templars the
element 'temple' has survived in many
place-names indicating where they had
preceptories or land – Temple Cloud
(Somerset), Temple Bruer (Lincolnshire)
and Temple Guiting (Gloucestershire).

The canons

While we may be impressed by the
reforming zeal of orders such as the
Carthusians, Grandmontines and
Cistercians, and marvel at the ruins and
engineering abilities displayed, particularly
at the sites of the last, their monasteries by
no means formed the bulk of the new houses
established in the post-Conquest period; that
numerical supremacy belongs to the orders
of the canons. Their origins are more
obscure than the orders discussed so far but
separate groups can be recognized at a

number of monasteries in France from the
late eleventh century at such sites as, for
example, St Ruf near Avignon. They were
by definition priests, unlike many monks,
following the Rule of St Augustine (of
Hippo) and they spent some time in the
community looking after the spiritual well-
being of lay people. For this reason many
houses of canons, particularly those of the
Augustinians, were seen as an ideal choice to
continue the role of the clergy in the old
pre-Conquest minster churches. Others
resembled certain orders of monks in their
austere lifestyle, such as the
Premonstratensian canons; yet others
continued the hermit tradition. There were
also several orders of canonesses.

The largest group by far were the
Augustinian canons, who were established
first at Colchester (by 1106) then at Holy
Trinity, Aldgate, London (1107–8) and
Huntingdon (1108). Other houses followed
at Merton (1114–17) and at Llanthony (after
1108) (see Fig. 66), together with an
important group in the north – Bridlington
(1113), Guisborough (1119), Embsay (1120)
the forerunner of Bolton Priory, Nostell (by
1121) and Kirkham (about 1122). By 1135
there were some forty-six Augustinian
houses in England and Wales on a variety of
sites from urban and suburban to isolated
rural retreats. Altogether over two hundred
of their priories were founded together with
a handful of wealthy and influential abbeys
such as Cirencester, Leicester, Waltham and
Northampton. Almost every part of the
country has at least one Augustinian house,
although they are most closely settled in
East Anglia and the Midlands.

Within their ranks were several
important, virtually separate, sub-orders.
These include the Victorines (founded at St
Victor in Paris) with houses at Wigmore and
Wormsley (Herefordshire), St Augustine's
Bristol, Keynsham, Woodspring (Fig. 48)
and Stavordale (Somerset); the Arrouasians
(founded at the abbey of St Nicholas,

48   *Woodspring Priory (Avon). A small Augustinian house of the Victorine group. Part of the church and a large barn remain; the site may have begun as a hermitage.*

Arrouaise near Bapaume in northern France) had houses at Dorchester on Thames (Oxfordshire), Hartland (Devon), Lilleshall (Shropshire), Notley and Missenden (Buckinghamshire), Lesnes (Kent) and Owston (Leicestershire); a third group, the canons of the Holy Sepulchre, had a few houses – at Warwick and Thelsford (Warwickshire), Caldwell (Bedfordshire), Thetford (Norfolk) and Newstead near Stamford (Lincolnshire). The Arrouaisian houses were meant to be self-sufficient and were often in isolated situations, as were some of the Victorine houses.

The Premonstratensians were founded by St Norbert at Prémontré near Laon in northern France, and were closely related to the Cistercians in their lifestyle and choice of isolated sites for their houses. The earliest was founded at Newsham (Lincolnshire; 1143), where there was a concentration of Premonstratensian houses.

The only English order, the Gilbertines, founded by Gilbert of Sempringham also in Lincolnshire, returned to the double houses of men and women which had existed in Anglo-Saxon England, although most houses had only men. Double houses include Alvingham, Bullington, Catley, Haverholme, Sixhills and Tunstall, all in the founder's home county of Lincolnshire (Fig. 49).

Patronage

The foundation of many of these houses of canons seems to have been random, depending on the interest of the founder and the patrons' family and connections, and one patron might found houses of several different orders. Fashion influenced some patrons while some sort of contact with, or affection and admiration for, a particular order seems likely with others, as well as a need to demonstrate clearly the ability and willingness to found monasteries. Status and prestige are certainly of importance but the site selected and the estates donated or sold to the monastery, and hence making up its endowment, depended on the disposition of the lands of the founder, which were themselves probably randomly acquired. As with the other new orders, the patronage of particular kings (especially Henry I) and their court officials was particularly important.

Much of this is demonstrated by the monasteries founded by William Marshall (?–1219). Rising from virtual obscurity, William marked his success at court in 1189–90 by founding the Augustinian house of Cartmel on his estate in Cumbria (Fig. 50). David Crouch remarks 'by 1190 it was beginning to be nouveau riche to advertise power by setting up a monastery; there was

49 *Watton Priory (Yorkshire). One of the best known of the double houses of the Gilbertine order. The air photograph from the north-east shows the extensive earthworks within the precinct while the plan (right) shows the excavated layout of the two monasteries.*

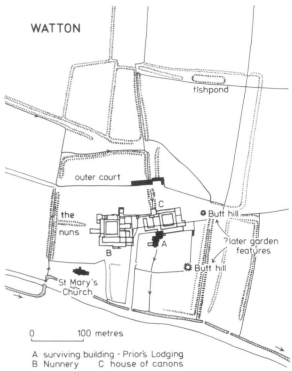

WATTON

fishpond

outer court

the nuns

C

Butt hill

?later garden features

B

A

Butt hill

St Mary's Church

0   100 metres

A surviving building - Prior's Lodging
B Nunnery   C house of canons

a surplus of religious houses and men of quite low station, mere county knights, were scraping together resources to found tiny and often short-lived priories on corners of their estates'; it was still, however, a respectable thing to do. In 1200 William founded both Tintern Parva Abbey 'in fulfilment of a vow he made when caught for a day and a night in a storm at sea before safely making Wexford harbour', and Duiske Abbey, both Cistercian and both on his estates in Leinster in Ireland.

The friars

By the early thirteenth century the foundation of houses of these newer monastic orders had, by and large, ceased. It was becoming difficult to separate the Cistercian houses from the older Benedictine and Cluniac sites in terms of the way they operated and although there were still lay brothers, from the middle of the thirteenth century there was little to

distinguish the estates of the various orders and how they were organized.

The friars represented another attempt, the final one of the Middle Ages, to return to the austere lifestyle of earlier religious groups. Houses for them began to be provided from the early thirteenth century onwards and considerable numbers were eventually established, particularly in the more important towns and cities. They concentrated on teaching and preaching and so centres of population were of more use to them than were isolated rural sites. They had a mission to look after the spiritual well-being of lay people while attempting to remain poor and without possessions themselves. In general they were given a site and buildings which they did not actually own. Frequently these were in the suburbs or even on the margins of major towns, and not uncommonly in marshy or poorly drained situations. Sometimes they moved to new sites as time went on. As relative latecomers to the topography of medieval

50 *Cartmel Priory (Cumbria). An Augustinian priory founded by William Marshall, originally a 'jobbing' soldier, as a thank offering after he had been made Earl of Pembroke in 1189–90.*

towns they had to fit into existing property boundaries, but as the land often reverted back to the town authorities at the Dissolution, the blocks of land on which friaries were built can sometimes be traced in the post-medieval topography (Fig. 51).

The most numerous friars were the Franciscans (Grey Friars, also known as the Friars Minor or the Conventual Friars) and the Dominicans (Black Friars or Preaching Friars). The former order was founded by St Francis of Assisi in Italy in the early thirteenth century. There is little doubt that they arrived in England with a preconceived plan of campaign; within a matter of weeks of their arrival (in 1224) they were to be found in Canterbury, London, Oxford (see Fig. 72), Cambridge and Northampton – the archiepiscopal centre, the capital, the two

university towns and the major market centre of the Midlands. By 1230 there were also houses at Bristol (see Fig. 72), Gloucester, Hereford, Kings Lynn and most of the other major medieval towns.

The Dominicans were founded by St Dominic, a Spaniard, in southern France; they arrived from Italy around 1221 and settled at Oxford. Most of their foundations are slightly later than the Franciscans, in the decade 1230–40, but they also centre on the main medieval towns; some of their earliest houses were at York (1227), Shrewsbury (1232), Northampton (1226), London (by 1224) and Exeter (1232). Because of the importance of poverty to the friars they never acquired landed estates; their impact on the rural landscape was therefore virtually non-existent. However, within

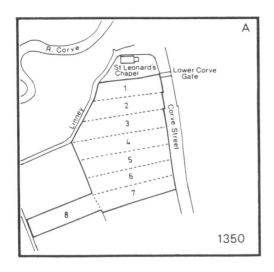

A

R. Corve

St Leonard's
Chapel

Lower Corve
Gate

Linney

Corve Street

1
2
3
4
5
6
7
8

1350

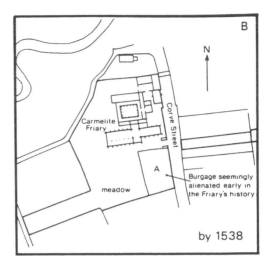

B

N

Carmelite
Friary

Corve Street

A

meadow

Burgage seemingly
alienated early in
the Friary's history

by 1538

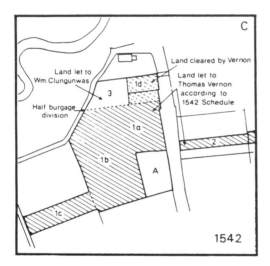

C

Land cleared by Vernon

Land let to Wm. Clungunwas

Land let to
Thomas Vernon
according to
1542 Schedule

3

1d

Half burgage
division

1a

2

1b

A

1c

1542

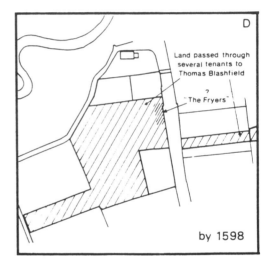

D

Land passed through
several tenants to
Thomas Blashfield

?
"The Fryers"

by 1598

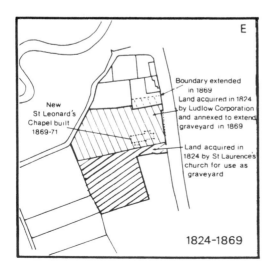

E

Boundary extended
in 1869

Land acquired in 1824
by Ludlow Corporation
and annexed to extend
graveyard in 1869

New
St Leonard's
Chapel built
1869-71

Land acquired in
1824 by St Laurence's
church for use as
graveyard

1824-1869

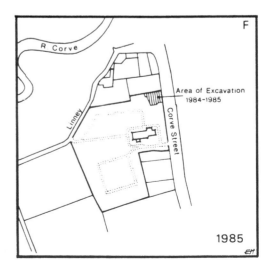

F

R Corve

Area of Excavation
1984-1985

Linney

Corve Street

1985

EH

towns the precincts of their houses could be extensive and significant.

Some groups of the earliest friars were much more like hermits and sought out isolated places, rather in the way the Cistercians had a century before. The Carmelites (or White Friars), for example, seem to have begun as hermits on Mount Carmel in Palestine in the mid-twelfth century. They received a rule from Albert of Vercelli, patriarch of Jerusalem, in around 1210 and as hermits migrated to Cyprus, Italy, Sicily and Spain. When they were brought to Britain in the early 1240s the first sites they chose reflected these hermit ideals. At Hulne (Fig. 52), for example, a group was established in one of the parks attached to Alnwick Castle, still an isolated and remote spot today. Others were established at Aylesford (now restored to the Carmelites) and Losenham (Kent), Burnham Norton (Norfolk) and at Chesterton (Cambridge-shire). They were reformed under Dominican influence by St Simon Stock (?–1265), the English general of the order, who relaxed the severity of the hermit lifestyle in favour of communal life and work in the cities. They became indistinguishable from the other groups of friars, and their later houses are all in towns.

The Austin or Augustinian Friars, officially known as the Order of Hermit Friars of St Augustine, were established by the pope in 1256 when several disparate groups were amalgamated. They had a constitution like the Dominicans but retained the spiritual tradition of hermits. Some of the earliest Austin friaries were sited in isolated places. One of the first

52 *Hulne Priory, Alnwick (Northumberland). One of the earliest Carmelite friaries established in a park attached to Alnwick Castle in 1242. The small group of buildings is fortified with a strong tower (foreground) and curtain wall. This is still a remote and inaccessible place today and reflects the original aspirations of the Carmelites as hermits.*

foundations (*c*.1250) is at Woodhouse on a remote uncultivated hillside site east of the Titterstone Clee in Shropshire. The earliest foundation was at Clare in Suffolk (1248), where the surviving buildings were restored to the Austin Friars in 1953. Most of the major medieval towns had an Austin friary.

Many towns and cities acquired at least one friary and some had houses of all four groups – Dominicans, Franciscans, Austin Friars and Carmelites – including, in England, Berwick on Tweed, Newcastle upon Tyne, York, Lincoln, Boston, Stamford, Kings Lynn, Norwich, Northampton, Cambridge, Oxford, London, Canterbury, Bristol and Winchester, and in Scotland, Aberdeen, Perth and Edinburgh. In many ways this is a good reflection of the main urban centres of the thirteenth century.

At Newcastle all the friaries were on the edge of the built-up areas of the city against the city wall. Three of the friaries at Kings Lynn were to the south and east of the built-up area, though still within the town

51 *The Carmelite Friary (Whitefriars), Ludlow (Shropshire). As a result of recent studies, the plans of this part of the town before the friary was founded in 1350, during its occupation by the friars, and subsequently through to the present day have been elucidated.*

bank and ditch. The Franciscans were within the town defences at Lincoln, but significantly the other houses were in the suburbs to the north, east and south (Wigford), whereas at Oxford the Franciscan friary was built across the city wall in the south-west of the city, the Dominican house was built beyond the south wall in marshy land by the river, while both the Austin and White friars were beyond the town wall to the north, almost in the fields. At York all four friaries were on the periphery of the town, though all were within the town wall – the Dominicans in the south-west, the Franciscans in the south, the Austin Friars on the banks of the river Ouse and the Carmelites on the banks of the Foss. In London, the Dominicans were in the extreme south-west of the walled area, the Franciscans in the north-west, the Austin Friars in an empty area in the north-east, while the Carmelites were outside the defences to the west on the north bank of the Thames. At Norwich three of the friaries were central but two of these, the Austin and the Dominican friaries, were on low-lying river meadow land; the fourth, the Carmelite friary, was in the extreme north-east of the walled area.

New monasteries in the landscape

With the exception of the friars, who were only important in an urban context, the impact of these new orders on the landscape can be seen to have been very considerable. This was partly because of the sheer number of new institutions which came into existence in the space of a relatively short period – from about 1066 to the 1240s – certainly less than two hundred years. In that time the number of houses had grown from some sixty to perhaps ten times that number. Although the population had risen over that period, by some estimates quite dramatically, there were fewer people in a

larger number of more recent monastic houses than there had been earlier in the smaller number of older and larger houses – perhaps less than 10,000 monks, nuns, canons and friars by 1250.

The sites chosen for this galaxy of new monasteries were not determined by the physical layout of the landscape, be it in town or country. The real reasons why particular sites were chosen can be explained best with reference to the land ownership and tenurial arrangements existing in the eleventh, twelfth and thirteenth centuries.

If a map of any locality at the time of a monastic foundation could be reconstructed to show who owned the land and the extent of tenancies, it would be easy to appreciate the 'social landscape' that was the real determining factor in the choice of order, choice of site and layout of buildings. As the status of the founders of monasteries moved down from the Crown, in the pre-Conquest and early medieval periods, to the higher and then the lower levels of the baronage, so the choice of site became less of an easy option. The foundation process went from a wide variety of extensive lands from which to choose, to more a case of finding somewhere reasonable in the locality. Perhaps the movement of sites in the twelfth and thirteenth centuries reflects more the limited choice in the 'landscape of ownership' available to monk-planners than to any great physical difficulties.

As well as the houses of the new orders, Benedictine and Cluniac monasteries continued to flourish through to the end of the Middle Ages, when the general trend of all orders was towards less asceticism and more comfort. It is easy to forget that along with the success of the new orders, traditional forms of monasticism continued to expand; Benedictine monasteries increased from around 48 in 1066 to 345 in the mid-thirteenth century, Benedictine nunneries from 12 to 140, and Benedictine monks from around 850 to perhaps 6000.

6 Monastic precincts

While the claustral buildings next to the church were certainly the most important in the religious and domestic life of monasteries, many other buildings and structures were important for the economic life of the community. These other buildings and structures were grouped in courts and enclosures around the main buildings in an area which can be called the 'precinct' – the central monastic enclosure. Since there are often substantial archaeological remains of precincts, either in the form of isolated or ruined buildings or as extensive earthworks, they form an important aspect of the immediate landscape of most monastic sites.

Elements in the precinct

It is possible to divide the features found most frequently in monastic precincts into several functional groups, contained in the inner and outer courts and a home farm, if there was one. Buildings associated with guests, visitors, pilgrims and people in receipt of alms, would include guest-houses, stables and barns and the almonry. Those structures concerned with the prodigious amount of supplies required for even a modest-sized house would include storage buildings of a wide variety of types and sizes, especially barns, but including animal houses – cattle sheds, pigsties, dovecots and so on. There would also be buildings for

food processing, barns and granaries for storage of grain and breweries and bakehouses for its processing. There would be more of such buildings if a farm was attached to the monastery, as there so often was. Then there were the buildings associated with the construction and maintenance of the complex structure that many large monasteries became – the builders' yards with sheds for stone working, lead working, making tiles, mortar mixing and so on. Also, many sites had some sort of industrial component. This might well have involved a watermill for grinding corn but equally there might be forges for ironworking, or wool and cloth processing establishments. As well as these ranges of buildings there were usually enclosures and gardens for vegetables, herbs, fruit and vine growing, as well as ranges of fishponds for fish breeding and storage.

Surveys of monastic precincts, especially those made around the time of the Dissolution in the sixteenth century, are sometimes detailed enough to list individual buildings. At Rievaulx, for example, 27 buildings are described in the inner and outer courts including a fulling mill, an iron smithy and a corn mill, a tannery and houses for a plumber, tanner and smith. There were also houses for tenants or 'corrodians'. Glyn Coppack discusses other useful surveys which have survived and it is clear that the size and layout of the precinct depends on

53 *Alnwick Abbey (Northumberland). The stone-built conduit house supplied fresh drinking water to the abbey which was on the flat land beyond the surviving gatehouse. The river in the trees beyond was diverted into channels which flushed out the drains and the latrines.*

the wealth of the house, what land and outlying granges and manors it possessed and whether or not it had a home farm.

When a new site was chosen, careful consideration was given to the layout of the precinct and the position of the buildings within it. One of the factors of prime importance was the provision of an adequate water supply and drainage system; this required springs, from which the former could be taken, and a site that was convenient for the use of streams. The ideal in practice meant a gentle south-facing slope with a stream running below. The church could then be built to the north of the cloister, with the stream draining the claustral ranges of buildings to the south. In reality there was often great ingenuity employed in laying out the buildings to make the best use of the locally available water supply, with many examples of the claustral plan being reversed, with the

cloister on the north side of the church, if this meant that a more efficient drainage system could be devised.

Benedictine precincts

The earliest English depiction of a monastic precinct is a map of Canterbury Cathedral Priory made in the mid-twelfth century when Prior Wibert had the water supply installed (Fig. 54). This shows very clearly not only the ranges of buildings, gardens and so on but also the elaborate water supply system. A wall runs round the whole complex within the city wall. Two cloisters are shown to the north of the large cathedral priory church. To the west is the main cloister with ranges for the cellarer, the refectory and the dormitory. The chapter house is shown on one side and, off the cloister, an elaborate lavatorium or washing place. Nearby is the guest-house with a great gate leading into the outer court. The other cloister links the church with the infirmary and the necessarium or latrines; nearby is the bath-house. In the outer court is the main gate, a new hall, bakehouse, brewhouse and granary.

The water supply came from a spring outside the town wall to the north-east. Before going through the town wall, the water passed through four settling tanks, and incidentally through a corn field, vineyard and orchard, and across the town ditch on an aqueduct. Inside the precinct, pipes led to a water tower, which still exists on the south side of the infirmary cloister, and to the washing place in the main cloister. This incoming supply is shown in

54 *Canterbury Cathedral Priory (Kent). The twelfth-century plan of the precinct (redrawn by James Bond) showing details of the precinct and the water system installed by Prior Wibert.*

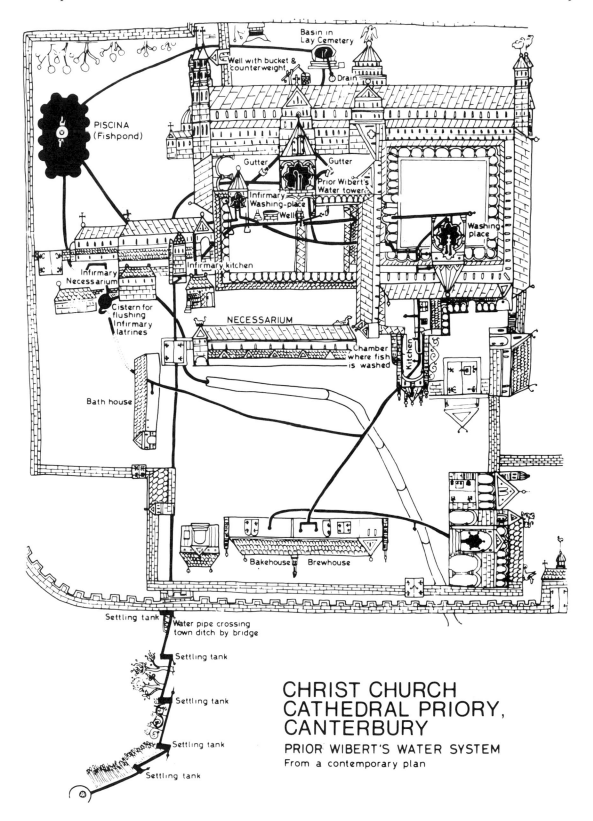

Basin in
Lay Cemetery

Well with bucket &
counterweight

Drain

PISCINA
(Fishpond)

Gutter

Gutter

Prior Wibert's
Water tower

Infirmary
Washing-place

Well

Washing
place

Infirmary kitchen

Infirmary
Necessarium

Cistern for
flushing
Infirmary
latrines

NECESSARIUM

Chamber
where fish
is washed

Kitchen

Bath house

Bakehouse   Brewhouse

Settling tank

Water pipe crossing
town ditch by bridge

Settling tank

Settling tank

Settling tank

Settling tank

CHRIST CHURCH
CATHEDRAL PRIORY,
CANTERBURY
PRIOR WIBERT'S WATER SYSTEM
From a contemporary plan

blue-green on the map. The water is led around the buildings, in pipes shown in red, to a number of named buildings and other structures. Thus the supply runs to a great basin in the lay cemetery next to the bell tower, and to an elaborate piscina or fishpool near the monks' cemetery. Elsewhere the infirmary and its necessarium are supplied, the latter with a cistern for flushing the latrines. Pipes led also to the infirmary kitchen and the refectory, and the kitchens and guest-house of the main part of the monastery. A branch crosses the outer court to the brewhouse and bakehouse and a basin in the new hall. The waste water is gathered after the necessarium into what seems to be sectional pipes and led away to the north-west beyond the town wall in the direction of the river Stour.

Many of the older Benedictine houses, although founded originally in thinly populated areas, had by the early Middle Ages become the focus of towns of various sizes. Unless a generous area had been laid out for a precinct from the start, expansion of the area at the expense of surrounding properties might prove difficult. The layout of the later buildings might in any case be greatly affected by the disposition of earlier structures.

At Ely the inner court lay to the south of the church and cloister, covering an area roughly 300 by 200m (1000 by 700ft) (Fig. 55). This was entered by a gate at the south end and included stores, granary, gardens and guest accommodation as well as an orchard, vineyard, lay cemetery and yards for the sacrist and the almoner. At Peterborough the whole precinct was considerably larger, being some 600 by 250m (2000 by 600ft), running south from the town and market to the river Nene. Vineyards, orchards and cemeteries lay to the north and east of the claustral buildings, with the great court to the west. On the south side was an extensive area of moats, ponds and gardens, altogether occupying almost half of the area. Durham is probably one of the largest and most complete of the Benedictine urban sites. On a great southward projecting spur within a meander of the river Wear, a large precinct was laid out in the eleventh century. This not only included the cathedral priory, with the Priory Garth and Great Gate, guest hall and granaries to the south, but also, to the north, Durham Castle, the home of the prince bishops of the Durham Palatinate.

Chertsey Abbey in the Thames valley in Surrey has hardly survived at all but early excavations and surveys enable the precinct to be reconstructed on paper. The claustral buildings lay within a moated and walled enclosure, of some 200 by 150m (650 by 500ft), outlined by the Abbey river and the Black Ditch, and they were approached from the west via gatehouses and the outer court. To the west was a further moated enclosure with numerous linear ponds, and the site of the abbey's home farm and barns. The church for the lay people was situated to the south at the T-junction of the medieval town nearby.

Rather more typical of a less important monastery in a rural situation is the precinct of St Benet of Hulme Abbey (Fig. 56) out in the middle of East Anglia, next to the river Bure in the Norfolk Broads. The monastery was founded in the ninth century at a time when probably little attention was paid to the best siting for the precinct. The isolated mound by the river has all the hallmarks of a site selected for its isolation by a group of hermits. The church and claustral ranges occupy a very small part of the large precinct area which is enclosed by a bank and ditch and was formerly walled. The precinct was approached along two causeways, one from the west where there was a hospital of St James, and the other from the village of Ludham to the north. To the east was a ferry across the river Thurne. A great gate, which still survives although it is blocked by a later brick windmill, leads to Stable Court with

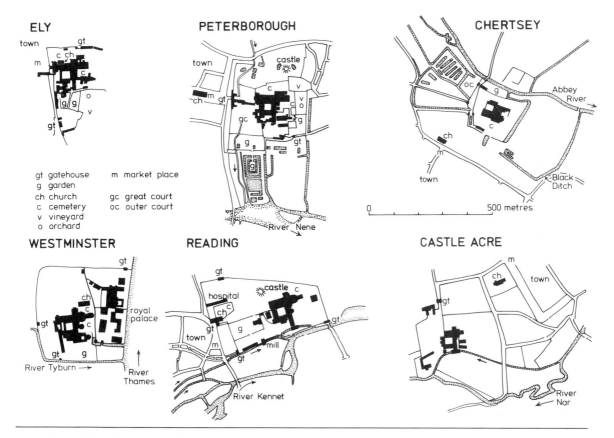

55 *Plans of Benedictine and Cluniac monastery precincts: Ely; Peterborough; Chertsey; Westminster; Reading; and Castle Acre.*

56 *St Benet of Hulme Abbey (Norfolk). Vertical air photograph of the monastic precinct beside the river Bure. The claustral buildings occupy a small area in the centre while all around there are enclosures, yards, gardens and fishponds.*

stables and the almonry along the riverside. There is a 'swan pit' nearby, presumably where swans were kept, and outside the gate a dock leads off the river.

The careful attention to water in this low-lying situation is best shown in the very elaborate set of fishponds and tanks which occupy the north-west quadrant of the precinct. Along the riverside to the south are situated a barn, brewery, bakery and the steward's office. Beyond is the complex of the abbot's hall and chambers. To the east there are gardens for the abbot, cellarer, prior and the infirmary. Elsewhere in the precinct are numerous enclosures, stock yards, a stack yard and more fishponds.

Cluniac precincts

Reading Abbey, though not a Cluniac foundation attached to the abbey of Cluny in Burgundy, was nevertheless staffed by Cluniac monks and run on the same lines as Cluniac monasteries. The site chosen by Henry I was on a peninsula between the river Thames to the north and the Kennet to the south. The abbey was sited to the east of the town on the end of the peninsula; it was thus possible to have the gates and the outer court to the west of the abbey buildings, with the mill and leat system to the south in channels running eastwards. Excavations have revealed indications of the leats, the wharfs on the waterfront of the Kennet, together with remains of the medieval mills. On the west side a block of properties seems to encroach on the precinct near St Laurence's church and the Compter gate. These properties may have been built as a speculative development by the abbey as they front on to the market place; a similar urban development, perhaps the best known, can be seen at Tewkesbury and there must be many others.

At Montacute (Fig. 57), the precinct of the Cluniac monastery had considerable impact on the local topography. It was founded in the late eleventh century between the castle of the Count of Mortain to the west and an embryonic town, Bishopston, to the north. The local church of St Peter seems to have been taken over as the first monastic church; later a new church, the present St Catherine's, was built to the north of the abbey. A roughly square precinct seems to have been laid out to the south of

Bishopston. In the thirteenth century when the town was expanded, a new series of plots and a market place were laid out around the east side of the precinct. The roads still follow a tortuous pattern through these urban developments and around the former precinct even though there is no trace of the claustral buildings.

At Castle Acre (Norfolk) (see Fig. 55) a Cluniac priory was built to the west of the town within a very generous precinct. There was plenty of room to lay out the buildings in the correct orientation, with a leat off the river Nar passing through the reredorter to the south of the cloister. The main gate to the north led to the outer court to the west of the claustral buildings.

The Cistercians

Many of the most impressive precincts remain around Cistercian monasteries. I began my career many years ago looking at the earthworks associated with Bordesley Abbey near Redditch (Worcestershire) (see Figs 44 and 45). Research since then has clarified and amplified details of the precinct. Excavations have been carried out on the precinct bank and ditch, the chapel of St Stephen at the gate and the mills and drainage system of the precinct, as well as on the abbey church itself.

Perhaps the finest surviving rural monastic precinct in Britain is that at Fountains Abbey (Yorkshire) (Fig. 58). The

---

57 *Montacute (Somerset). The site of the Cluniac priory (the open space bottom left) surrounded by the town; Bishopston to the north was laid out before the priory in the eleventh century, the new borough to the east, around a square market place, in the thirteenth century. Montacute house which succeeded the priory in the late sixteenth century, and which probably used its stone, is top right.*

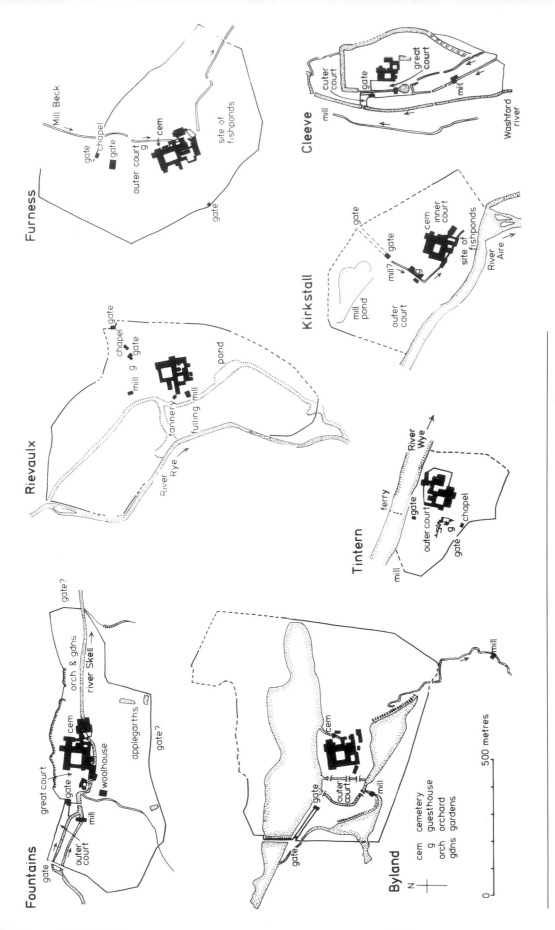

Fountains

gate?
orch & gdns
river Skell
gate?
great court
cem
gate
woolhouse
mill
outer court
applegarths

Rievaulx

chapel
gate
mill g gate
pond
tannery
fulling mill
River Rye

Furness

Mill Beck
gate
chapel
gate
cem
g
outer court
gate
site of fishponds

Cleeve

outer court
gate
great court
mill
mill
Washford river

Kirkstall

gate
gate
cem
inner court
mill?
g
site of fishponds
outer court
mill pond
River Aire

Byland

cem
gate
outer court
mill
ferry
gate
g
chapel
gate

Tintern

River Wye
gate
outer court
g
chapel
gate
mill
mill

cem   cemetery
g   guesthouse
orch   orchard
gdns   gardens

N

0   500 metres

58 *Plans of precincts of Cistercian abbeys: Fountains; Rievaulx; Furness; Byland; Tintern; Kirkstall; Cleeve.*

abbey was built on the north side of the river Skell, where it flows through a narrow, almost gorge-like section of the valley. To the west, upstream, the valley is wider where a stream joins from the south-west. In this area were laid out many of the buildings of the outer court including a watermill, one of the most elaborate to have survived (Fig. 85), and a woolhouse recently excavated by Glyn Coppack (Fig. 59). Altogether the precinct was 1000m long and up to 400m wide (3300 by 1300ft), with the main gates to the west. It was surrounded by a large wall and had within it fishponds and orchards. A large enclosed park abutted the precinct on the south-west side and there were the lands of the granges of Swanley to the north and Morker to the south.

The precinct at Rievaulx Abbey was as elaborate. We have already seen how the drainage pattern of this part of the valley of the river Rye was altered; the final course of the river defined the west side of the precinct, with walls on the north and east sides. The area within was some 1000m long by 400m wide (3300 by 1300ft), and included extensive areas of meadow and enclosed fields as well as ponds, old river courses and canals, leats and mill sites. The outer court with the stables, guest-house and chapel were to the north-east between the inner and outer gatehouses.

The precinct at Furness is similar in layout. An area 800 by 450m (2500 by 1400ft) was enclosed by a wall with outer and great gates to the north with a chapel, and a gate to the west. The outer court lay to the north of the claustral buildings, while to the south were the fishponds and a quarry. The water supply system was very elaborate with leats feeding the cloister from the north and west. Channels fed the monks' and lay brothers' latrines, the abbot's house (which had been the infirmary), the new infirmary and the guest-house. The stone sluices are very well preserved.

At all three of these sites a section of the river valley was walled in, but since the walls run along the crests of the valley on each side there can have been no intention of defence, only of enclosure.

At Byland the layout and development of the precinct, as already mentioned (see Fig. 47) is associated with other major landscape changes in the vicinity. A wall ran round the roughly rectilinear area of the precinct of some 800 by 700m (2500 by 2200ft), with part of its course running along the top of a massive earthen dam of one of the fishponds. There were inner and outer gatehouses controlling access to the precinct from the west. These led to an outer court with guest-houses, mill, granary, forge, bakehouse, brewhouse and dovecot, all of which have disappeared. The claustral buildings of the abbey were built on a ridge of glacial debris, to the north of which a large lake was developed which supplied water to the mill and the drains. The overflow fed two other irregular ponds and two more mills. The whole scheme was an ingenious way of draining the site while at the same time supplying the monastery with water and feeding ponds and mill sites. The water left the precinct at the south-east corner heading south-eastwards, the natural course for the numerous small streams in this area, and went into the scheme already described (p. 80).

At Tintern, where magnificent claustral buildings also survive, the precinct displays many similar points (see Fig. 6). The river Wye forms the northern boundary and a later road cuts across the precinct cutting off the gatehouse site with the chapel from the main buildings. Not only do long lengths of precinct wall survive but also the water gate by the ferry on the river Wye. There are extensive remains of buildings in the outer court. An early plan of 1764 shows the outline of the precinct clearly and excavations have demonstrated that the outer court had a succession of guest-houses, the earliest aisled, a smithy and

59 *The woolhouse at Fountains Abbey (Yorkshire) after excavation. These are the remains of a large and complex building of several phases used for the processing of cloth.*

other buildings for industrial activities including cupellation and bell-founding. Excavation of a building in the outer court at Fountains Abbey proved to be a probable woolhouse (Fig. 59), which was aisled and used for the fulling and finishing of cloth, while another at Beaulieu seems to have been a fulling mill and woolshed.

At Kirkstall Abbey, in the suburbs of Leeds, while the buildings of the monastery survive virtually complete, the precinct area, 700 by 400m (2200 by 1300ft), has been broken up by more recent developments. A road now cuts across the site so that the outer gatehouse and the former mill pond are divorced from the claustral buildings. The river Aire on the south side is probably more or less in its original course but the definite delineation of the precinct boundary is only certain in a couple of places where it has survived in the form of property boundaries. Within the precinct area there is an inner court with the abbey buildings, while to the west there is an extensive outer court occupying half of the area. Here, there was a mill with its pond and a guest-house, which has now been excavated and laid out on display, but there must have been many more structures and buildings in this area, of which there is now no surface trace.

Cleeve Abbey (Somerset) (see Fig. 3) is not so well known as those discussed above but it has a very well preserved claustral area and many earthworks and features associated with the precinct. This lay in the valley bottom and was evidently walled; on the west the precinct wall survives along the stream, and there is an outer court with a fine gateway. The stream seems to have been canalized and moved to the west side of the valley so that the buildings could be laid out on the wide flat valley floor. A leat from the south evidently fed the latrines and other buildings while a further leat to the west fed one of the mills. There were several fishponds to the north.

All of these sites have substantial buildings, indeed they are some of the best in Europe, and considerable detail of the precincts around can be seen. They are most useful in helping our understanding of the less well preserved sites where there may be only a few ruins, but where extensive areas of earthworks covering other structures survive. Such sites are much less obvious to the visitor but are of great interest to the landscape archaeologist. Frequently the few building fragments and areas of earthworks that do survive make it possible to attempt a reconstruction of the layout of the precinct and the buildings within it.

Such a site is Kirkstead (Lincolnshire) (Fig. 60), where only one tall pinnacle of masonry survives, formerly part of the church, together with the chapel at the gate. However, there is a vast area of well-preserved earthworks indicating the foundations of buildings and other features. Air photographs taken in low sunlight emphasize the mounds and hollows on the site and from these a reasonable interpretation of the layout can be made. The precinct was defined by a moat within which a bank supported a wall. The main monastic buildings were in the south-east quadrant of the roughly square precinct enclosure, while the north-west was given over to a series of long linear fishponds.

Foundations of walls and ditches show that the rest of the precinct was divided into several large enclosures.

The sites of the abbeys of Stanley (Wiltshire) (Fig. 61) and Meaux (Humberside) are similar, except that at these sites there are no standing remains at all. Nevertheless, the basic layouts can be worked out. At Stanley an extensive precinct is defined by a bank and ditch, within which there were numerous ponds, a mill leat to a documented fulling mill, and the claustral buildings. The site was evidently approached from the south, along a causeway lined with drainage ditches running alongside a further pond. Meaux is today represented by a very large area of complex earthworks (see Fig. 42). The site of the church and cloister can be picked out and the approximate outline of the precinct suggested, but there are many other earthworks which are difficult to interpret.

Whitland Abbey (Fig. 62), begun in 1151 near Carmarthen, was the foremost of the Welsh Cistercian houses but there is very little left of the monastic buildings. The earthworks around, however, show very clearly how the abbey was sited on a ridge

60 *Kirkstead Abbey (Lincolnshire). This air photograph shows the rectangular precinct (top) with extensive earthworks of the Cistercian abbey buildings; only one substantial piece of masonry remains. In the foreground is a series of fishponds.*

between the Afon Gronw and its tributary, the Nant Colmendy, the latter manipulated to supply leats for ponds and mills and the drains of the monastic buildings. Part of the complex relates to a later forge.

Sometimes there is very little to go on. At Dunkeswell (Devon) (see Fig. 62) a nineteenth-century church has been built on the site of part of the monastic church; nearby are the remains of a gatehouse and

61 *Stanley Abbey (Wiltshire). Air photograph of the earthworks of the claustral buildings. The church was in the centre, with the cloister to the right of the small building. Beyond is the mill leat and main drain and the river Marden.*

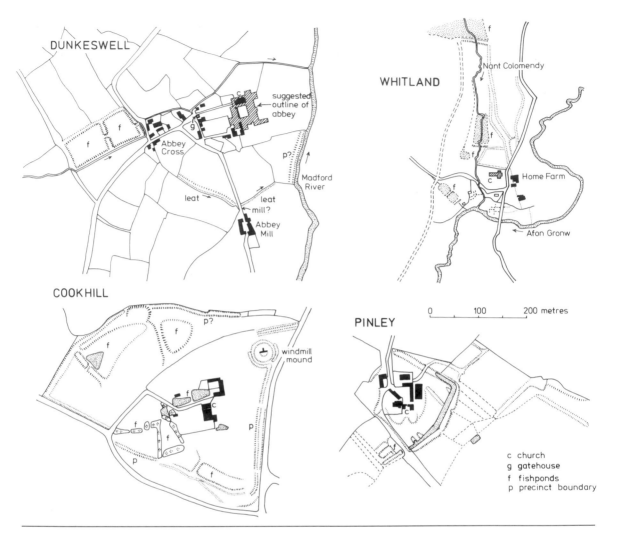

62   *Plans of Dunkeswell Abbey (Devon); Whitland Abbey (Dyfed, Wales); and the nunneries at Cookhill (Worcestershire) and Pinley (Warwickshire).*

there are fine earthworks of fishponds in the valley. But there are few earthworks and so the general position of the site has to be used to suggest the monastic layout. The claustral buildings lay to the south of the church on a north-east facing spur between the Madford river to the east and a stream to the north. There may have been a leat off the river passing through the buildings along a contour canal but a more likely supply was the stream, flowing around the fishponds and then into the precinct from the west.

There was a mill to the south and this can only have been supplied off this stream via a canal along the contours from the fishponds. Fieldwork around the site, looking at the landscape to see how it might have been best organized and used in the past, suggests all sorts of possibilities for the way the precinct was laid out.

A similar outline can be provided for Hulton Abbey near Stoke-on-Trent. Recent excavations have provided a great deal of information about the church and the claustral buildings which were on its south side. Here the water-supply leat must have been led off the stream to the south of the site and along the contours to the buildings, which are on a west-facing spur with the probable outer court to the west.

Rather more typical are the smaller precincts with less elaborate water control schemes and slighter earthwork remains. Two Cistercian nunnery sites in the Midlands, Pinley (Warwickshire) and Cookhill (Worcestershire), demonstrate this well (see Fig. 62). Both sites have small precincts surrounding claustral buildings in which timber was used extensively. At Cookhill the roughly triangular precinct area is outlined by ditches and banks. The claustral buildings were in the middle and there arc fishponds in the southern half and to the north-west. It is not clear where the gate was but, unusually, a medieval windmill mound survives in the north-east corner on the hill. At Pinley the area of the precinct was very small, confined within a moated enclosure. There was probably no room for more than the small claustral ranges and a few gardens. The farm buildings and gatehouse were probably on the north side near the gate; beyond the moat were other enclosures and fishponds.

Carthusian precincts

Carthusian priories had layouts which were considerably different to those of the other orders. The large cloister with cells and gardens around and the few and generally small communal buildings are distinctive and make predicting what should be on a Carthusian site fairly easy. Little or nothing is known of the precincts of some sites, while others, as with so many monastic sites, were overlaid with gardens and later houses in the post-Dissolution period and the earlier arrangements obscured. Recent work, however, has shown the layout of

some clearly. At both Hinton Charterhouse and Beauvale earthworks and standing buildings enable the layout to be easily understood. At both, the large cloister with cells was surrounded by an outer wall and there are areas of earthworks beyond. At Beauvale these include a fishpond and possible coalpit, while at Hinton there are building foundations of a probable later farm, and quarries. At Sheen near Richmond (Surrey), on the site of what was the largest and most magnificent of the English charterhouses, there are only the most enigmatic of earthworks mixed up with the greens and bunkers of a golf course. Despite parchmarks in the grass and a magnetometer survey of part of the site, the best reconstruction so far has been achieved by John Cloake working from the early surveys and documents.

At Mount Grace (Yorkshire) the precinct of a charterhouse survives almost complete. As well as the great cloister with the cells around, there is another enclosure, the inner court, with the service buildings. There was formerly a further enclosure to the west, the outer court, with the farm buildings and the guests' accommodation. The water supply and drainage system is particularly well preserved, with no less than three conduit houses on the hillside to the east feeding both a large conduit in the middle of the cloister and a channel to the rear of the gardens which drained the latrines. Such a system is depicted in a rare medieval map for the London charterhouse, though little now survives there on the ground. There is also a mill leat at Mount Grace with the stone foundations of the mill in what was the outer court (Fig. 63).

Grandmontine precincts

Of the three priories of the Grandmontine order, two, Alberbury and Craswall, have very interesting precincts both from the

63 *Mount Grace Priory (Yorkshire). One of the three conduit houses which supplied both water to the great conduit in the centre of the cloister for drinking water and, via the stone gutters, water to flush the latrines.*

point of view of surviving earthworks and for the fortunate survival of an early map for Alberbury. Alberbury (Shropshire) (Figs. 64 and 65) was founded as an Augustinian priory some time before 1226 but in about 1230 was granted to the Grandmontines. In 1441 it was bought by Archbishop Chicheley and granted to All Soul's College, Oxford by Henry VI. The map of the precinct and the area around made in 1579 still belongs to the college and this, together with later maps and air photographs, enables us to reconstruct the former arrangements at the site. The precinct was surrounded by a bank and moat ('the great dicke or moate about the abbey'), the latter fed by several watercourses on their way to the river Severn. An offshoot fed a large pond within the precinct ('an olde pounde or mylne pole decayed') and then probably drained other

buildings ('a moate issuynge out of the mylne pole'). The precinct was entered at the south-west corner through a gatehouse ('a foundacion of a olde stone wale and a yate house'). Inside, the small church had a cloister to the south. There were other buildings scattered around, including a large barn, 50 by 10m (150 by 30ft) and a mill off the end of the pool ('a olde mylne place decayed'). By the time the map was drawn many of the buildings had been reduced to their foundations but the church remained, called 'the Black Abbey', and it still exists incorporated into the modern farmhouse.

At Craswall priory (Herefordshire) there are spectacular ruins in a deep secluded valley in the Black Mountains near Hay-on-Wye (see Fig. 40). The church remains almost to gable height, though buried, and much of the east range can be seen. The small stream that cuts across the south-west corner of the claustral buildings must formerly have drained the latrines beyond the dormitory and it probably drove a mill. Although it is difficult to trace a definite precinct boundary in the form of a bank and ditch, there are plenty of areas of earthworks indicating a dam and a large pond, building sites and water leats.

Precincts associated with the canons

The wide range of orders of canons, the different types of localities selected and the huge number of houses formerly in existence make it a daunting task to select examples of their precincts.

Some sites were very similar to those of the Cistercians. Thus the abbeys of Alnwick, Shap and Halesowen, founded for Premonstratensian canons, each have sites laid out in a similar fashion to those of the white monks, in secluded situations with considerable attention paid to the management of the local water resources. At Llanthony, an Augustinian house in the

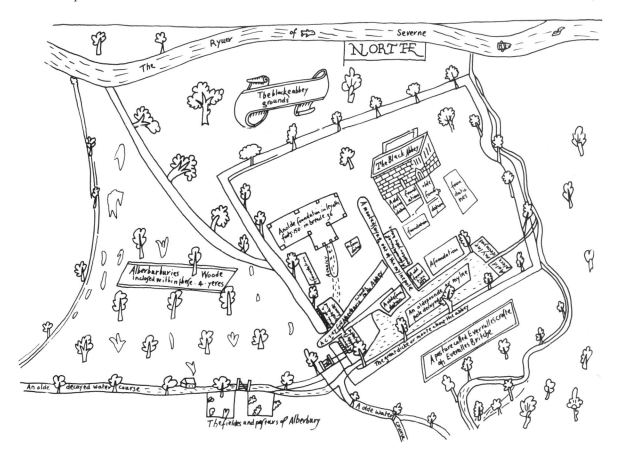

64 *Alberbury Priory (Shropshire). Plan of 1579 (redrawn) showing the precinct of this small Grandmontine priory. Within the moat, the church remains standing (The Black Abbey) while all around the surveyor, Robert Harding, has shown the foundations of other monastic buildings. To the south is a mill pool with the site of the mill shown.*

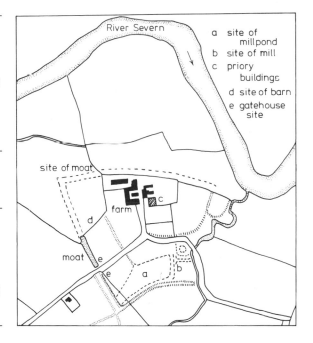

65 *Alberbury Priory (Shropshire). Plan of the earthworks as shown on recent air photographs and existing on the ground. The outline of the precinct is lost except for one piece of the moat and some property alignments. The mill pool is ploughed over but several areas of earthworks remain.*

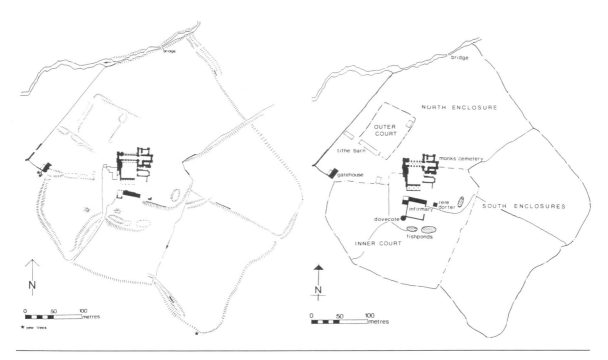

66 *Llanthony Priory (Gwent, Wales). Plan of the precinct showing the earthworks and the original arrangement of the buildings within it.*

Black Mountains, the isolated priory had a well-defined precinct with a bank and ditch around (Fig. 66). A gatehouse leads into the outer court, now a field but formerly accommodating a large barn, while beyond this are remains of the inner court with a dovecot. The water system cannot be traced but must have been tapped off the stream to the north.

At other isolated sites there are also substantial remains of the precinct. Kirkham (Yorkshire) has a fine gatehouse at the entrance to the precinct on the east side of the river Derwent. Air photographs, taken in frost and melting snow, have shown up previously unsuspected buildings within the precinct. Rather more survives in the way of buildings at Maxstoke (Warwickshire) (Fig. 67) and Ulverscroft (Leicestershire) (Fig. 68). At the latter the claustral buildings were surrounded by a moat, a feature that can be seen at several of the smaller monastic

houses. The roughly square precinct at Maxstoke is surrounded by a substantial wall with both outer and inner gatehouses; there are fine remains of a watermill.

The extent of many monastic precincts is indicated by earthworks. A good example which has been surveyed in detail is Thornton Abbey (Lincolnshire). Beyond the ruins in the guardianship of English Heritage, earthworks remain of the inner and outer courts and the home farm – 'one of the best preserved monastic complexes in England'. A less impressive but rather more typical example exists at the small Victorine priory of Stavordale (Somerset), while nearby at Maiden Bradley (Fig. 69) recent survey has shown what is probably the early leper house as well as the site of the canons' enclosure.

Perhaps the most thorough archaeological examination of an Augustinian house is at Norton Priory near Runcorn (Cheshire) (see

Fig. 109). Although little remains above ground level, excavations over several years have resulted in a detailed knowledge of the claustral buildings and much has been learned of the water supply and drainage system. The layout of the precinct and the disposition of the buildings within it have also been demonstrated; eighteenth-century maps show a rectangular enclosure surrounded by moats with a pond and a watermill on Bannerstich.

Another well-studied site, by contrast in an urban context, is Waltham Abbey (Essex). Over a number of years rescue excavations have enabled much of the plan of the abbey and its precinct to be recovered. Adjacent to the claustral buildings was a moated enclosure, while to the north was a group of fishponds in Veresmead and the

67 *Maxstoke Priory (Warwickshire). This air photograph shows the roughly square precinct with the gatehouses in the foreground. Beyond are the earthworks of the claustral buildings with one large piece of the church crossing tower remaining.*

68 *Ulverscroft Priory (Leicestershire). Plan of the remaining buildings within the moated enclosure, with associated fishponds.*

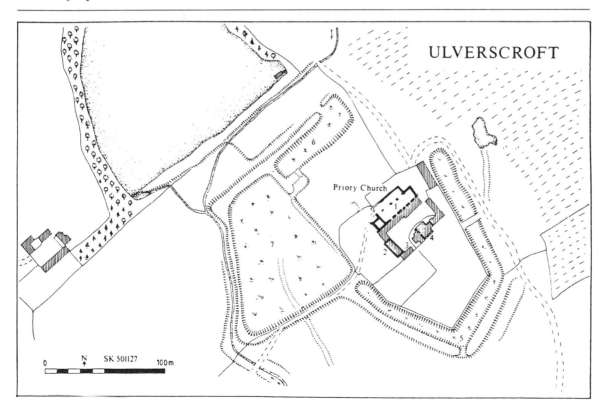

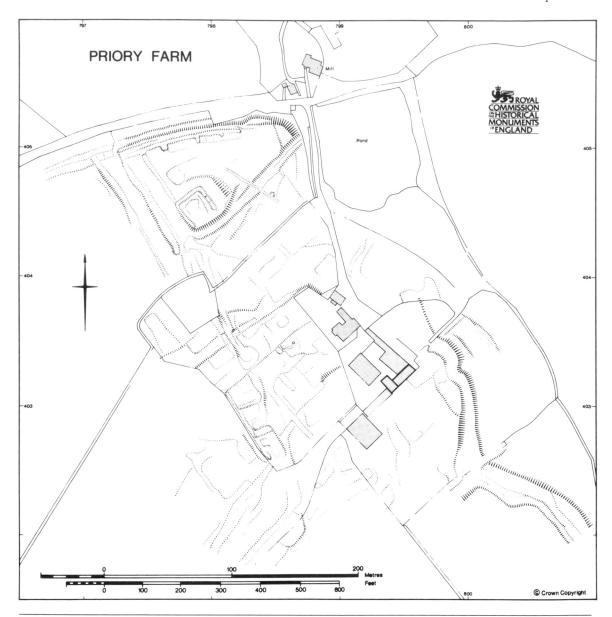

PRIORY FARM

69 *Maiden Bradley Priory (Wiltshire). Plan of the earthworks with the priory to the bottom right (east), and the possible leper settlement to the north, top left.*

home grange with its farm buildings and enclosures. The latter included a twelve-bay timber-framed barn close to a dock on the Cornmill stream, a timber-framed hay barn and a forge. Nearby was an aisled hall and two dovecots. Some of this has been lost

under a roundabout and a new road but there is still much to see north of the abbey.

The site of Lanthony Priory at Gloucester (Fig. 70) has been studied largely from documentary evidence. Although there is little left of standing buildings and

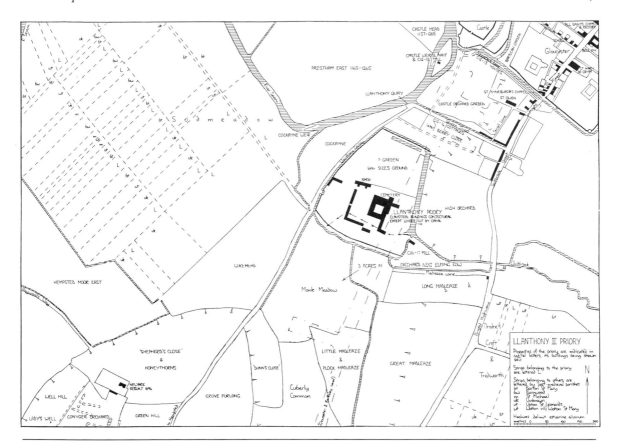

70 *Lanthony Priory (Gloucester). Plan of the precinct of the Augustinian house built to the south of
Gloucester. The area is now built up and the Gloucester canal and docks partly cut through the site. This plan is
the result of detailed documentary research by John Rhodes who has managed to resurrect on paper the lost
landscape around the monastic buildings.*

structures, it has been possible to produce a
useful plan of the precinct relating it not
only to later changes, which include the
construction of a canal across the site, but
also to the medieval town of Gloucester and
surrounding features such as common fields
and gardens. The precinct was moated, with
the gate to the west; there was ample space
for the outer court, gardens and fishponds.

Many other sites could be discussed,
although in general there has been less study
of the precincts of the canons' sites. An
unusual site is Watton (Yorkshire) (see Fig.
49), which was a Gilbertine 'double' house
of nuns and canons. The unusual plan of the

claustral buildings with its two cloisters and
two churches was excavated many years ago
and there are plenty of earthworks on the
site as well as the surviving 'Prior's lodge'.
Because of the way the monastery was
organized there were, in fact, two conjoined
precincts. The smaller westerly one
surrounded the nuns' buildings and was
defined by a watercourse on the east side and
ditches and banks on the west and north
sides. That of the canons' lay to the east and
was larger; it was defined by a moat, hedge,
ditches and a wall. As both halves of the
claustral buildings were linked by galleries
the division of the precincts was at the

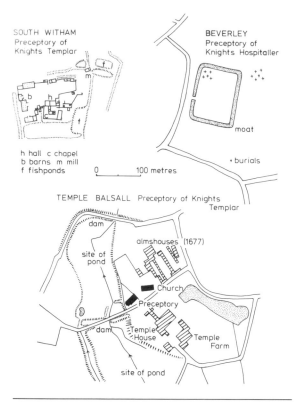

SOUTH WITHAM
Preceptory of
Knights Templar

BEVERLEY
Preceptory of
Knights Hospitaller

moat

· burials

h hall c chapel
b barns m mill
f fishponds

0   100 metres

TEMPLE BALSALL Preceptory of Knights Templar

dam

almshouses (1677)

site of
pond

Church

Preceptory

dam

Temple
House

Temple
Farm

site of pond

71 *Precincts of the Military Orders: South Witham Knights Templar Preceptory (Lincolnshire); Beverley Knights Hospitaller (Humberside); and Temple Balsall Knights Templar (Warwickshire).*

meeting of the two communities, at the 'window house'.

Precincts of the military orders

The establishments of the military orders in England, the Knights Templar and the Knights Hospitaller, consist rather more of farms than proper monasteries, and as such they seem to have poorly defined precincts. Some are well preserved, such as Temple Balsall (Warwickshire) (Fig. 71), where there is possibly a moated enclosure with a hall and church, or Quenington in the Gloucestershire Cotswolds with a church, gatehouse and moat, but at others nothing

survives. The preceptory of the Knights Hospitaller at Beverley (Yorkshire) (Fig. 71) was one of the wealthiest in the country at the time of its dissolution in 1540, but there is nothing visible now. The moated enclosure survived as a pesthouse and then a garden through to the eighteenth century but it was finally obliterated in the construction of a railway station and sidings.

The site at South Witham, near Stamford (Lincolnshire), has been completely excavated and the entire plan of the Knights Templar preceptory revealed (Fig. 71). Within a rectangular enclosure, defined by banks on three sides and by the river Witham, fishponds and a mill site on the east, was a chapel, halls, kitchens, barns and various kilns and workshops. The complex looks like the outer court of a large monastery, or a grange or monastic farm.

Houses of the friars

Most of the friaries of the thirteenth century were founded in urban situations with the same sort of problems of space and layout as have already been noted with the older Benedictine houses. At Oxford, for example, the Greyfriars were founded just inside the town wall in the south-west part of the town, but the rebuilding of the church necessitated breaching the town defences and extending on to the low-lying land to the south (Fig. 72). Nearby the Blackfriars laid out their buildings on a less restricted site but it was nevertheless on the low-lying land next to the Thames. Both the Greyfriars and the Blackfriars have also been examined at Bristol. For the latter substantial buildings remain and it looks as if the precinct was a rectangular area of the

72 *Plans of Bristol and Oxford with the sites of the friaries.*

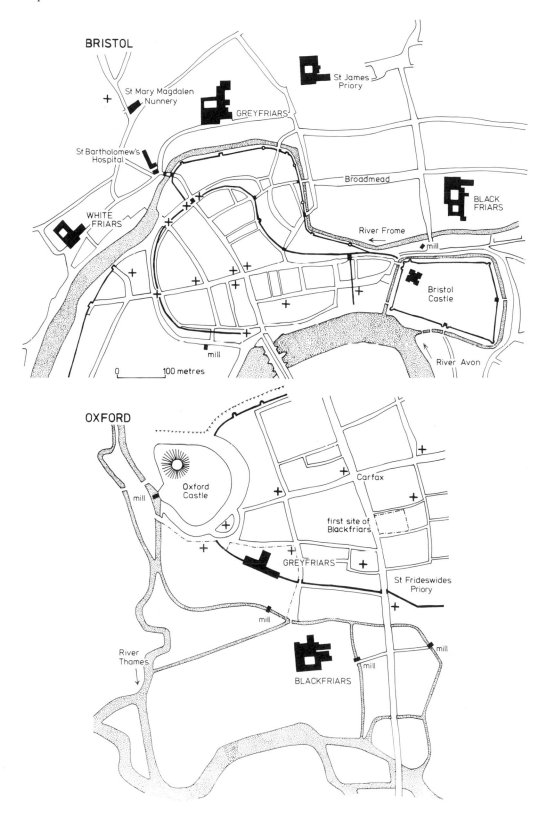

BRISTOL

St James Priory

St Mary Magdalen Nunnery

GREYFRIARS

St Bartholomew's Hospital

Broadmead

BLACK FRIARS

WHITE FRIARS

River Frome

mill

Bristol Castle

mill

River Avon

0   100 metres

OXFORD

Oxford Castle

mill

Carfax

first site of Blackfriars

GREYFRIARS

St Frideswides Priory

mill

mill

River Thames

mill

BLACKFRIARS

new town, which was developed to the north of the castle near the river Frome, between Rosemary Street, Merchant Street and the Broad Weir stream. Greyfriars, which has been excavated, was hemmed in between a sandstone cliff to the north and the river Frome to the south. The exact extent of the precinct is not apparent but the friary was surrounded by other monasteries: St Bartholomew's Hospital and St Mary Magdalene's nunnery to the west and the Benedictine priory of St James to the east.

Finally, an example of a small walled precinct can be seen at the early Carmelite friary of Hulne in the park at Alnwick (see Fig. 52). This is no more than 100 by 100m (330 by 330ft) but is surrounded by a stout wall, with a gatehouse on the south side, and sited on a bluff ideally suited for fortification. Inside, small spaces are allocated to gardens, an orchard, a cemetery and a small court with a late medieval tower. The whole stands in contrast to the vast Cistercian precincts and seems to owe more to the early monastic enclosures of Wales and the west than to most medieval precincts.

The landscape of monastic precincts

What general points can be learned from this study of a selection of monastic precincts? Is there perhaps a 'characteristic' size, layout of buildings, disposition of water supply and drainage features or means of demarcation? It seems clear that, in general, the wealthier the monastery the larger the precinct, although there were always restrictions in urban sites. The layout of buildings seems always to take into account the flow of water through the precinct. At Gloucester, for example, the Fullbrook was led across the north side of the town defences, through the claustral buildings of St Peter's Abbey, now the cathedral, to the north of the church, through the abbey mill, and then on through the precinct of St Oswald's Priory before

being discharged into the old river Severn. Such arrangements are typical.

The construction of the precinct boundary seems to depend on the wealth of the particular monastery involved. The larger and wealthier houses eventually constructed stone walls and elaborate gatehouses, while the smaller ones had banks and ditches, and no doubt timber palisades, as their boundary. A great variety of buildings remain, have been excavated or are recorded in documents in monastic precincts. Although the general outlines are similar in many cases, the length of time that monastic sites were used, with attendant periods of building and renewal, means that there are infinite differences in detail.

The precincts around medieval monasteries not only enclosed and protected the main monastic buildings, providing an area of peace and detachment from the world, but they also enclosed a variety of buildings and structures which tell us a great deal about the everyday life of the religious community and those whose job it was to support them. They demonstrate that monasteries were not only religious institutions – even if this was their main purpose, or even architectural masterpieces – which many of them are, but that they were also economic organizations involved in a variety of activities designed to support the people within them and the charitable work they did for lay folk. We may be impressed by spectacular architectural remains but often we forget all the ancilliary structures on such sites. It is usually not too difficult to see something of the precinct around and the features and structures within it, thus enhancing our understanding of the significance of monastic sites in the landscape. Monasteries could not operate successfully without an income and this usually meant land and the products from it. Their estates were the means by which monasteries supported their activities and it is to these that we must now turn.

7 Monastic estates, lands and buildings

All monasteries depended for their continued existence on the proper management of their estates. This could either be done directly, with the land being worked by the brethren and the goods produced consumed by the community itself, or by the leasing out of the land for rent, with the income thus produced being used to purchase food, goods and services as required. In practice a variety of different strategies was employed, depending on the order concerned, the period covered and the involvement of particular abbots and monks. Some sought to build up the estates of their houses by judicious purchase of land, although much might have already been given by founders and patrons. Once the estate was consolidated, production could be increased by careful management of the resources available. To be successful in a predominantly agricultural economy, monasteries depended for their prosperity on the exploitation of their land. After the initial grants of lands by the founders and any subsequent purchases by the religious house, any improvement in production would have had to come from the efforts of the community itself.

Three types of information about medieval monastic estates are available to us. The first is the multitude of names on the map which have some sort of monastic connotation to them – 'abbots', 'monks', 'priors' or the like – attached to villages, woods, mills or even whole parishes. While such elements are for the most part quite reliable and indicate that the land was held by some ecclesiastical institution in the Middle Ages, caution is needed about others. 'Grange' for example can indicate a monastic farm, but in later times it was used more often for any large Victorian mansion with no monastic connection whatsoever and can therefore be very misleading. Examples of such names are legion and are found in every corner of the country.

Secondly there is the wealth of surviving monastic estate buildings scattered the length and breadth of the country in farms, villages and towns. The most obvious of these monuments are the large barns, invariably but wrongly called 'tithe barns', of which there are some very spectacular surviving examples. These were used for the storage of the demesne produce from an entire manor or several manors and are unlike tithe barns, which were used for the storage of one tenth of the grain produced from a manor for the support of the parish church and are usually quite small. Examples of large barns in the care of English Heritage (EH) and the National Trust (NT) include Bradford-on-Avon (Wiltshire; EH) which formerly belonged to the nuns of Shaftesbury; Great Coxwell (Oxfordshire; NT) (Fig. 73) belonging to the Cistercian monks of Beaulieu; Prior's Hall Barn, Widdington (Essex; EH); Leigh Court Barn (Worcestershire; EH) of Pershore Abbey; Buckland Abbey barn

73   *The Great Barn at Great Coxwell (Oxfordshire). The early thirteenth-century barn on the grange here belonged to Beaulieu Abbey in Hampshire.*

74   *The dovecot at Kinwarton (Warwickshire). This fourteenth-century circular dovecot belonged to Evesham Abbey.*

(Devon; NT); Coggeshall Grange barn (Essex; NT); Ashleworth, (Gloucestershire; NT) belonging to the canons of St Augustine's Abbey, Bristol; Middle Littleton (Worcestershire; NT) of Evesham Abbey; and the barn at West Pennard Court (Somerset; NT) of Glastonbury Abbey.

Also well represented are dovecots or pigeon houses, the possession of which was a medieval prerogative of manorial lords like monasteries; a good example survives at Kinwarton (Warwickshire; NT) (Fig. 74) formerly belonging to the monks of

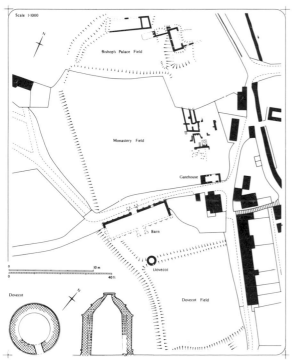

75 *The grange at Llantwit Major (Glamorgan, Wales). Plan of the ruins and the earthworks and excavated buildings, together with an artist's reconstruction of the barn and the dovecot (above).*

Evesham Abbey. There are also substantial numbers of manor houses or parts of former monastic granges surviving, often encased in later rebuilding schemes. Good examples include Monknash, a grange of Neath Abbey, and Llantwit Major (Glamorgan) belonging to Tewkesbury Abbey (Fig. 75); Frocester Court and Standish (Gloucestershire), both properties of St Peter's Abbey, Gloucester; Tisbury Place (Wiltshire) (Fig. 76) belonging to Shaftesbury Abbey; and Meare (Somerset), a manor of Glastonbury Abbey.

Many aspects of these buildings remain to be studied by historians and archaeologists. It would be useful to know, for example, if the size of the barns was related to the area of an estate and how it was exploited. The date of construction of many needs to be more closely defined using techniques such as dendrochronology. It is not at all clear, without detailed study of individual estates, what proportion of the original number of them is left in the landscape. There were, for example, two large barns on the estate of Glastonbury Abbey at Shapwick (Somerset) but both were demolished in the early

76   *Tisbury (Wiltshire). The gatehouse of the grange farm which belonged to the Benedictine nuns at Shaftesbury Abbey in Dorset. The house survives as well as a magnificent great barn.*

nineteenth century. Only with detailed research on the estates of a particular monastery from a topographical point of view will such questions be answered.

Thirdly, there is an abundance of historical material about the activities of monasteries in the countryside. The burcaucratic nature of these institutions meant that many documents were compiled and maintained; the numerous chronicles, cartularies and surveys that have survived provide a wealth of topographical detail of estates and the activities undertaken on them. From these sources a number of themes can be examined, which occur again and again in the activities of monasteries. These include colonization of new land and the extension of cultivation; clearance ('assarting') in the forests and woodlands; the draining of fen and marsh and reclamation along the coast; the control of the sea and fresh water by canals, embankments and dykes; and reclamation of the uplands. Also we must not overlook the fact that many of the estates of the older monasteries had belonged to them for generations by the time of the Norman Conquest. During the late Saxon period, the growth of village settlement and the development of the common field system had taken place, often it seems planned and carried out by monastic landowners. Their lands were intimately associated with the lands of the lay people and most of this land, all through the early Middle Ages, was concerned with the production of crops.

The monastic grange

Monastic farming was conducted from farms in the countryside, often referred to as 'grangia' in the documents, and which have come to be called granges, whether they were part of the village fabric or isolated in the countryside. These granges consisted of the normal range of farm buildings, even if on a rather larger scale and perhaps more elaborately built than elsewhere. Apart from the farmhouse there would often have been a chapel; one or more large barns were provided for storage and there was often a dovecot. Apart from animal sheds there may have been fishponds and a mill. The whole complex might be moated or surrounded by a wall with a gatehouse.

Granges might be sited in villages, with the monastic lands mixed with those of the peasants, or in villages but on their own land, or away from villages at the centre of a monastery's own lands, like those of the Cistercians. Granges tend to be viewed as separate establishments but in most cases the land of the monks or canons was intermixed in common field systems with that of the villagers and the grange was an integral part of the village structure. The historical definition of a grange tends to reflect the former – a consolidated block of land from which all common rights have been excluded – while the archaeological viewpoint sees granges as groups of buildings from which an estate was worked, regardless of the style of landholding.

Little archaeological research has been carried out on grange sites; in 1969 Colin Platt was able to cite only a few which had been examined, although at a number of others he noted medieval buildings remaining. Since then Dean Court, one of five granges in Cumnor parish near Oxford

belonging to Abingdon Abbey (Fig. 77), has been excavated. Apart from a house for the reeve, or farm manager, there were barns, a cowshed, a dovecot, fishponds, a smithy, other farm buildings and cottages for the farm workers. A grange belonging to Garendon Abbey, Holywell Hall outside Loughborough, has also been examined. The moated house survives as a farm, while beyond there are earthworks of a fishpond and enclosures with extensive ridge and furrow of field systems, as at Dean Court.

Other sites survive as earthworks and there are probably more of these about than has previously been recognized. Many of the granges belonging to the great Cistercian abbeys of Yorkshire have earthwork remains of moats, fishponds and enclosures. Frequently there are also settlement remains of the peasant hamlets that accompanied the grange and which housed the labourers who worked the monastic estates alongside the lay brothers. Examples of granges with good earthworks which belonged to the Welsh abbeys of Margam and Neath include Marcross and Monknash, while the well-preserved remains at Llantwit Major belonged to the abbot of Tewkesbury (Figs 14 and 75). Widespread examples include those belonging to Garendon and Leicester abbeys in Charnwood Forest (Leicestershire) and the group in the former forest of Feckenham, such as Holloway, belonging to Bordesley Abbey. On Levisham Moor on the North York Moors a sheep farm of Old Malton Gilbertine priory survives as well-preserved earthworks and there are others at Griff Grange (Rievaulx Abbey) and Melsonby Grange (Jervaulx Abbey).

A recent landscape and archaeological study of great interest is that of Roystone Grange in the White Peak area of Derbyshire (Fig. 78). This was one of a number of granges in the area belonging to Garendon Abbey – others were Biggin and Heathcote nearby – and although it was established as

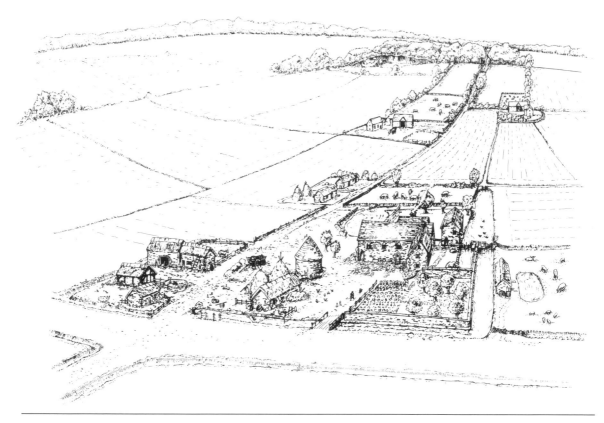

77   *The Grange at Cumnor (Oxfordshire). A reconstruction based on the evidence recovered from recent excavations by Tim Allen and the Oxford Archaeological Unit. It belonged to Abingdon Abbey.*

an upland farm in the twelfth century, recent survey has shown that there had been occupation on the site for several thousand years before that. The farm continued in the post-medieval period through to the present day. The buildings of a typical grange were excavated here but of equal interest was the location of the fields of the medieval grange surviving among the rest of the field boundaries, some of which go back to the prehistoric period. Nearby were numerous other monastic granges – Dunstable Priory's grange at Mouldridge, as well as granges of the abbeys of Combermere, Darley, Leicester, Lilleshall, Merevale, Roche and Rufford.

Any monastery might have a range of different granges. At Guisborough Priory,

for example, there seem to have been separate isolated granges at Brotton, Ugthorpe, Loftus and perhaps Skelton and Moorsholm, whereas at North Loftus there were 15 messuages and 19 tofts with 28 bovates and 30 acres of land – evidently this estate was part of a village.

The Gilbertine priory of Malton had a number of granges in the rich land of the Vale of Pickering – Wintringham, Swinton, Sutton and Rillington – on which arable farming was very important. That these were farms working land in the nearby villages, presumably intermixed with other villagers' land, is suggested by 14 bovates of land at Thorpe being worked by Rillington grange half a mile away and the grange at Swinton probably working the 12 bovates at

Arable farming

There is a growing body of evidence that many villages and their fields were carefully laid out in the centuries between 900 and 1200. Some researchers see this as an aspect of careful estate management in the centuries either side of the Norman Conquest. If this was the case the major Benedictine abbeys could be considered as the sort of 'improving' landowners who might be involved in village and field planning. At present it is very difficult to prove that this planning definitely occurred at any particular place, but there is some indication that abbeys like Glastonbury might have been involved in laying out villages in Somerset, such as those on the Polden Hills for example.

The ancient Benedictine abbeys had become highly efficient farmers by the beginning of the Middle Ages. It has been estimated, for example, that 55 per cent of the arable land in Kent in 1086 was in ecclesiastical hands. With more compact estates, continuity of institutional ownership, together with careful administration, efficient production and careful division of farming on their lands, the Benedictines became specialists in cereal farming. Canterbury Cathedral Priory reached its peak of grain production in 1306–24, the period of 'High Farming', which was marked in the thirteenth and early fourteenth centuries by rising production, capital investment on a large scale, technological improvement and flexible rotation of crops. Typical was Prior Eastry of Canterbury, who acquired rented property, made improvements to farm buildings and invested heavily in watermills and windmills, land drainage, marsh reclamation and soil improvement. A similar situation can be seen on the estates of Westminster Abbey. The remarkable farm at Alciston (Sussex), formerly belonging to Battle Abbey, with its barn (Fig. 79) and

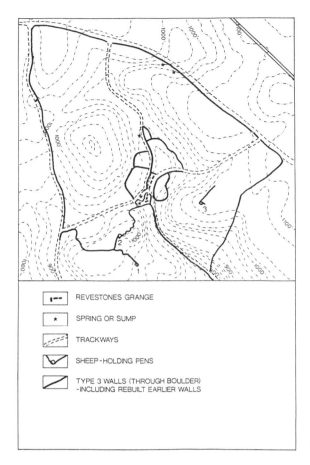

78 *Roystone Grange (Derbyshire). This plan which forms part of the long-term research project on the farm at Roystone shows the new walls and farm added to form a grange in the twelfth century for Garendon Abbey in Leicestershire. The land had already been settled and farmed from prehistoric and Roman times and has continued to be farmed right up to the present day.*

REVESTONES GRANGE

SPRING OR SUMP

TRACKWAYS

SHEEP-HOLDING PENS

TYPE 3 WALLS (THROUGH BOULDER) -INCLUDING REBUILT EARLIER WALLS

Amotherby and the 34 bovates at Broughton which the priory owned. The priory continued to acquire land in the Vale and build up the estates of the monastery. Some time between 1223 and 1234 it acquired the grange at Ebberston and by 1301 this had become the richest of all its granges.

79   *Alciston (Sussex) the interior of the barn.*

fourteenth-century manor house, 'is a fitting record of the entrepreneurial efficiency and foresight which established a farming regime unmatched generally in England until 400 years later'. In the later Middle Ages the growth of the renting economy, with the leasing out of the demesne land, led to the almost total disappearance of this type of direct demesne farming.

Without any surviving buildings, it is usually not possible today to distinguish such monastic arable farming from that of the peasantry at the time; the great barns are the main witnesses. As Christopher Taylor says of the Dorset Benedictine estates, 'There is no evidence, however, that any of these monastic estates were exploited or worked differently from the adjacent lay estates. Much of the land was leased, though there were also grange farms worked by lay brothers. In this sense the effect of these houses on the landscape was negligible'. Nevertheless, when we look at the arable fields of medieval settlements we are in

many cases looking at the land which was managed, and in some cases worked, by generations of monastic officials and servants.

Many of the sites selected for the Benedictine monasteries founded in the seventh, eighth and tenth centuries had shown some preference for isolated and wild surroundings, cutting off the monks from the temptations of the world. Marshes, fens, wooded and forested landscapes, and to a lesser extent mountain areas, were often chosen. By the twelfth century, attitudes had changed so that the wild areas, originally chosen to provide isolation, were seen as areas to be improved and exploited for the greater benefit, and wealth, of their monastic owners. This was also true of those houses, both of the old and new orders, founded in the twelfth and early thirteenth centuries; no sooner had they settled in their wild lands than they set about clearing woods, draining marshes and exploiting the countryside for greater material and financial gain.

Forests, woods, assarts and clearance

Although it is possible to overemphasize the amount of wooded land in Britain in the early Middle Ages and the degree to which it was exploited, there is no doubt that great changes were engineered in the twelfth and thirteenth centuries, in both the north and the south of the country, and that large areas were cleared of trees and brought into cultivation. This was undertaken by the existing Benedictine communities, as well as the newer orders and a large number of lay people.

There have been few attempts to see how much trace is left on the ground of this clearance activity, even though a lot of it is recorded in the documents, which have been extensively studied by economic historians. It is easy to get the impression that the impact of the monasteries was greater in the north, especially Yorkshire, than in the south and that most of the activity was in the twelfth and thirteenth centuries rather than earlier. However, there were great changes in the well settled and exploited areas of the south of the country and much of this must have taken place in the largely undocumented centuries before 1100.

For example, Peterborough Abbey must have been clearing land on a large scale before the documents of the twelfth century enable us to see the process in detail. Fines were paid for assarting in Werrington, Cottingham, Oundle and Great Easton in 1162–3 and 1166–7. The sacrist of the abbey created a whole new estate of 240 ha (600 acres) at Paston (Huntingdonshire) between 1175 and 1225 by assarting and clearance in an area under Forest Law. The abbey also cleared much of Oundle woods, an area 7 by 5 km (4 by 3 miles) in the period 1163–7; by 1189 there were 160 ha (400 acres) of assarts. The abbey's manor here, called Novum Locum, is now Biggin Grange situated 2 km (1 mile) west of Oundle – a new manor carved out of forest land. Clearance was also going on between 1175 and 1225 in north Northamptonshire, to the west of Peterborough at Longthorpe, Walton, Castor and Ailsworth. A grange was established in the manor of Castor and new assarts in Nassaburgh are now represented by Belsize in the same parish.

In Hertfordshire, St Alban's Abbey was active in the period up to 1250 in clearing land in the west of the county, estates which in some cases had been granted to the abbey by Offa in 793. In the post-Conquest period the abbey expanded its own manors rather than letting assarts to sub-tenants. In Oxfordshire, Eynsham Abbey was clearing land in Wychwood forest, while in Suffolk, Bury St Edmund's Abbey was engaged in the assarting of Bradfield in the eleventh and twelfth centuries. Many other examples could be cited in all parts of southern England. Extensive forest clearances in the counties of Shropshire, Sussex, Northamptonshire, Warwickshire and Hertfordshire can be instanced from the activities of the abbeys of Shrewsbury, Battle, Ramsey, St Albans and the cathedral priory of Ely.

Thus when the new orders arrived on the scene, much dramatic change in the landscape was already underway. The predilection of these orders to seek out areas with few settlements, and thus few feudal ties, meant that grants of woodland were very acceptable to them; however, clearance and cultivation quickly followed. The intention seems to have been to acquire land with no restrictions so that it could be farmed directly rather than there being an interest in wooded or wild places for their own sake. The amount of forest clearance achieved was prodigious, leaving a lasting impression, especially in connection with the Cistercians, that the monks of the newer orders were the greatest land clearers of the early Middle Ages. Gerald of Wales wrote of them in the twelfth century:

settle the Cistercians in some barren retreat which is hidden away in an overgrown forest; a year or two later you will find splendid churches there and monastic buildings, with a great amount of property and all the wealth you can imagine.

The true explanation is more likely to be that they were energetic in the exploitation of *any* land free from manorial restrictions and that such land tended to be the relatively less exploited forest, marsh and hill country.

In order to create these conditions of unrestricted exploitation they were not above removing existing settlements and the white monks quickly acquired an unenviable reputation for this; it was, however, not a prerogative confined to the Cistercian order. By contrast, new villages were sometimes created and many granges had settlements of lay people attached to them. It has usually been assumed that evictions indicated a complete change from feudal settlements to farms run exclusively by lay brothers. While the latter certainly existed and there were also some evictions, the creation of many granges may have been more of a change from village or hamlet to grange farm and labourers' hamlet, with the feudal tenants becoming paid servants working alongside the lay brothers. There were probably never enough lay brothers overall for the work that was needed and peasant labour would always have been necessary to run the estates, especially at harvest time and for such tasks as ditch digging. The earthworks at many sites seem to show this (Fig. 80), with settlement remains being found next to grange sites at Griff, Braithwaite and Cayton, while the documents suggest numbers of lay people on the staff of granges together with the hiring of part-time labour at certain times of the year.

In Yorkshire, it is clear that there was a lot of underused land in the twelfth century at the time that many monasteries of the new orders were founded in the county. Not only were the uplands largely unused, and the valleys full of woodland, but many of the settlements which had existed had been destroyed by William the Conqueror 'harrying the north', destroying crops and houses to deter rebellion in the late eleventh century. Much of this land was still derelict and unused by the early twelfth century and therefore available to be granted to monasteries of the new orders. There are also many indications that woodland was extensive in the Dales in the twelfth century and later and that it was first exploited by the monasteries.

It is not difficult to show that virtually every Cistercian monastery was engaged in such colonizing and clearance activities. At Byland, Kirkstall, Combermere, Tintern and Stoneleigh, assarting was carried out from the foundation of the abbeys.

Fountains was clearing at Long Marston, South Stainley and Wheldrake, and around the early granges of Brimham and Bradley. Near to Bradley the monks received assarts in Kirkheaton and at least one was bounded by woodland on one side. Rievaulx was given 8.5 ha (21 acres) of woodland and uncultivated ground at Bolton in Wensleydale in 1173–4 and 4 ha (10 acres) in Pilley to assart in 1150–7; it was also granted two woods in Farndale by Roger de Mowbray before 1155 – Middlehead and Dowthwaite – which were cleared. Kirkstall was creating clearings along the river Aire and its tributaries and there were many assarts to the south of the abbey at Bramley and near the grange of Bessacar.

Further south, Warden Abbey (Bedfordshire) was clearing land in Paxton and Diddington. It also assarted the wood of Ravenshoe for arable, as well as the wood of Pirie (East Perry in Huntingdonshire) which it then enclosed with a ditch and fence. Dieulacres Abbey (Staffordshire) cleared land at Pulford for assarts and in 1314 there is mention of the newly tilled land of Stanley Abbey at le Mershe in Chippenham (Wiltshire). Pipewell, established in a heavily wooded area in Northamptonshire, was involved in the clearance of woods to provide tillage; Rawhaw, Barrowdykes, Askershaw, Little Haws and Monks Arbour woods were all cut into, Cooeshawe, Rahage and Otha woods were entirely cleared, and Wilbarston and Pykemede woods had gone by 1237.

The same sort of activities can be traced in Wales, for as Gerald of Wales said of the Cistercians in the late twelfth century, 'give them a wilderness or forest, and in a few years you will find a dignified abbey in the midst of smiling plenty'. Licences to the monks to fell trees and bring land into cultivation were granted to the abbeys of Dore, Strata Florida and Whitland. At both Neath and Tintern there were granges called 'Assart'. Tintern probably cleared much of

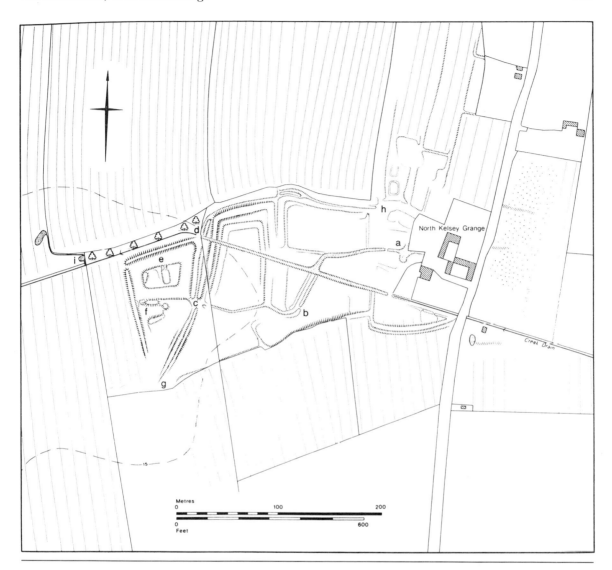

80 *North Kelsey grange (Lincolnshire). Plan of the grange earthworks of the Gilbertine priory of North Ormsby, showing the lay hamlet at 'h', to the east of the farm buildings. The earthworks to the west are fishponds.*

the parish of Newchurch in Gwent when it developed its manor of Plataland, and it was involved in assarting right down to the fifteenth century. It paid fines following the clearance of Royal Forest land, the major assart resulting in the grange of Ashwell in Tidenham. Basingwerk was involved in clearance of land on its English estates in the Peak District and near Glossop. The land

near Strata Florida has been shown by pollen analysis to have changed from woodland to arable in the late thirteenth and early fourteenth centuries.

Most of these assart areas were usually held individually as separate enclosed fields, although some became part of the local common fields and their identity as monastic clearance was lost. One advantage of assarted land was that it was free of tithes. Some of it was cleared by lay brothers alone, but elsewhere work might have been carried on with the collaboration of local peasants.

The legacy of this activity is still there in the landscape with its host of field clearance names, farm and grange sites and pieces of remaining woodland. Sinuous roads and holloways and serpentine field boundaries, often very rich in shrub species, reflect the piecemeal and unplanned nature of the clearance and the way the landscape evolved.

Fen, marsh and coastal drainage

Many monks had retreated to the marshes originally for solitude, but from at least the late Saxon period, and to judge from the documents particularly in the twelfth century, they set about draining and improving these areas. They attempted to make them more useful agriculturally, more productive and more like the rest of the countryside. The change is reflected by the thirteenth-century monk Matthew Paris writing about the Fens:

Concerning the marsh a wonder has happened in our time; for in the years past, beyond living memory, these places were accessible neither for man nor for beast, affording only deep mud with sedge and reeds, and inhabited by birds, indeed more likely by devils as appears from the life of St Guthlac who began to live there and found it a place of horror and solitude. This is now changed into delightful meadows and also arable ground. What does not produce corn or hay brings forth abundant sedge, turf and other fuel, very useful to the inhabitants of the region.

What had happened to the earlier ideals?

The main centres of this drainage were in the Fens of eastern England (see Fig. 25), due to the activities of the abbeys at Peterborough, Ramsey, Crowland, Ely and Spalding, and the Somerset Levels,

associated with the abbeys of Glastonbury, Muchelney and Athelney. Other areas were also tackled, such as the north coast of Kent by Christ Church Cathedral Priory, Canterbury, and the marshes of Holderness in the East Riding of Yorkshire by Meaux Abbey. Other non-monastic institutions were also active; in the Somerset Levels, for example, much of the drainage was engineered by tenants of the bishops of Bath and Wells.

The Fenlands and the Somerset Levels were drained to provide rich pasture. Peterborough Abbey was active in the reclamation of the fen at Eye to the north-east of the abbey. The abbots seem to have created a new park at Eyebury and new farms were also developed at Northolm, Eyebury and Oxney. The abbots of Thorney were also involved; the whole area to the east of Peterborough was clearly being developed in the twelfth and thirteenth centuries with the areas next to the 'highland' being the easiest to reclaim and any areas of higher ground, the 'islands' like Oxney, forming the focus for new farms.

In Somerset the abbeys set about land reclamation by working outward from the 'islands' in the Levels, such as the new ground taken in around Sowy (now Westonzoyland, Middlezoy and Othery), and Brent Knoll, in the thirteenth century. As well as digging ditches and building dykes, rivers were diverted and canals built. The whole drainage pattern was dramatically altered with the diversion of the river Brue. This formerly ran north from Glastonbury through the gap in the hills at Panborough into the waters of the river Axe. There was frequent flooding around the 'island' of Glastonbury so an ambitious plan was put into operation some time between 1230 and 1250. This involved the canalization of much of the waters of the former river Brue into a new channel taken out to the river Parret through a cut at

Highbridge. Water which formerly went
through the gap at Bleadney to the valley of
the Axe now fed the new river and the
Pilrow cut (Fig. 81), a thirteenth-century
canal running north from the Brue to the
Axe at Rooks Bridge nearer its confluence
with the Severn estuary. These waterways
acted as both drainage ditches and canals and
they must have facilitated the movement of
heavy goods far inland from the coast. The
great mere or pool at Meare, which was
2km (over a mile) across and more than 8km
(5 miles) round at its greatest extent (see
Figs. 32 and 84), formed part of this system,
whereas the river Siger, which had drained
much of the western part of the Levels,
seems to have had its headwaters cut off.
This drainage together with the build up of
sand dunes along the coast led to the
disappearance of the river.

Elsewhere, the extensive pasture in the
open Levels gave rise to frequent disputes
over use. Glastonbury Abbey and the
bishops of Bath and Wells were often at
loggerheads and several times arguments
were solved by the construction of banks
and dykes to define areas of ownership.
Hartlake Rhyne was dug to separate their
lands and in 1327 after a famous prolonged
argument, which included violent clashes
between the servants on each side, the
Bounds Ditch (Fig. 82) was dug on the
border of the parishes of Wedmore
(belonging to the bishop) and Meare
(belonging to the abbot).

In east Yorkshire the wide marshy valley
of the Hull, running south to the Humber,
was tackled by the monks of Meaux Abbey,
founded on an island in the valley in 1150.
They began to dig canals around 1160,
initially to provide water transport between
their properties but as time went on these
became increasingly important for drainage
(Fig. 83). Eschedike (1160–82) linked the
abbey to the Hull river; Monkdike (1210–
20), which was 6m (20ft) wide, diverted
some of the water of the Lambwath (one of

81   *The Pilrow Cut, Rooks Bridge (Somerset).
This thirteenth-century channel served as both a canal
from the river Axe to Glastonbury and as a drainage
ditch diverting much of the water of the river Brue.*

82   *Bounds Ditch, Meare and Wedmore (Somerset).
This seemingly ordinary ditch in fact marks the
boundary between the lands of the bishop of Bath and
Wells in Wedmore and those of the abbot of
Glastonbury in Meare. It was dug after a dispute in
the early fourteenth century.*

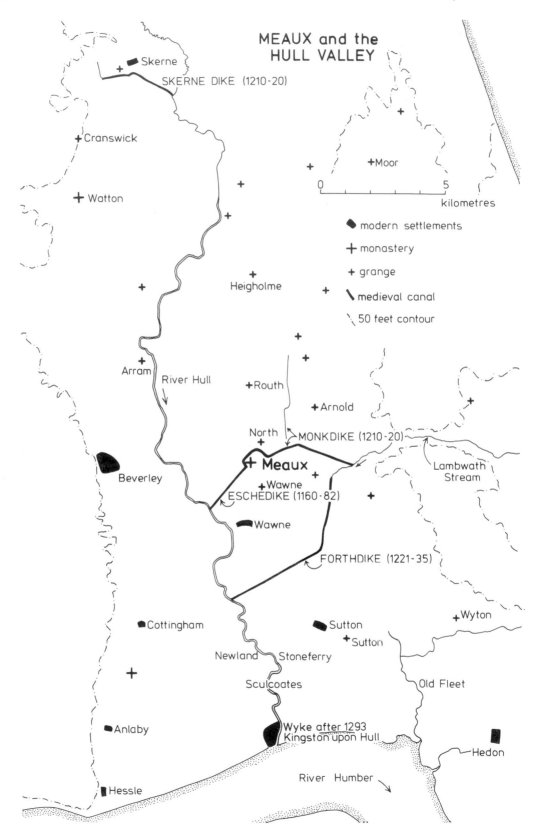

MEAUX and the
HULL VALLEY

Skerne
SKERNE DIKE (1210-20)

Cranswick

Watton

Moor

0 _____ 5
kilometres

● modern settlements
+ monastery
+ grange
▬ medieval canal
⸝ 50 feet contour

Heigholme

Arram

River Hull

Routh

Arnold

North

MONKDIKE (1210-20)

Lambwath
Stream

+ Meaux

Beverley

Wawne
ESCHEDIKE (1160-82)

Wawne

FORTHDIKE (1221-35)

Cottingham

Sutton

Sutton

Wyton

Newland   Stoneferry

Sculcoates

Old Fleet

Anlaby

Wyke after 1293
Kingston upon Hull

Hedon

Hessle

River Humber

the main Old Fleet tributaries) through the abbey grounds into Eschedike; Forthdike (1221–35), 5m (16ft) wide, improved an old fence-ditch between Wawne and Sutton and carried much of the Lambwath water; Skernedike (1210–20) served a grange in the north of the valley. The 'clows' or sluices were frequently blocked and little improvement to the land came about until after the Middle Ages. Nevertheless, the early drainage pattern has been overlain by many other, more recent, improvements, but the names and to some extent the lines of the Meaux dikes survive in the present landscape.

Along the coast of the Humber, the abbey was also reclaiming land; farms called Saltheugh, Keyngham and Tharlesthorpe were established on newly reclaimed land, only to be lost in later flooding and replaced by more farms built further inland. Bridlington Priory was also involved in drainage in the Hull valley. At Brandesburton the priory made a fosse around a marsh called Witheland and farms called Hempholme and Hollytreeholme were created.

Elsewhere in Yorkshire, there are several cases of the draining of marshes and their use for farming in the moors and carrs of the Vale of Pickering. Reclamation of the marshland of Pickering Waste had already been undertaken by Rievaulx Abbey. Later the monks had two granges in the central vale at Loftmarsh and Kekmarsh with extensive and valuable lands – in 1274 Kekmarsh had 120 ha (300 acres) of arable and 120 ha (300 acres) of pasture. There was also much land in Thornton marshes. In the

same area the Gilbertines at Malton had several granges – Ryton, Kirby Misperton and Edston – as sheep or cattle stations.

The engineering and drainage skills of the monks were considerable by the twelfth century. The examples outlined above are merely some of the best known but countless other schemes can be detected from the documents and careful fieldwork. Much of the drainage could not have been achieved, of course, without the construction of canals and dykes, often of impressive proportions. Examples include the new sea defences of Pevensey (Sussex) built by the Benedictines of Battle Abbey. There Abbot Ralph (1107–24) organized the reclamation of Barnhorne in Romney Marsh and the subsequent fields yielded good crops of cereals. The sea was kept out by the Crooked Ditch and its embankment, raised further in the fourteenth century. As Peter Brandon says, 'for several hundreds of years the Abbey carefully defended its marshland against flooding and its chequerboard pattern of ditched fields . . . making it a fine "period piece" of early medieval landscape shaping'. Similar work was going on elsewhere along the main rivers: in 1342 the abbot of Byland had built up the banks of the river Derwent in the Vale of Pickering into levees at Rillington to protect his pasture. These banks were broken by men of the nearby villages and the pasture was flooded causing great loss.

Upland pasture

In the north of the country there were vast areas of wild upland in the early Middle Ages, hardly used except as rough pasture. Over the centuries these areas were improved and developed with the building of farms and granges, the improvement of pasture with grazing and the development of mineral resources. The greatest use of such areas was for sheep pasture, and to a lesser extent as cattle farms.

83 *Meaux Abbey and the Hull valley (Humberside). A map showing the site of the abbey founded in 1150 together with the canals constructed to link its granges to the main rivers. A number of granges are shown, those belonging to Meaux being named.*

In 1127, Furness Abbey was established in a deep valley in Cumbria. It was granted two large estates – the plain of Furness, rich fertile lowland with deposits of iron ore, and High Furness, a vast area of forest and sheep pasture. Following local land disputes, in 1163 it became necessary to define the abbey's lands more precisely so that the ownership of land in the Furness Fells was clear. This resulted in confirmation to the abbey of a block of land around the monastery, together with Walney island, and the high land of Furness Fells between Coniston and Windermere. The monks also held Borrowdale, which they had bought in 1209 from Alice II de Rumelli. Fountains Abbey also held land in the area, so in 1211 the ownership was clarified there as well. A third block of land in Upper Eskdale came to Furness Abbey in 1242 when they exchanged Forse or Monkfoss near Bootle for it, giving them some 5700 ha (14,000 acres) of sheep pasture. Around 1290 the monks were given licence to enclose the pastures of Brotherkild and Lincove with a wall or dyke. Furness developed a whole range of granges in the Fells at, for example, High Furness, Lawson Park and Parkmoor, and at Hawkshead Hall Grange where the gatehouse remains. There were also several parks including New Park by the abbey's west gate. Other monasteries also held land in the Fells of Cumbria including Shap, which had land east of Ullswater, and Byland owned part of Westmorland Borrowdale.

With increased attention to the use and value of these uplands it became more and more necessary to define ownership more closely and, as noted above, agreements over rights had to be arranged. Thus in the twelfth century Upper Nidderdale was divided between Fountains and Byland abbeys, with both creating farms and granges on both old and new settlement sites. In the thirteenth century the Cistercian abbey of Newminster in Northumberland owned vast areas of upland sheep pasture in Upper Coquetdale, with the bare fells and scree of Kidland and all the hills between the river Coquet and the Scottish border. In 1181 when they were granted grazing rights in Kidland, the boundaries are carefully described – 'between Alwin and Clennell and thence by the Kidland Burn to the south as far as the great road of Yarnspeth by the wood to Yarnspeth Burn'. Even in the wild country near Windyhaugh it became necessary in the thirteenth century to define the western limits of the abbey's grazing estate; the stone bank and ditch constructed at that date on Barrow Law and Barrow Cleugh can still be seen.

Small-scale schemes and agreements over pasture were widespread. For example, in 1254 Guisborough Priory partitioned the waste of Ugthorpe in Yorkshire with Handale nunnery nearby, with the intention of converting the waste to arable although much of the land was above 180m (600ft). Most of these uplands were developed as sheep pastures and the valleys between were settled with granges which became some of the greatest sheep farms of the Middle Ages. Sheep were, however, important on all monastic estates, whether these were in upland or lowland environments, or belonged to old established Benedictine monasteries or those of the newer orders.

Sheep farming

The impression has developed that sheep farming was a prerogative of the newer orders and particularly the Cistercians. It is easy to overlook the importance of sheep for wool production, not only to the older Benedictine monasteries but also to the great lay estates and the millions of small peasant producers. As Robin Glasscock remarked: 'Sheep farming as a source of wealth was the oldest of all forms of commercial farming, and retained its importance to such great monastic houses as those of Ely, Peterborough, Glastonbury, Crowland and Canterbury Cathedral Priory' and as Robin Donkin cautions,

only Fountains among the Cistercian houses ever possessed anything like 15000 sheep (the number owned by the bishop of Winchester in 1208–9). The Cistercians were probably more deeply committed to wool growing, and certainly to supplying the overseas trade, than any other monastic order, but they by no means overshadowed all contemporary producers. At best, they supplied only three to four per cent of all the wool exported at the close of the thirteenth century.

The Cistercians were privileged in a number of ways which favoured wool production. Pope Honorius III in 1221 commanded the rectors of parishes in which they pastured sheep not to take tithe from them. They were also exempt from various tolls, free from forest regards and so on – and so it is perhaps not surprising therefore that sheep farming became so important to them.

Something of the production of wool, and hence the number of sheep and the extent of pastures and estates, is known from a very interesting early fourteenth-century source. Francesco Balducci Pegolotti, an Italian merchant and member of the merchant house of Bardi, represented the firm in England from 1318 to 1321. He made a list of monastic suppliers, which included many Cistercian monasteries, and recorded the numbers of sacks to be supplied. On the basis of 200 fleeces to the sack, the approximate size of the sheep flocks can be suggested. This produces enormous figures for the Yorkshire abbeys, for example, some of which can be verified from other evidence.

Rievaulx is reckoned to have had 12,000 sheep, Byland 7000, Whitby 6000 and the Augustinian priories of Bridlington, Kirkham and Guisborough respectively 10,000, 6000 and 4000; the Gilbertine house at Malton had 9000. Not all of this may have been their own wool and there are other caveats in addition to other lists supplying information. It does seem, however, that the monasteries became the centres of extensive trade and that the figures are to a large extent indicative of the sort of production that was achieved. In the north-east, for example, monastic sheep farming reached a predominant position over every other sphere of monastic activity. The size of the flocks was very large, especially on the Cistercian estates (notably at Rievaulx). There were not less than fifty to sixty thousand sheep belonging to the monasteries in the area in the thirteenth century.

Thus the great Yorkshire abbeys, and particularly those of the new orders, were heavily involved in sheep farming, with many of their estates noted for wool production. These were to be found particularly on the North York Moors, near the coast, in the Dales with their adjacent moorland and on the southern margins where there was even more extensive moorland. This is indicated in such documents as the Inquisition of the Ninth of 1341 and in the *Valor Ecclesiasticus* of 1535. The sheep were on the high moorlands in the summer but kept in the valleys for shelter in the winter. Monastic landowners concentrated their flocks to the north of the Vale of Pickering. The small nunnery of Rosedale had 2000 sheep in Middleton parish in 1308 and the larger houses had even more. From Ryedale to the coast there were large numbers of granges and the sheep numbers and values were high. Behind were extensive moors – Rievaulx had large areas of pasture in Farndale, Bransdale and Bilsdale. Guisborough Priory concentrated its sheep granges and sheepcotes in Eskdale; Whitby had most sheep in Hackness Dale and Rievaulx made Bilsdale its main centre with five granges and many associated sheepcotes.

Nevertheless the main sheep farms were on the estates of the older Benedictine houses. An indication of the scale of production and the importance of the enterprise to the monks can be seen from the activities of the Benedictine abbey of Winchcombe (Gloucestershire), at its Cotswold manor of Sherborne. There were extensive sheep pastures on its upland manors of Snowshill, Hawling and Charlton Abbots and the abbey's flocks were clearly moved about throughout the year. The shearing, however, took place at Sherborne and was attended each Easter by the abbot and his servants, who consumed a great deal of the manorial produce at that time. 'The abbot and his retinue did not come simply to enjoy an annual outing, although in this district the shearing must have been as festive as the harvest'. In 1468 we hear that 1900 sheep were washed and shorn, in 1485, 2900 sheep. The wool was weighed and it took four days to put it into sacks.

Cattle farming

Cattle farms or 'vaccaries' were as important as the sheep farms ('beccaries'). Cattle were grazed by the older Benedictine houses on the Somerset Levels, the Fens and areas like Romney Marsh and the Isle of Thanet. Elsewhere the new orders had cattle farms around the Pennines. There were fifteen in Wyresdale, several in Nidderdale belonging to Fountains Abbey, and others in Wensleydale attached to Jervaulx Abbey. Cattle were also kept in the Pennines, North Wales and in the forests and chases of Cumbria and the Pennines. They were moved about from lowland to upland pastures within the estates of the main houses as pasture became available. The produce could be used at the monastery, although, at least in the early centuries, the meat was probably sold rather than consumed, as most monks were largely

vegetarian. Milk and cheese were produced and there was much demand for the leather for a variety of purposes – shoes, harness and so on. As a result tanneries are important establishments at many abbeys.

Fisheries

Most monastic sites have at least one fishpond and there are frequently large numbers of them, often surviving now as dry grassy hollows, both within the precinct and on the estates (see, for instance, Figs 30, 44, 55, 60 and 62). Recent research suggests that there were very large numbers of medieval fishponds in the landscape, with a bewildering variety of shapes and sizes. Contrary to popular belief, very many of these are associated with baronial and peasant settlements rather than monastic sites. All tend to display the engineering skills which have already been discussed in connection with medieval water systems; often fishponds were linked to systems of water supply, drainage and mill complexes in elaborate water control and management operations.

As well as fishponds many monasteries possessed river and sea fisheries, usually in the form of weirs and fishtraps. Some rivers like the Severn were well endowed with them and there was some modification to the local topography as problems with reconciling the needs of mills and navigation were solved with by-pass channels. The yields, usually in eels, are recorded in Domesday Book (1086) for both river fisheries and for fen areas such as the Somerset Levels.

Vineyards

In Domesday Book there are also numerous references to vineyards. These are widely distributed in the southern counties, with

84 *Meare Fish House, Meare (Somerset). This small building housed the fishermen, their nets and equipment on the abbot of Glastonbury's manor at Meare, an estate named after the vast lake which existed nearby.*

85 *Watermill at Fountains Abbey (Yorkshire). The large corn mill within the precinct was built in the twelfth century and altered in the thirteenth. The size and elaborate architectural treatment of this building demonstrates both the wealth and the long-term investment by monasteries in economic activities on their estates.*

four or more being recorded in Wiltshire, Suffolk and Somerset; most were in Essex and Middlesex. The remains of the vineyards at Hampton, which belonged to Evesham Abbey, and Panborough, belonging to Glastonbury Abbey, have been recognized and both are on gently sloping sites with little trace of terracing. There are later references to vineyards, but with superior wine from western and southern France available from the mid-twelfth century onwards there was little need for home-grown produce.

Industrial activity

The main 'industry' of the Middle Ages was, of course, agriculture, and a number of establishments were developed to process its products. The production of wool also generated what can be called 'industrial establishments' such as the woolhouse at Fountains Abbey (see Fig. 59). Early on, the

development of the fulling mill was readily adopted by monastic houses – the first recorded is on an estate of the Templars by 1185. Stanley Abbey (Wiltshire) had a fulling mill by 1190, Thame (Oxfordshire) in 1197 and Newminster (Northumberland) by 1200. These were all Cistercian houses, and by 1300 others are known at Kirkstall, Meaux, Combermere, Flaxley, Beaulieu and Quarr.

Quarrying and mining

With the grants of large areas of land to monasteries it was inevitable that they would acquire good sources of stone and metal as well as mineral deposits and sources of coal. Their exploitation of these resources, however, is not particularly obvious from the documentary sources; as William Hoskins says of the sixteenth-

86   *Windmill at Rievaulx Abbey (Yorkshire). There were many windmills on monastic estates though they were never as profitable or reliable as watermills. This carving shows a postmill on a mound.*

century sources: 'There was an almost entire absence of revenues from mineral wealth. This has led to the belief that the monastic houses were sitting passively on top of untold wealth for later and more commercially-minded owners to develop'. There is some truth in this, but with a little searching it is not difficult to show that many monasteries were involved in the exploitation of materials on their estates. However, it is often difficult in the field to distinguish the medieval activity from later reworking of quarries and mineral deposits, as this was usually much more intensive.

Stone

The availability of a plentiful supply of good quality stone, along with other building materials, was a prime consideration while a monastic house was being built, as it was both heavy and was required in very large quantities. Sometimes it was available close at hand and could be dug out with the

minimum of work and transport costs, as at Fountains and Roche where the valley sides near the monasteries were exploited. Elsewhere there were deposits not far away which could be easily worked and where the difficulties of transport would have been minimal. Glastonbury Abbey used the famous stone from Doulting, while Cleeve Abbey dug the sandstone from nearby on its estate. At Rievaulx Abbey the nearest sources of stone were a little way from the abbey up the river valley; the quarries worked at different dates are reflected in the building phases in the abbey church and the stone may have been brought to the abbey along purpose-built canals (see Fig. 46).

Where there was no good local stone a supply had to be exploited which did not involve crippling transport costs, particularly if the quarries were at some distance from the abbey site. Transport was easier and cheaper by sea or river so that often a distant quarry was used in preference to a source which was nearer to hand but more difficult to reach by water. Caen stone from France was used in Kent and south-east England, for example, where there were few good building stones. Elsewhere, the most successful quarries in the medieval period were those close to water transport, by coastal shipping (as from Purbeck and Portland) or by river (Barnack near Peterborough, Tadcaster in Yorkshire). There were also large numbers of earlier, particularly Roman, structures that could be pillaged, even in the twelfth century.

At the famous Barnack stone quarries in Northamptonshire several abbeys had concessions and strips of land, and stone was taken from a wharf on the river Nene nearby to Ramsey, Crowland, Peterborough, Bury St Edmunds and Sawtry abbeys (Fig. 87). At the latter there was a canal called the Monks' Lode, which went from the old course of the Nene to bring in the stone. The best of the Bath stone in the Middle Ages came from Hazelbury near Box (Wiltshire) where several monasteries had rights to dig stone, including the Cistercian abbey of Stanley.

Research has now begun in locating the sources of the various stones used to build medieval monasteries. Such work will not only indicate something of the exploitation of the different quarries in the Middle Ages but also demonstrate the problems of transporting the stone over what were, in some cases, considerable distances.

Coal

William Hoskins says that 'many houses in the coal-bearing districts like Tyneside, Furness and the Forest of Dean had been digging coal for generations and using it lavishly for their own needs. This valuable "invisible" income naturally does not appear in the *Valor*' (*Ecclesiasticus* of 1535), but it should be allowed for on the estates of monasteries lying over coal measures. Little has been done to identify this aspect of the monastic economy; there are some documentary references but it is likely that fieldwork could locate examples of coal exploitation if those houses situated on exposed coalfields were studied. Examples of known medieval coal working include the monks of Finchale in Durham who derived around £30 a year from their coal mines, and the priory at Tynemouth which leased a mine in 1530 for £20 per year. The Cistercian abbeys of Newminster and Flaxley had coal on their land, as did the Carthusian priory of Beauvale in Nottinghamshire. Several of the Welsh houses also exploited their coal deposits – Neath and Margam for example. In Leicestershire, Garendon Abbey received land with coal mines in 1270 from Ralph Bozun, while in the fifteenth century Leicester Abbey clearly owned a coal mine of some depth at Oakthorpe. It is clear from these references that coal mining was more widespread than has so far been appreciated.

87 *Sawtry Abbey and the Monk's Lode canal (Cambridgeshire). The site of the claustral buildings can be seen as earthworks in the centre of this air photograph. Running away to the north (top) is the Monk's Lode, the canal linking the abbey to the river Nene.*

Iron

Iron was possibly an even more valuable commodity for monasteries where it occurred on their estates. In Yorkshire, the existence of iron ore and woodland in the Dales led to the development of iron working there on the estates of the monasteries with land in the area, including the abbeys of Fountains and Byland. Guisborough Priory had iron workings at Glaisdale in Eskdale. The same is true in the Forest of Dean; before 1154 Flaxley Abbey had an iron works at Elton near Westbury. Two oaks a week were allowed to fuel this before it was commuted to a grant of Abbots Wood in 1258. In the Lake District there were iron deposits in the High and Low Furness areas but these do not seem to have been worked on a large scale. Nevertheless, the Furness fells have a lot of remains of medieval bloomeries on them and it would seem that the monks were bringing iron ore from their mines in Low Furness by pack animal, and perhaps boat, to be smelted using the timber on the High Furness. Ore also seems to have come from Eskdale, from where it was taken to a bloomery in Langstrath, where Greenup Gill joins the main stream – probably a Furness or Fountains Abbey venture.

Although it is clear that there were a few mines of some depth in the Middle Ages most iron, as well as coal, lead and other minerals, would have been dug out of the ground from shallow pits with short radiating galleries. This type of mining results in a 'doughnut-shaped' mound of spoil around a shaft – called a 'bell-pit' – and these occur in clusters or lines across the landscape. Some of these are medieval but the technique persists through to the nineteenth century. One group which has been claimed to be medieval and the result of iron working by Byland Abbey exists as fine earthworks at Bentley Grange in west Yorkshire. It now seems possible, however, that they may not be medieval in origin but a little later and hence were not worked from the monastic grange.

Lead

Lead occurs in far fewer localities than coal or iron, but in the Middle Ages several sources were owned and exploited by monastic houses. It was needed in large quantities for roofing and pipework. On the Mendips, for example, land with lead and silver deposits were held by both the bishop of Bath and Wells and the Carthusian monasteries of Witham and Hinton Charterhouse. Each of these had a grange on the plateau, Charterhouse on Mendip for the former and Green Ore, or Greenworth for the latter; there is, however, little evidence for extensive lead working even though

Witham was granted the right in 1283 'to work all mines of lead which they might find in their own several ground and to take and have for their own use the profits accruing from them'.

Gough comments that 'no information is available to throw any light on the subsequent career of the mines under Carthusian control: in fact, we hear scarcely anything further about this district until a century or more after the dissolution'. By contrast, in the Yorkshire Dales Roger de Mowbray granted rights to mine iron and lead to Fountains Abbey in the manors of Bewerley and Dacre and to Byland Abbey in Stonebeck Up and Down, upriver from Greenhow and Pateley. Disputes arose where the lands of the two abbeys met on Coldstones on Greenhow and in 1225 the mines were divided between them. At that time veins were being worked underground, the lead was smelted near Brimham and Bishopside and marketed through York, Richmond, Ripon, Barnard Castle and Kirkby Malzeard. None of the lead mining in the Peak District at this time seems to have been carried out by monasteries.

The foundation of towns

The monastery gate had the same power to draw traffic to it as the gate of a castle, palace or hunting lodge. Tenants, suitors and litigants had occasion to come to the courts of the abbot when abbots became great landowners; and the

---

88 *St Alban's (Hertfordshire). This vertical air photograph shows the former abbey church (now the cathedral) within its extensive precinct. To the top right is the long, thin triangular market place (infilled) of the tenth-century market town developed by Abbot Wulsin.*

monastery had a further attraction for visitors if it became a place of pilgrimage, especially if its church became the centre of a popular cult.

So Maurice Beresford sums up the dilemma of many monasteries, perhaps founded in isolation, possibly desiring solitude, but finding that as powerful and wealthy institutions they needed a variety of goods and services and therefore could not avoid contact with hosts of lay folk.

Many sites in the pre-Conquest period were founded away from centres of population but later acquired or developed towns at their gates; this is the case with Abingdon, Evesham, Glastonbury, Hartlepool, Pershore, Peterborough and Whitby. Even if towns existed in 1066, 'it is very difficult at this early period to distinguish between the natural attraction of commerce to the monastery gate and its deliberate stimulation . . .' Some examples of early monastic town planning, rather than haphazard 'organic' growth are, however, clear. The town at St Albans (Fig. 88) adjacent to the abbey seems to have been developed as a triangular market place surrounded by urban properties by Abbot Wulsin around 950; the foundation of Durham cathedral priory in 1003–6 was accompanied by the development of a town; Burton on Trent Abbey, founded 1002–4, converted a village into a borough, which itself had suburban extensions by the mid-thirteenth century; and at Bury St Edmunds (Fig. 89) the town which developed outside the precinct was described in Domesday Book (1086) – 342 houses had been built over cornfields since the Norman Conquest. The town plan which still survives at Evesham shows the process well: the pre-Conquest unplanned market place at Merstow Green contrasts with the regular grid system of the new borough laid out in the twelfth century.

The incentive to town foundation was the profit that could be made from rents, market tolls and so on. It was not long after the foundation of Battle Abbey (Fig. 90) on the site of William the Conqueror's victory that the monks laid out the market place and burgages of their new town. Elsewhere, Tavistock Abbey (Devon) developed a borough out of the manor at its gate some time between 1108 and 1185, St Ives was developed by Ramsey Abbey and Baldock, or 'New Baghdad' was developed by the Templars in Hertfordshire.

With the Cistercians it was somewhat different. Although they eventually had property in some 40 English and Welsh towns, the statute of 1134 prohibited them from building their monasteries in towns – only the late and exceptional houses at Oxford and London were near to towns. However, 'the Cistercians' business sense was too acute for them to remain aloof from such a profitable venture as town plantation, especially since their active work as colonists would make them well aware of the necessity for augmenting existing market facilities'; they nevertheless were not involved much in the process in England and Wales. A rare exception was Kingsbridge (Devon) founded by Buckfast Abbey – a market was granted in 1219 and there was a borough by 1328. Perhaps the most successful Cistercian plantation, however, was Wyke upon Hull founded by Meaux Abbey on the fields of its grange of Myton. This was taken over by Edward I and is now Kingston upon Hull.

Within some towns there are buildings which serve to remind us of the involvement

89 *Bury St Edmunds (Suffolk). Vertical air photograph of the abbey in its extensive precinct to the right, and the grid plan of the new streets and properties of the abbot's town to the left. Despite later rebuilding the outline of the eleventh-century town being developed at the time of Domesday Book (1086) can still be clearly seen in the townscape.*

90 *Battle (Sussex). In the foreground can be seen the remains of the important abbey founded by William the Conqueror as a thanksgiving for the successful conquest (1066). Beyond the large gatehouse is the triangular market place with the lines of burgage plots along the street founded by the monks in the 1070s.*

of monasteries in town life. In Winchcombe, for example, the George Hotel was developed by the abbey there as a hostel in the late fifteenth century when several properties in the town were taken over and redeveloped. In Norton St Philip another inn, the George (Fig. 91), belonged to the monks of Hinton Charterhouse priory and seems to have been at various times their wool store and hostelry. Many other such buildings survive up and down the country.

The topography of monastic estates

The study of monastic lands from the point of view of their topography and field archaeology is a fairly recent development although historical studies of monastic estates have been undertaken for over a

91 *The George Inn, Norton St Philip (Somerset). This fine building belonged to the Carthusian monks of nearby Hinton Charterhouse. It has been used as a woolstore, guest-house and inn at various times.*

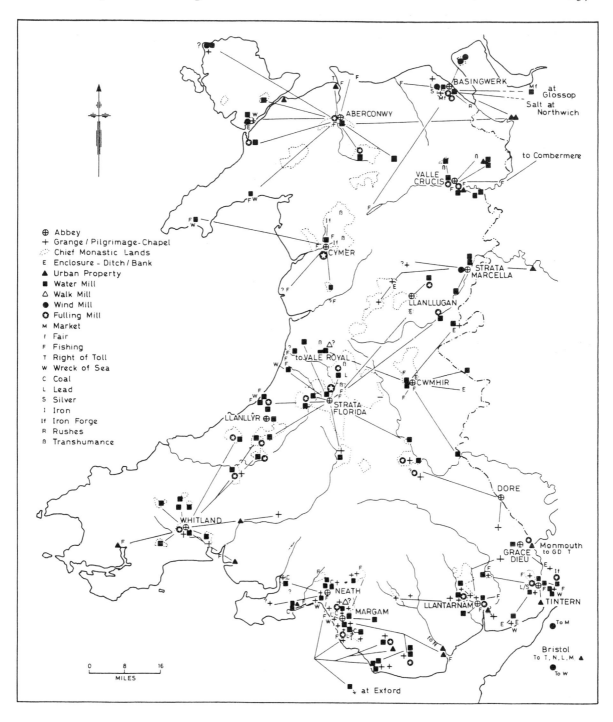

92 *The estates and resources of the Cistercians in Wales. David Williams' map represents the most successful attempt so far to demonstrate the impact of the Cistercian monasteries over a wide area. Not only are the abbeys shown with the extent of their grants of land, but also all the landscape features which existed on these estates.*

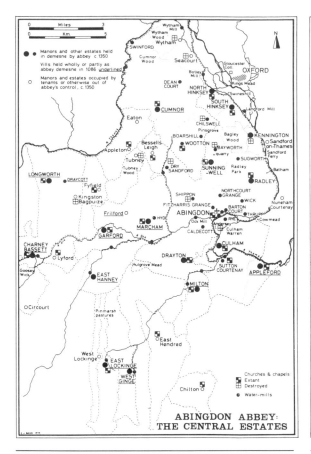

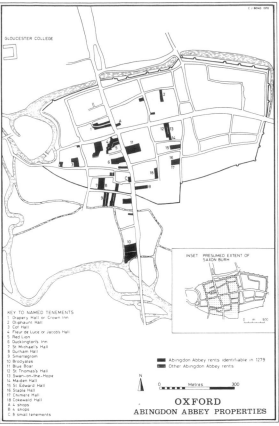

93 *The central estates of the Benedictine abbey of Abingdon. James Bond's map shows the concentration of manors and other property held by the abbey in north Berkshire in the Middle Ages, together with some of the topographical features to be found on them.*

94 *The estates of Abingdon Abbey in the medieval town of Oxford. This map shows the extent of the urban holdings of the abbey in Oxford as recorded in medieval documents. Abingdon was a pre-Conquest abbey and it is noticeable how much of its property was within the presumed extent of the Saxon burh at Oxford.*

century. Perhaps the most extensive and comprehensive piece of work, or series of works, is that by David Williams on the Cistercian lands in Wales (Fig. 92). Not only have all the estates been mapped for the country, down to apparently the smallest piece of ground, but many features reflecting aspects of the economy of each monastery have been located. These include watermills, fulling mills and windmills, fishing rights and weirs, market and fair rights, and possession of deposits of coal, lead, silver and iron. A very large number of

the outlying granges have also been located and mapped.

For the topography of the estates of individual monasteries, however, there has been nothing as extensive as the pioneering studies carried out by James Bond on several Benedictine abbey estates – Evesham (Worcestershire) and Abingdon (Berkshire) (Fig. 93) have been mapped and work is in hand on the estates of Glastonbury Abbey (Somerset). He has been able to locate the

95 *Welburn Grange, near Kirbymoorside (Yorkshire). The site of the grange belonging to Rievaulx Abbey in the Middle Ages is still occupied by a farmstead, albeit with much later buildings.*

estate centres from the readily available documentation and to catalogue the features such as manor houses, barns, dovecots, corn mills, fulling mills, river fisheries, fishponds, stone quarries, parks, warrens and woods. For Abingdon, the urban properties in Oxford have also been located (Fig. 94).

The Abingdon estates clustered in the Vale of the White Horse, west of Abingdon across to Newbury, and on the Berkshire Downs, but there were important outlying estates as far away as Windsor to the south-east and the Cotswolds, south Warwickshire and north Gloucestershire to the north-west. The lands of Evesham Abbey adjoined Abingdon's in that area. Although they clustered around the town of Evesham and the villages to the east of it, there were other estates on the Cotswolds and in south Warwickshire; outliers could be found in Northamptonshire and Worcestershire.

It can be seen from these examples that many Benedictine estates consisted of predominantly villages and associated lands, and the abundant documentary material that has survived shows that, although the home farm on these estates would have been a separate complex from that of the peasants, the lands of the demesne and the tenants were often intermixed. A wide variety of field archaeological monuments is associated with these estates, from the remains of the grange buildings themselves, through barns and dovecots to moats, fishponds, mill sites and vineyards.

Conclusion

In every area of agricultural and industrial activity the monasteries predominated. Sometimes they were initiators, as in the settlement of the moorland and marshland, and sometimes they consolidated and organized what they had been granted. Their settlements and agriculture were carefully adapted to the environment in which they found themselves. In fact, the capacity of monastic houses to adapt and to follow long-term policies was largely responsible for their success and influence. Monastic estates were widespread and the impact of the monasteries on the landscape in general was considerable. This was achieved by working through the system of granges.

The system of grange farming was invented by the Cistercians and copied by the other orders – it was invariably the unit of 'exploitation'. It was supremely well equipped for the development of the less intensively settled areas, such as the forest lands, marshlands and uplands of many parts of Britain. It was a flexible instrument for it could be an administrative, pastoral, arable, or industrial unit depending on the area in which it was situated – granges specializing in fishing, salt manufacture and iron mining existed in Yorkshire for example. In some areas of dispersed settlement, many farms still occupy the exact sites on which the monks built their granges, and the farmer still tills the land which the monks broke up and ploughed eight hundred years ago (Fig. 95). Part of the success of monasteries in farming was that as institutions with a variety of land at their disposal to manage in the most efficient and productive way, they could organize their estates in relation to the rest of their lands. Arable and pastoral estates were run together, each deriving benefit from the other.

Monasteries were perpetual corporations with a continuity in policy and administration. Their abbots and priors could look at developments in the long term and plan accordingly. They felt it was worth investing in buildings and such expensive items as mills because their value would be appreciated beyond the lives of the current community in the monastery. They also had extensive privileges in markets and ports and their land was often wholly or partly exempt from tithes. Their property was frequently legally protected from any kind of violation or intrusion. They had power, organization and resources which enabled them to acquire monopolistic positions and to act on a large scale.

We have thus moved a long way from the idea of monks as hermits and recluses living away from the world and seeking to subsist on very little. Instead, the thirteenth and fourteenth centuries were times of macro-economics, estate management, almost medieval agri-business in the areas of land under monastic estate management, with the production of crops, cattle and sheep in great quantities. The wealth, influence and power this engendered, as well as the envy, together with the widespread lay feeling that this was not what monasteries should be about, led to their increasing unpopularity and eventually to their undoing.

The later Middle Ages and the Dissolution

The later Middle Ages

By the time of the Black Death in 1348–9 monasteries had reached their zenith, both in terms of number of houses and the monks, nuns, canons and friars in them. There were nearly a thousand houses, including about 200 friaries and 150 nunneries. Something like 14,000 men and 3000 women were following the religious life.

Not many new monasteries were established in the fourteenth and fifteenth centuries, while a number were disbanded, their lands being reallocated to, for example, colleges at the universities. Some orders expanded or developed, such as the Observant Franciscans and the Carthusians, and a few new orders appeared.

One of the most interesting developments of this period involved these new and austere groups. The greatest expansion in the number of Carthusian monasteries, from two to ten, took place in the later Middle Ages while several others were planned but never built, at Horne (Surrey) and near Exeter for example. Six houses of Observant Franciscans were built, two more houses of Bonshommes and a house of Bridgettines – a new austere order founded by St Bridget of Sweden in 1346. Like several Carthusian houses, the house of Celestines, an order of eremitical monks founded in Italy in the fourteenth century, was never built; these developments reflect both the religious needs of the time for greater sanctity in its

monks and nuns, as well as the difficulties of finding the endowments and the will to get the projects started.

Sheen and Richmond

In 1414 Henry V began to build a great palace and religious complex at Sheen, now Richmond, on the river Thames, west of London (Fig. 96). A large Carthusian house intended for forty monks was started in 1414, laid out around a great cloister with an impressive perpendicular church. On the other side of the Thames at Twickenham a house of the new order of Bridgettines was begun in 1414 and moved to Syon, opposite Richmond, in 1431. This was a vast establishment with a double monastery – up to sixty nuns in one, and a number of priests and lay brothers in the other. Henry V intended also to found a house for the new Celestine order and a start may have been made on the buildings. The project was abandoned in 1415 following financial difficulties and the ensuing wars with France, from where the monks were to have come. Later, Henry VII established a house of Observant Franciscans near to Richmond palace in about 1500. If all these houses had survived and developed they would have formed an impressive display of the newer austere monastic orders and provided a powerful reservoir of prayer and holiness for the royal family in what would have been

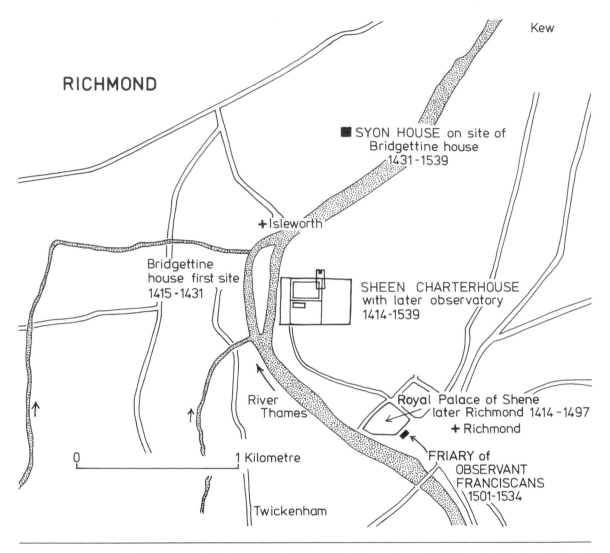

96   *Richmond on Thames (Surrey). The group of monasteries founded in the later Middle Ages by Henry V.*

virtually a late medieval monastic landscape.

Elsewhere, few areas of new land were acquired and no new estates were developed. Land was often leased out to lay people and little new major building or rebuilding work was undertaken, with a few notable exceptions. Although almost everywhere religious life seems to have been at a low ebb, with attention to comfort and good living being the aim of many members of religious communities, this may be more

a reflection of the sources of information which tend to emphasize this condition, rather than the true situation.

'Holiday homes'

This laxity is reflected in one of the characteristic developments of the later Middle Ages, from the fourteenth century onwards. On the estates of many monasteries, provision was made for 'holiday homes' where a period of recreation ('seyney' or 'minutio') could be taken, often after monks had been bled – a process thought to be good for their health. Thus, Winchcombe Abbey had a manor house at Corndean on the Cotswolds, and Canterbury had Caldecote, east of the city, where the monks might 'breath the fresh country air after blood-letting'. The 'minuti' (monks who had let blood) of Spalding took 'seyneys' at the prior's grange of Wickham and the monks of St Albans used the Hertfordshire 'seyney house' of Redburn Priory. The best known is perhaps Finchale Priory used by the monks from Durham (Fig. 97). Evesham Abbey used the manor house of Badsey; this is now called the Manor House but, significantly, was formerly the Seyne House.

97 *Finchale Priory (County Durham). This small Benedictine house was used as a 'holiday' retreat by the monks of Durham cathedral priory in the later Middle Ages. Much of the present arrangement of the buildings at the site reflects its use as accommodation for visiting monks.*

The Dissolution of the Monasteries

Between 1530 and 1540 a major revolution took place in the landholding and estates of the monastic sites in England and Wales. Not only were hundreds of institutions swept away and their buildings sold off, altered or demolished, but all their lands, estates and other enterprises were sold or leased out on a vast scale. The hundreds of monasteries that had existed, in some cases for well over five hundred years, all disappeared in less than a decade and were replaced by secular estates in a secular landscape. It is not the purpose of this book to look at the reasons for this change, however, as it has been well studied by historians, but rather to draw attention to what can be seen of it in the landscape.

There were about 848 religious houses in 1534. The Dissolution in 1536 of the houses worth less than £200 per year closed down a total of 243, about thirty per cent of the total number in England and Wales. None of the 187 houses of friars were closed and 176

houses worth less than £200 were allowed to continue, some after fines had been paid.

Between 1537 and 1540 the rest of the monasteries, including the larger, wealthier and older established, gradually surrendered their sites and lands to the king's commissioners. The friaries were closed in 1538. The last monastery to go was Waltham Abbey which surrendered on 23 March 1540; by then the wealth of the monasteries was in the hands of Henry VIII. The Court of Augmentations was set up to run the estates of the monasteries before they could be leased or sold off.

What happened to all these monasteries and their lands? Generally it is not difficult to find this out as there are abundant leases of monastic sites and lands surviving for the decades following the Dissolution and all the lands were eventually sold off. The historical documents emphasize the acquisition of many of the sites by members of the king's court, Dissolution officials and the 'nouveau riche' anxious to improve their social standing and develop landed estates for their future generations.

The rapid changes of ownership in the early years also shows a lot of speculation and capitalizing on investment at a time of high inflation. Around London, for example, Holy Trinity, Aldgate, was bought by Thomas Audley, St Bartholomew's Priory, Southfield, by Sir Richard Rich, the London charterhouse by Sir Edward North, later Duke of Norfolk, and Bermondsey Abbey by Sir Thomas Pope, treasurer to the Court of Augmentations. The important royal foundation of St Mary Grace's passed quickly through the hands of Sir Christopher Morice, the king's master gunner (1539–42), Sir Arthur Darcy, commissioner of the Court of Augmentations (1542–60) who also purchased Jervaulx Abbey in Yorkshire, and then to Edward Brasshe, first General Surveyor of the Victuals (1560–75), at which point the site became a naval victualling yard.

Demolition of monastic buildings, or at least parts of them (such as the churches), was often swift, certainly to make money from the building materials, but also probably to make it impossible for any change of policy to restore the sites to the religious communities. Removal of the roof seems to have been a condition of sale in some cases.

Houses and gardens

It is clear as a result of much recent field archaeological work, particularly by Christopher Taylor and Paul Everson of the Royal Commission on Historical Monuments (England), that the majority of monastic sites were in some way transformed into secular mansions, often with elaborate conversions of the monastic buildings being undertaken to make them

into comfortable residences. The evidence for this comes not so much from the buildings themselves, although there are numerous good examples – such as Titchfield (Hampshire) (Fig. 98), Flaxley (Gloucestershire), Newstead (Nottinghamshire), Buckland (Devon) and Mottisfont (Hampshire) – but from the new interest in the history and archaeology of gardens. Although some post-medieval formal garden schemes have survived to the present day, it is now realized that very large numbers were abandoned in the past and only exist today as earthworks, reflecting earlier arrangements of lawns, parterres, terraces, prospect mounds and ponds.

A large proportion of the earthworks that survive on monastic sites actually relate to such later gardens, although in the past it has generally been assumed that they reflect the monastic arrangements, especially where there is no standing masonry (Fig. 99). For example, David Wilson's analysis of the sites in Lincolnshire from air photographic evidence showed that only seventeen sites had earthworks which related to the medieval monastic sites beneath. At a further 67 sites the earthworks were not related to the monastic phase of the site at all; of these five were definite gardens, 31 were possible gardens and 31 were uncertain. He concludes:

These observations should not be unexpected. Probably the most usual fate of religious houses at the Dissolution was to provide the site and the materials for constructing a residence for the new owner. . . . In reality we should regard any monastic site as potentially holding the remains of a later house and garden.

In practice it seems that those sites with good monastic earthworks are rarer than was formerly thought.

At Warden Abbey (Bedfordshire), for example, the Goswick family built a house on the site of the abbey in 1540, surrounding it with formal gardens; only a fragment of

98 *Titchfield Abbey (Hampshire). The nave of the monastic church was converted into a Tudor mansion after the dissolution of the monastery in December 1537. The work was commissioned by Thomas Wriothesley, one of Thomas Cromwell's assistants, who had been granted the monastery, and was so speedily carried out that it was recorded as finished by John Leland in 1542.*

99 *Thornholme Priory (Humberside). Air photograph of the extensive earthworks on the site of the Augustinian house. Most of these features, however, relate to the post-medieval use of the site for a great house and its gardens.*

this house now remains. Elsewhere the Royal Commission has shown that there are garden earthworks over the charterhouse sites at Witham (Somerset) (see Fig. 4) and Axholme (Lincolnshire) and adjacent to that at Hinton Charterhouse near Bath (see Fig. 39). Air photograph evidence shows a similar situation at Brooke Priory and Burton Lazars medieval hospital (both in Leicestershire), while early earthwork surveys suggest that sites like Watton (Yorkshire) are covered with later garden features (see Fig. 49).

Dynasties

Eventually many monastic sites and their estates came into the hands of families which would retain them for generations. Not infrequently such ownership lasted through hundreds of years, and even occasionally to the present day. Longleat, which began as a small Augustinian priory in Wiltshire but was rebuilt as a palatial mansion after 1572, still belongs to the Thynne family, and Wilton, site of the rich Wessex nunnery, to the earls of Pembroke. Lacock Abbey, a house of Augustinian canonesses, now belongs to the National Trust, but descendants of the Sharrington family who acquired it at the Dissolution still live there. The Tracys who acquired Hailes Abbey lived there until comparatively recently. There are very many other examples from all over the country.

At many sites the post-medieval architectural developments remain. At rather more they can be seen from prints and drawings made in the sixteenth and

100   *Hailes Abbey (Gloucestershire). View of the ruins and the west range 'Abbot's House', around 1748, by Thomas Robins the Elder. This shows how the monastic range has been converted to a house, for the Tracy family, with the cloister used as a garden. The ruins of the monastic church are to the right.*

seventeenth centuries before later demolitions. A fine series for Hailes Abbey (Gloucestershire) (Fig. 100), for example, shows a substantial house built out of the abbey ruins, which has itself now gone as the site has been cleared to make it into an ancient monument; some of the foundations at the site only make sense in terms of this post-medieval mansion.

Following initial conversion, the whole complex was demolished at a lot of sites and a newer more fashionable house erected in the seventeenth, eighteenth or nineteenth centuries. Rebuilding was invariably accompanied by the landscaping of the land around the house into an elaborate park so

that there is little, if anything, left of either the monastic buildings, the precinct or features of the estate around the original monastic site. Examples are legion from the well manicured landscapes of the post-medieval period, some of the best are: Calke Abbey, Syon House, Wilton House, Amesbury Abbey, Welbeck Abbey, Combe Abbey, Stoneleigh Abbey and Garendon Abbey. At the majority of sites, however, following the initial demolitions, the ruins remained disarticulated among the buildings of succeeding farmsteads.

Out on the estates, the granges in the villages and in the countryside survived as farmsteads. Many had already been leased out by the time of the Dissolution and some were acquired by the tenant farmers. Others were purchased by the former abbey officials who had in many cases been running the estates anyway, knew how they worked and, perhaps more importantly, how much they were worth. Ledston Hall (Yorkshire) began as a grange of the Cluniac priory of St John at Pontefract but after the Dissolution it was gradually transformed into a fine country house by the Witham family. Another splendid example is Mells (Somerset) (Fig. 101), an estate of Glastonbury Abbey, which came to the Horncr family, one of whom was land steward to the abbey at the Dissolution; the 'plum' of the 'Little Jack Horner' nursery rhyme is a reference to the rich Mells manor.

101 *Mells (Somerset). The manor belonged to the great Benedictine abbey at Glastonbury; at the Dissolution in 1539 it was acquired by the Horner family, who had been stewards of the manor for the monastery. One of them is the 'Jack Horner' of the nursery rhyme and the 'plum' is said to be this rich manor.*

New cathedrals and surviving churches

The Dissolution was not entirely an event of decay and destruction. Throughout the Middle Ages a number of monastic communities had existed alongside the retinue of bishops in the cathedral priories. While the communities were dissolved in the 1530s, the buildings and precincts continued as the establishments for the new deans and chapters of the cathedrals. These cathedrals, such as the Benedictine examples at Worcester, Rochester, Ely, Winchester, Canterbury, Norwich and Durham, and the Augustinian at Carlisle, still give a very good impression of what the major monastic churches, claustral buildings and precincts of these large institutions were like in the Middle Ages, even though there has been some demolition and a lot of later building.

Other major monasteries survived almost intact because they were transformed into new cathedrals in the 1540s. Of the former Benedictine abbeys, Gloucester (Fig. 102) Chester, Peterborough and Westminster became cathedrals, although the last did not persist after 1554. The Augustinian monasteries of St Frideswide and St Augustine's became the cathedrals of Oxford and Bristol. These sites provide a very good picture of the precincts of major medieval monastic institutions, which unlike the cathedral priories, were not complicated with bishops' residences.

The monastic church was retained at other sites for use by the local parish, either because they had purchased it from the Crown or because they had some rights in the church before the Dissolution. Sometimes, following purchase, the whole of a large monastic church has remained; examples include Selby, Tewkesbury, Great Malvern, Little Malvern, Christchurch, Cartmel (see Fig. 50), Boxgrove, Blythburgh, Blyth, Dorchester-on-Thames, Brinkburn and Romsey. At Sherborne and Malmesbury (Fig. 103) the local parish churches used by the lay people were demolished when the grander monastic churches were acquired, although at the latter only the nave was retained.

103   *Malmesbury Abbey (Wiltshire). The former abbey church was acquired by the people of the town for a parish church, but only part of the nave was retained. The former parish church to the south was demolished except for the tower.*

102   *Gloucester Cathedral. This had been the Benedictine abbey of St Peter's but was converted into a cathedral for the new diocese in 1541.*

Elsewhere, a whole monastic church proved too large for local requirements, so only a fragment of the church was retained, as at Abbey Dore (Fig. 104), Pershore, Malton, Margam, Bolton, Waltham and Blanchland. Where the local lay population had rights in only part of the church, this was often retained at the Dissolution while the section used by the monastic community was demolished; examples include Bolton in Wharfedale, Leominster, St James in Bristol, Thurgarton, Malton, and Wymondham.

Where a monastic community had built a church for the use of lay people adjacent to their abbey in the Middle Ages, this was invariably retained at the Dissolution, whereas the abbey, its church and

conventual buildings, were demolished. This is the case at the Benedictine abbeys of Muchelney, Bury St Edmunds, Evesham, Abbotsbury, Much Wenlock, Whitby and Reading. At a number of Cistercian abbeys the 'capella ad portam' – the chapel near the main gate provided for lay people – remains, still in use, while the monastic church has gone or is ruined. Examples are at Kirkstead, Hailes, Rievaulx, Merevale and Furness.

It is perhaps noticeable how many of the surviving monastic churches are from Benedictine and Augustinian houses, and conversely how few there are from monasteries of the newer orders. This, to some extent, must reflect not only the more isolated sites chosen by the latter but also the fact that their churches were not needed by post-Dissolution lay communities.

Demolition was so complete on many sites that nothing at all remains to show the outline of buildings and the precinct. At West Dereham (Norfolk), where not quite everything was demolished, cropmarks visible from the air give the only clue to the extent and layout of the site. The same is true of the Cistercian abbey of Robertsbridge (Sussex). Cropmarks in cereals at the completely demolished

104   *Abbey Dore (Herefordshire). Only the east end of the former Cistercian monastic church survives as the parish church. Around 1633 Lord Scudamore restored this, adding the rather incongruous square tower.*

Cluniac site of Mendham (Suffolk) show the normal claustral arrangements together with a large detached moat, probably representing a garden or fishponds. No doubt more details of lost monastic sites will be discovered from this sort of evidence, which is some of the most ephemeral in the landscape. For example, cropmarks have recently revealed the site of the Cistercian abbey at Faringdon (Fig. 105), the precursor of Beaulieu, to where the community moved after only a few years; the Faringdon site then became a grange of the 'new' abbey.

Ephemeral revival

When Mary came to the throne in England in 1553 Catholicism was restored and an attempt was made to re-establish monasticism. But the demolition and dispersal of monastic sites and property had been so thorough in the previous quarter century that little was achieved; Westminster Abbey was refounded and a start made on the charterhouse at Sheen. Five years later with the death of Mary monasticism ended for around three centuries in England and Wales.

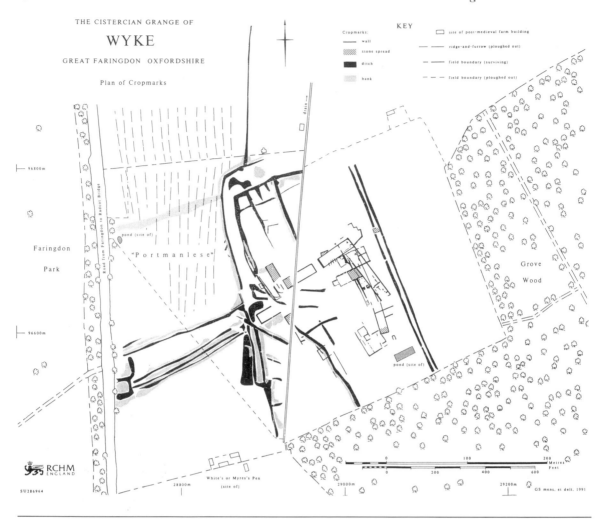

105   *Faringdon (Oxfordshire). A plan of the cropmarks of a monastic site near the town. This is almost certainly the Cistercian site founded by King John in 1203. The community moved to Beaulieu in 1204 and this then became a grange site.*

The removal of so many buildings, the construction of mansions and the laying out of new gardens and parks meant that the physical appearance of many parts of the country in 1550 was considerably different to what it had been in 1530. The patterns of ownership had been transformed totally. While there may have been little immediate change on individual estates, as farming continued in the traditional manner, farmers looking up from their work in many parts of the country would have been very aware

that a profound change had taken place in their surroundings. Where there had been churches as big as cathedrals in the Somerset Levels at Glastonbury, Athelney and Muchelney, or in the Dales of Yorkshire at Fountains, Rievaulx, Byland and Roche, there were now ruins or open spaces. On hilltops at Malmesbury and Shaftesbury, where there had once been monastic churches to rival Salisbury cathedral, there were now only 'bare ruined quires'.

9 From the Dissolution to the present day

Monasteries never lost their fascination for lay people. Not long after the Dissolution early antiquaries began to collect the documents from monastic archives and to study the ruins. Some of these ruins were preserved both for their Catholic associations and because they could be used as follies in an age that became fascinated with the gothic.

It is interesting to note that we owe the survival of some of the most spectacular monastic ruins in the landscape to their being used, or rather retained in an age of demolitions, as follies and gothic ruins. This is certainly the case with the dramatic remains at Tintern (see Fig. 6), Fountains and Rievaulx (see Fig. 58), but it is probably an under-appreciated aspect of other sites as well.

The romantic ruins of Tintern were visited regularly by picnickers as early as 1781. In 1732 Samuel and Nathaniel Buck produced an engraving of the ruins and archaeological interest began when the Duke of Beaufort prevented further neglect by clearing some of the ruins. The site was painted by the young J.M.W. Turner on several occasions between 1792 and 1798 and it was made the subject of a poem by William Wordsworth in 1798. In the 1790s Tintern was at the height of its 'Romantic' appeal and was the subject of organized visits by boat from Chepstow.

Fountains Abbey (Fig. 106), which now seems to us so complete, was pillaged for its

stone between 1598 and 1611 when the adjacent Fountains Hall was built by Stephen Proctor. However, in the late seventeenth and early eighteenth centuries the Messenger family, who were Roman Catholics, protected the ruins with reverence. When the site was sold on to William Aislabie in 1742, not only had it been saved from further demolition but there was also by then a new significance attached to such ruins – they were seen as attractive features enhancing the landscaping schemes being carried out at the time. From 1720 John Aislabie had begun to landscape the valley of the river Skell here with ponds and terraces. In 1742 his son William completed the scheme by purchasing the abbey ruins and developing the approach from the east, together with the spectacular 'Surprise View' of the abbey from 'Anne Boleyn's Seat' in the woods on the south side of the valley. The ruins thus became an integral part of the landscaped garden along with the classical temples, canals and cascades. The effect is captured in the paintings of about 1760 by Balthazar Nebot.

Retention for a folly, however, was not always a good thing for the survival of the ruins. Glyn Coppack cites the case of Roche Abbey where 'Capability' Brown reorganized the estate of Lord Scarborough at Sandbeck Park in 1774, work which included the demolition of part of the cloister buildings – presumably to make them more picturesque! Parts of Halesowen

106 *Fountains Abbey (Yorkshire). View of the abbey ruins in about 1760 by Balthazar Nebot; they are depicted as part of the gardens of Studley Royal developed by John and William Aislabie.*

Abbey (see Fig. 2) were removed to make a folly by William Shenstone (1714–63) in his gardens at The Leasowes nearby.

Absentee landowners and the remote situation of the site helped to preserve the ruins of Rievaulx Abbey through the sixteenth and seventeenth centuries. There was no attempt to convert the abbey into a house or pull it down for building stone. In 1687 the local estate was sold to the wealthy goldsmith and banker Sir Charles Duncombe, eventually descending to Thomas Duncombe III in 1746. The house at Duncombe Park with its terrace was built in the early eighteenth century but in 1758 a second terrace was built to overlook the ruins of the abbey. The intention seems to have been to follow Aislabie's use of Fountains as an eyecatcher and a stopping place on a tour of the garden. The whole scheme combined 'the classical with romantic views of authentic Gothic ruins in one of the most naturally splendid settings in Yorkshire'.

At Furness the site of the impressive remains of the former Cistercian abbey was also acquired by a Roman Catholic family, the descendants of John Preston. The last of these, Thomas Preston, became a Jesuit and before he died in 1709 he attempted unsuccessfully to leave the abbey on trust to the Jesuit Order.

These are some of the most spectacular examples of the retention of abbey sites but no doubt the gradual growth of interest in the picturesque and ruins, followed by genuine interest in antiquity, helped to preserve other sites in the eighteenth and nineteenth centuries.

New monasteries in the nineteenth century

In the nineteenth century new abbeys were built, partly to reflect the interest of Catholic converts but also as refuges for religious communities from Europe driven out by

107 *Downside Abbey, Stratton on the Fosse (Somerset). The main house of the modern English Benedictine Congregation was established in 1814 in the mansion (right centre) to which a church was attached (left). In the foreground are the buildings of the public school; behind are the extensive nineteenth- and twentieth-century buildings of the monastery.*

anti-religious feelings long after the Reformation. The legislation of 1829 formalized the tolerance of Catholicism that had developed since at least the French Revolution (1789) when large numbers of French priests as well as English monks and nuns living abroad came in as refugees. The community at Downside Abbey (Somerset) (Fig. 107), for example, was re-established in England in 1794 having been at Douai in northern France since 1607. It moved to its present site in 1814, taking over a house and extending it. In 1872 a grand plan was drawn up for the development of the abbey which included the enormous church which stands today. From the air the great complex of abbey and public school rivals the grandest precincts of medieval abbeys. The community at Ampleforth Abbey (Yorkshire) began in 1802, having fled from

Dieulouard in Lorraine where they had been since 1608. As at Downside, the community acquired a large house which they extended. A church was built in 1857, the monastic buildings in 1894–8 and the present church was constructed between 1922 and 1961.

By contrast Belmont Abbey outside Hereford was created by F.R. Wegg-Prosser, a recent convert to Catholicism, and offered to the Benedictines. Building lasted from 1854 to 1882. Mount St Bernard, the only modern English Cistercian monastery, was founded in 1835 by Ambrose de Lisle, another Catholic convert, and Bishop Walsh from Melleray in Ireland. De Lisle was loaned £4000 by the bishop to buy 200 acres, Tin Meadow, in Charnwood Forest. A small monastery was built, later to be enlarged to the present complex. It gives a good impression today, in its somewhat remote situation, of what many medieval Cistercian houses must have been like.

It is noticeable that some of these monasteries were founded, as in earlier times, with the active involvement and financial backing of patrons and supporters and that this was essential to get the communities and buildings started.

Monasteries today

There are many monastic institutions in existence in Britain today. Most of them bear little relationship to the sites of earlier times discussed in the bulk of this book; certainly many of them do not look how monasteries are supposed to look – large gothic structures – and the way they are organized and supported is different to earlier institutions. And yet many of their activities, their services, their charitable works, their teaching and their scholastic endeavours would have been entirely appropriate in earlier monasteries.

A visit to a modern monastery, if only for a day, will show just how much has remained the same in monastic communities for over a thousand years. The dress of the religious certainly marks them out from the rest of the world – the black habits of the Benedictines of Downside Abbey for example, the white habits of the Prinknash monks or the white woollen habits of the Carthusians of Parkminster. The monastic day is still made up of periods of prayer and meditation, even if the times of the services are not the same everywhere. And meals are still taken in most houses in communal refectories, in silence, while a reading is made from the pulpit (nowadays with microphones and speakers), with guests and visitors invited in. The libraries of many monasteries attest to their academic interests, while a number of recent monks have become well known historians, such as

David Knowles and Aelred Watkin, carrying on the tradition of Bede.

It is difficult to be precise about the exact number of modern orders and hence of modern monasteries; this is particularly true with nunneries. Monasteries are closed down through lack of novices and the increasing age of the monks or nuns in them, or because the community moves to a new site. It is possible, however, to identify the main monasteries in Britain and show how they relate to the modern landscape.

There are several 'congregations' of Benedictines within the Catholic church. In England, the abbeys for monks at Downside (Somerset), Ampleforth (Yorkshire), Douai (Berkshire), Belmont (Herefordshire), Ealing (London), Buckfast (Devon) and Worth (Sussex) belong to the English Benedictine Congregation (with Downside as the senior house), as does Fort Augustus in Invernesshire, Scotland. The nunneries at Stanbrook (Worcestershire) and at Curzon Park (Cheshire) and Colwich (Staffordshire) belong to the same group. Quarr Abbey on the Isle of Wight belongs to the Solesmes Congregation, while Ramsgate (Kent), Prinknash (Gloucestershire) and Farnborough (Hampshire) in England and Pluscarden (Morayshire) in Scotland belong to the Congregation of Subiaco. At Cock-fosters in London there is a house of the Olivetan Congregation, founded in Italy for hermits in 1313. There are nunneries of these orders at Oulton (Staffordshire), Fernham (Oxfordshire) and Ryde (Isle of Wight).

There are Cistercian monks only at Mount St Bernard (Leicestershire) and on Caldey Island off the coast of South Wales. Sancta Maria Abbey, Nunraw, East Lothian is the only Cistercian house in Scotland. There are Cistercian nuns at Holy Cross, Hemel Hempstead, St Bernard's Convent, Slough (Berkshire) and Hyning, Carnforth (Lancashire). The only Carthusian monastery, or charterhouse, in the British Isles is at Parkminster (Sussex), for men.

All of the above are Catholic houses; there are, however, a few Anglican monasteries in England. There are Anglican Benedictine monks at Elmore (formerly Nashdom) and Alton (Hampshire) and nuns at Edgeware, West Malling and Burford. There is an Anglican Cistercian monk at Ewell (West Malling), and there are Anglican Cistercian nuns at Burnham, Slough (Berkshire).

Many new orders have arisen since the Middle Ages, involved in a range of activities from practical work, such as teaching and nursing to social work, and including the 'army' of the Jesuits who will turn their hand to almost anything. Modern monasteries have a wide variety of roles today. Several have large public boarding schools attached such as Downside and Ampleforth, while Buckfast has a preparatory school. Ampleforth and Belmont provide priests for large numbers of Catholic parishes, while at Downside, Ampleforth and Mount St Bernard there are farms attached to the monasteries, at the last worked by the monks themselves. Prinknash produces incense and pottery, Buckfast glass, tonic wine and honey and Stanbrook, along with others, cassette tapes of religious music. At Downside the community was once completely self-sufficient, with its own farm, waterworks, gasworks and slaughter house. They still have a market garden, orchard and herd of cows and they grow their own potatoes.

The abbey at Buckfast (Fig. 108) perhaps gives the best impression of what a medieval abbey would have been like. It is situated in the valley of the river Dart and the present buildings which were put up in the nineteenth century follow the foundations of the medieval abbey, which began as a Benedictine house and then became Cistercian. The layout is typical of traditional medieval monastic sites and includes a cloister and workshops. Monastic activities there include looking after bees and the production of honey; one of the monks

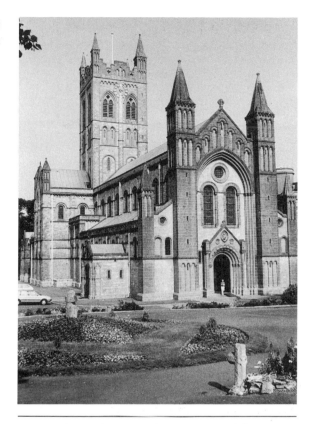

108 *Buckfast Abbey (Devon). One of only two revived modern Benedictine abbeys which stand on medieval sites, Buckfast was rebuilt in the nineteenth century. It had been a tenth-century Benedictine abbey and a twelfth-century Cistercian abbey in earlier times.*

is a world authority on bees. They do a lot to instruct visitors and have an impressive educational programme for schools. Only at Buckfast and Pluscarden are modern monasteries on the exact sites of medieval monasteries.

Monasteries in the modern landscape

There are of course numerous ruins of earlier monasteries that can be visited. English Heritage, Historic Scotland and Cadw (Welsh Historic Monuments) have a variety of remains in their care and at some there are

109   *Runcorn Priory, Runcorn (Cheshire). Within the area of the new town developed at Runcorn the priory site has been excavated, conserved and a superb display developed. This view shows the site of the church (left) and the cloister.*

now very good displays that attempt to put the ruins into their contemporary medieval social, economic, religious and topographical context. Particularly good examples can be seen at Tintern, Rievaulx, Fountains, Cleeve and Furness and Mount Grace charterhouse. More and more tourists are visiting these sites and presumably enjoying what is a difficult aspect of the past for the modern mind to grasp. In this respect the popular books of Ellis Peters about Brother Cadfael at Shrewsbury Abbey give

a good impression of monastic life, even if the criminal life of twelfth-century Shropshire is made to seem more exciting than it actually was!

Sites elsewhere are increasingly being redisplayed so that the visitor can see the context of the ruins in the landscape around; this is about to happen at Glastonbury Abbey and a very successful example already exists in an award-winning scheme at Norton Priory in Runcorn (Fig. 109), a site which also demonstrates another important aspect. Abbey ruins have taken on a new role since the 1960s in providing an historical identity for uprooted populations coming into the numerous new and expanded towns which have been built since the war. Several sites have been excavated, some have been laid out on display for visitors and a few now have visitor centres. Thus Norton Priory was excavated as Runcorn new town developed and what was in fact a rather ordinary Augustinian site, with little in the way of surviving buildings or ruins, has been turned into a major attraction for the area by careful excavation of the ruins, conservation of the remaining buildings and a superb display of monastic life. Within the area of Milton Keynes new town, Bradwell Abbey has been excavated and conserved as an attractive feature, while at Redditch new town in Worcestershire a long-term research excavation of the Cistercian abbey at Bordesley is being undertaken in land now set aside as a country park. The ruins are being consolidated gradually and interpretative materials provided.

Similar developments are taking place in the run-down industrial areas of the Midlands. At Stoke-on-Trent, Hulton Abbey is being excavated and will eventually be displayed, while at Sandwell in West Bromwich a small Benedictine priory has been excavated and laid out as one of the features of the country park and there is a monastic display in the nearby visitor centre at Sandwell Park (Figs 110 and 111).

To some extent these innovations show that monastic development has come full circle. Many monasteries always were fully integrated into their local communities, serving the needs and aspirations of the local lords and the populace. In earlier times this was achieved through the prayers and services which took place in them and the charitable works which were undertaken outside. In an increasingly secular and leisured age the role of monasteries has

110 *and* **111**   *Sandwell Priory, West Bromwich (Staffordshire). This small Benedictine priory has been excavated and conserved as a feature within the country park in the Sandwell valley in the heart of the Black Country. The south transept of the church contained numerous burials of the local lords; the most elaborate architectural treatment of the site was reserved for the eastward projecting apsidal presbytery and chapels.*

changed; where they are still operating as religious institutions they are also seen as both havens for retreats and as centres of scholarship; where they exist only as ruins they are utilized increasingly as tourist, recreational and educational resources. One wonders what Benedict, Bede or Bernard would make of it all.

Further reading

The Bibliography contains a large number of the most useful books and articles; many of them will be referred to in the references for the appropriate section of each chapter.

For the location of monastic sites in England and Wales see Knowles and Hadcock (1971), for Scotland see Cowan and Easson (1976), and for Ireland Gwynn and Hadcock (1970). Also useful is Midmer (1979).

Ordnance Survey Historical Maps include *Britain in the Dark Ages* (1966), which shows both bishops' seats and monasteries, this needs considerable revision now; and *Britain before the Norman Conquest* (1973) with sheets for north and south, which shows bishops' seats, cathedrals, monasteries and minsters. Many of the latter would probably now be interpreted as monasteries. The most useful maps are, however, *Monastic Britain*, north and south sheets (third edition 1976). Also useful is Hill (1981). For the current situation with the *Victoria County History* for England see Tiller (1992).

Chapter 1 *Monasteries in the landscape*

For the history of the landscape see in particular Hoskins (1988), Aston and Rowley (1974), Aston (1985), Beresford (1957) and Muir (1981) though few of these even consider the role of monasteries in the landscape.

Several book series contain useful background material to monasticism in various areas as well as brief accounts of monastic sites, precincts and their lands. See for example volumes in the *Making of the English Landscape* series from Hodder and Stoughton and the *Regional History of England* series from

Longmans. There are also very useful volumes in the series *Studies in the Early History of Britain* from Leicester University Press.

For the Middle Ages and the general background to medieval archaeology see volumes of *Medieval Archaeology* (1957 continuing), Bolton (1980), Clarke (1984), Darby (ed. 1976), Hinton (1990), Steane (1984) and Platt (1978). Settlements and field systems, etc. are covered in Beresford and St Joseph (1979), Taylor (1983) and numerous other volumes.

The role of patrons is discussed in Burton (1986), Cowley (1977), Hill (1968) and Wood (1955). For the relationship to castles see Thompson (1986). For a good study of the relationship between patrons and the changing fortunes of a monastery (Kirkstall, Leeds) see Barnes (1984).

The basic requirements for supporting medieval religious communities are discussed in Coppack (1990), Cranage (1926) and Dickinson (1961); there is much of interest for this aspect as for many of the topics in this book in Gilchrist and Mytum (eds 1989) See also Loades (ed. 1990 and 1991) and Greene (1992).

Monastic water supplies are discussed by Grewe (1991) and Bond (1989 and 1991). For monastic building see Morris (1979); for stone see Blair and Ramsay (eds 1991), Harvey (1975), Parsons (ed. 1990), Salzman (1952) and Senior (1989). Timber is covered in Rackham (1980) and Hewitt (1985).

For demonstrations of status in the Middle Ages see Cantor (1983), Dyer (1988), Le Patourel and Roberts (1978), Taylor (1989 and 1990), and Thompson (1986).

Chapter 2 *The earliest monasteries*

The best general history of monasticism is probably still Knowles (1969) but see also Zarnecki (1972); the background is covered in Chadwick (1967); for Britain see the incomparable volumes by David Knowles – 1940, 1948, 1955 and 1959 (with later editions). The best modern introduction is Lawrence (1984).

The earliest monasticism and monasteries, in Egypt, Syria, Palestine and so on, are discussed in Butler (1884), Chitty (1966), Watterson (1988) and White (1932 and 1933); also of interest are Meinardus (1961), Torp (1957), Walters (1974) and Wessel (1974).

For the Rule of St Augustine, see Bavel (1984); it is also discussed in Lawless (1987); for the rule of St Benedict see Parry (1984), Farmer (ed; 1980 a & b).

For monasteries in the West see Braunfels (1972); for Lérins Fletcher (1980). The quote about Lérins is from Lawrence (1984). The background to Britain is covered in Barley and Hanson (eds 1968), Thomas (1971a, 1971b, 1981), Morris (1989), Pearce (ed. 1982) and Edwards and Lane (eds 1992). In the latter Wendy Davies questions the whole concept of a 'Celtic' church being distinct from the early church in other areas. For Ireland see Norman and St Joseph (1969), Hughes (1966), Evans (1966); Ryan (1931) still has much useful material and has recently been reprinted. Scottish sites are covered in the volumes of the Royal Commission on the Ancient and Historical Monuments of Scotland. See also Radford (1967). For Whithorn see *Current Archaeology* 96, April 1985 and 110, July 1988, Hill (1987 and 1990) and Thomas (1967); for Iona see RCAHMS

1982; for Tiree and Mull RCAHMS 1980; Jura RCAHMS 1984. For a hermitage on North Rona, surely one of the most remote monastic settlements in Britain see Nisbet and Gailey (1960). For Wales and the West see Radford (1962) for earlier ideas which have now been largely superseded, Foster and Daniel (eds 1965), Pearce (ed. 1982) and Edwards and Lane (eds 1992). Wales is discussed in Bowen (1954 and 1977) and Johns (1960 and 1962) but is best covered in Davies (1982) with new material in Edwards and Lane (eds 1992). See also Nash-Williams (1950). Individual sites as well as general introductory accounts can be found in the inventories of historical monuments published for some counties by the Royal Commission on Ancient and Historical Monuments in Wales, see RCAHMW 1964 (Caernarvonshire Vol 3 West), 1937 (Anglesey), and 1976 (Glamorgan Vol I Part 3). See also James (1992) and James (1993). Gerald of Wales is from Kightly (1988).

For Cornwall see Pearce (1978 and (ed.) 1982) and Olsen (1982 and 1989). Tintagel is discussed in Thomas 1988 and 1993 and the Isles of Scilly in Thomas (1985).

Chapter 3 *Anglo-Saxon monasteries before the Vikings*

The background to this period is dealt with in Blair (1962), Godfrey (1962), Sawyer (1978), Southern (1970), Stenton (1943), and of course by Bede. See also Wilson (ed. 1976), Richards (1991). The *Anglo-Saxon Chronicle* (edited by Garmonsway, 1953) contains much of interest and importance. For monasteries in the north and Northumbria and its influence see Blair (1976); for Lindisfarne see Cambridge (1988).

See Dornier (1977) and Stafford (1985) for the East Midlands, Sims-Williams (1990) and Gelling (1992) for the West Midlands, for Surrey, Blair (1991), and Kent, Everitt (1986). There is much useful material in Hillaby (1987).

The survivals of fabric are detailed in Taylor and Taylor (1965) including Hexham and Ripon. Repton is reported in Biddle and Biddle (1992). Other archaeological evidence is discussed for: Jarrow by Cramp (1969 and 1976) (see

also Monkwearmouth, Cramp 1969); Nazeingbury by Huggins (1978), from where the quotes are taken; Flixborough by Tomlinson (1991) and *Current Archaeology* 126, 1991; Brixworth by Parsons (1977) and Sutherland and Parsons (1984) with quotes; Whitby by Rahtz (1976), Whithorn by Hill (1990) and Hartlepool by Daniels (1988), with quoted material. See also Carr *et al.* (1988) for discussion of another possible monastic site at Brandon in Suffolk.

For the contemporary lay settlements see for example Cowdery's Down in Millett and James (1983).

Abingdon is discussed by Lambrick (1968), from where the early description is taken, and in *Current Archaeology* 121, 1990. For dioceses and monasteries see Stenton (1943), Hill (1981) and the Ordnance Survey period maps. For Roman shore forts see Rigold (1977). For Dorchester on Thames see Cook and Rowley (1985). For sites in the Fens see Darby (1940 and 1983). Westminster is discussed in Hunting (1981), Chertsey in Bird and Bird (eds 1987) and Poulton (1988).

Anglo-Saxon estates are listed in Sawyer (1968) including those for Glastonbury Abbey. The latter are discussed in Costen (1992). For Glastonbury Abbey and its surroundings see Rahtz (1991 and 1993) where the Tor site is suggested as an early monastery; see also Rahtz and Hirst (1974) on the Beckery site outside Glastonbury.

Chapter 4 *Saxon and Norman monasteries*

As background to the early part of this period see Stenton (1943), Knowles (1940), Godfrey (1962), Parsons (ed. 1975) and Dumville (1992).

For Alfred see Keynes and Lapidge (eds 1983) and Garmonsway (ed. 1953). Shaftesbury is shown in Penn (1980) and Athelney in Aston and Leech (1977); William of Malmesbury is available in Thompson (1987).

The St Gall plan and its significance is discussed at length in Horn and Born (1979). For early developments at Cluny see Lackner (1972) and for Glastonbury and Cheddar see Rahtz (1979), Ramsay and Sparks (1988) and Dales (1988). The tenth-century monastic reform is dealt with by Knowles (1940), Hill (1981) and Parsons (ed. 1975). See also Yorke (ed. 1988) and Dumville (1992).

For the dates of monasteries see Knowles and Hadcock (1971); the Abingdon water systems are in Bond (1979); for Glastonbury see Radford (1981), Aston and Burrow (1982) and Aston and Leech (1977); for Winchester see Biddle and Keene (1976); work has recently been undertaken at Abingdon by Tim Allen for the Oxford Archaeological Unit; and at Eynsham by Graham Keevil for the Oxford Archaeological Unit; for Sherborne see Gibb and Gem (1975); for Jarrow see Cramp (1969 and 1976); St Oswald's, Gloucester see Heighway and Bryant (1986); Wenlock see Woods (1987). See also Blair (1992) for the topographical setting of contemporary minsters and Hillaby (1987) for a detailed study of Leominster.

Research on monastic estates includes Costen (1992) on Glastonbury and Barker (1988) on Cerne Abbas Abbey; Ely is discussed in Miller (1951) but see also Raban (1977) on Thorney and Crowland Abbeys in the Fens, King (1973) on Peterborough Abbey and Harvey (1977) on Westminster Abbey.

The impact of the Norman Conquest on monasteries as well as the values of monastic estates from data in Domesday Book (1086) are discussed in Knowles (1940), from which the figures are quoted.

Excavations at Winchester are reported in Biddle (1964–72), Exeter Henderson and Bidwell (1982), Wells in Rodwell (1981 and 1982).

The data for the new Norman monasteries, Cluniac priories, alien priories and cells are taken from Knowles and Hadcock (1971); the quotes are from Knowles (1940). There is much on Cluniac monasteries in the works of Joan Evans (1938 and 1950) (mainly on the art and architecture) and Rose Graham (1929). The Bec properties are discussed in Morgan 1946. Other foreign houses and their properties are discussed in Matthew (1962). For a local study of alien priories (Hampshire) see Hughes and Stamper (1981). The figures for monastic houses in 1100 and 1175 are from Knowles (1940).

Chapter 5 *The new orders*

The best general books on monasteries in the Middle Ages include Platt (1984), Coppack (1990) and Greene (1992); the latter two are the first books to look at the archaeology of monasteries from the fabric and excavated evidence. The general historical background is discussed in Knowles (1940 and 1948) and Lackner (1972). For hermits generally see Leyser (1984).

For the Carthusians generally see LGC (1984), Lockhart (1985), Aston (1993), and for the order in England Thompson (1930), and Farmer (1985) on St Hugh of Lincoln. For Somerset see Thompson (1895), Burrow and Burrow (1990) on Witham, Aston and Bettey (1990) on Hinton. Other houses: Beauvale – Hill and Gill (1908), Mount Grace – Bas and Hope (1905) and Coppack (1991). For the Grandmontines see Graham and Clapham (1926) and Hutchison (1989).

The literature on the Cistercians is voluminous so I have only picked those items with a good 'landscape' content. See especially Lackner (1972), Donkin (1978), Hill (1968), Norton and Park (eds 1986). Also Knowles and Hadcock (1971), Cowan and Easson (1976), Gwynn and Hadcock (1970) and the Ordnance Survey *Monastic Britain* maps. Butler (1981) discusses recent archaeological research on Cistercian abbeys.

The references to the 'desert' in the foundations of monasteries are derived from the Vulgate Bible – Deuteronomy 32: 10 *'invenit eum in terra deserta in loco horroris et vastae solitudinis'* and Isiah 21:1 *'onus deserti maris sicut turbines ab Africo veniunt de deserto venit in terra horribili'*.

For discussion on founders and patrons see Hill (1968), Burton (1986) and Barnes (1984). For sites and site moves see mainly Donkin (1978) but see also Platt (1969). For Wales see Cowley (1977) and Williams (1984).

Information on change in the landscape is widespread. For Bordesley Abbey see Aston and Munton (1976); for Rievaulx see Weatherill (1954) and Coppack (1990); for Byland see McDonnell (1981).

For the Military Orders see Burman (1986), Forey (1992) and Gervers (ed. 1982). See also Martin (1929) for a county study (Yorkshire) where a lot of land was held by the Templars.

For the Canons see the following: Augustinians – Dickinson (1950), Robinson (1980), Baugh and Cox (1988), Brooke (1985) and Herbert (1985); Premonstratensians – Colvin (1951), Bond (1993); Gilbertines – Graham (1901), Irwin and Irwin (1990).

For William Marshall see Crouch (1990) from which the quote is taken. For the Friars in general see Knowles (1955), Knowles and Hadcock (1971), Butler (1984 and 1987). Many studies of

historic towns include maps and references to friaries, and other monastic sites, within them; see for example Lobel (ed. 1975) for Bristol, Cambridge, Coventry and Norwich, and Lobel (ed. 1969) for Glasgow, Gloucester, Hereford, Nottingham, Reading and Salisbury; for Kings Lynn see Clarke and Carter (1977); for London see Schofield and Dyson (1980). The Carmelite friary at Hulne is described in Hope (1890).

Chapter 6 *Monastic precincts*

There is no single useful source on monastic precincts but see Knowles and St Joseph (1952), for water supply see Bond (1989 and 1991). For buildings in the precinct see Coppack (1990). For mills see Holt (1988) and Luckhurst (n.d.); for gardens see Harvey (1981); for fishponds see articles in Aston (ed. 1988), especially Bond.

Glyn Coppack discusses the precinct at Rievaulx in Coppack (1986). For Canterbury see Grewe (1991), Bond (1988), Urry (1967) and the map in Trinity College library, Cambridge. For Chertsey see Poulton (1988). For St Benet of Hulme see Snelling (1971). For Montacute see Aston and Leech (1977). For Bordesley Abbey see Aston (1972), Aston and Munton (1976). Much of the most useful material on individual abbeys is often in guide books or articles in journals. For the various Cistercian abbeys see Peers (1967) and Fry (1986) (Rievaulx), Dickinson (1965) (Furness), Harrison (1990) (Byland), Robinson (1990) (Tintern).

For Kirkstall see Wrathmell (1984), Moorhouse and Wrathmell (1987) and their reassessment of earlier excavations. For Tintern see Courtney (1989), Courtney and Gray (1991) and for the woolhouse at Fountains see Coppack (1986). For Cleeve see Gilyard-Beer (1990). Stanley is discussed in Brakspear (1908) but for Meaux there is no modern appraisal. For Whitland see James (1978) and for Hulton see Wise (1985).

For Carthusian sites: Hinton – Aston and Bettey (1990); Beauvale – Hill and Gill (1908); Sheen – Cloake (1977 and 1990); Mount Grace – Coppack (1991) and Grewe (1991); Alberbury – the map is in the Bodleian Library MS. DD All Souls C6, CTH 15/226.

Precincts of the canons: for Llanthony

in Wales see Evans (1984) and for Lanthony by Gloucester see Rhodes (1989). For Norton Priory see Greene (1989), for Waltham Abbey see Huggins (1972 and 1973) and for Watton in Yorkshire see Hope (1901).

Military orders: for Beverley see Hall (1982); South Witham in Lincolnshire see Selkirk (1968). The precinct of the London Temple is discussed in Godfrey (1953).

Precincts of the friars: the areas of the precincts concerned are mapped in the volumes of the *Historic Towns Atlas* Volumes 1 and 2 (Lobel (ed.) 1969 and 1975); in addition see for Oxford: Blackfriars – Lambrick and Woods (1976), Lambrick *et al.* (1985); Greyfriars – Hassall *et al.* (1989), for Bristol – Ponsford (1975). See also the excellent study of Ludlow Whitefriars – Klein and Roe (1987). The Carmelite friary of Hulne near Alnwick is discussed in Hope (1890).

Chapter 7 *Monastic estates, land and buildings*

For the general economic background see Darby (1973), Miller and Hatcher (1978) and Bolton (1980); see also Hinton (1990).

For monastic barns and dovecots see especially Bond (1973). There seems to be no good book or gazetteer of the surviving barns, dovecots and other monastic estate buildings though most are listed and discussed in the Pevsner *Buildings of England* (and now Wales and Scotland) series of county volumes published by Penguin. For a recent study of monastic barns on the Glastonbury Abbey estates see Bond and Weller (1991).

Despite the large number of monastic sites and the abundance of the documentary evidence which survives for many of them, including in particular cartularies (Davis 1958), there are relatively few studies of the economic and topographical aspects of monasteries and their estates. Some of the main ones are DuBoulay (1966) (Canterbury – the archbishop's lands), Dyer (1980) (Worcester – the bishop's lands), Harvey (1977) (Westminster Abbey), Hockey (1970) (Quarr Abbey), Kershaw (1973) (Bolton Priory), King (1973) (Peterborough Abbey), Miller (1951) (Ely), Morgan (1946) (Bec Abbey estates in England), Page (1934) (Crowland Abbey), Raban (1977)

(Thorney and Crowland), Raftis (1957) (Ramsey Abbey), Searle (1974) (Battle Abbey), Smith (1943) (Canterbury Cathedral Priory); much of the later detail is taken from these. The best recent archaeological and topographical survey of monastic estates is by Stephen Moorhouse (1989).

Granges are covered generally in Platt (1969) and Donelly (1954); local studies include monastic granges in Glamorgan by RCAHM Wales (1982) and Leicestershire by Courtney (1981). See also Bond (1973) and Butler (1981). For Dean Court see Allen (1986), for Llantwit Major see Nash-Williams (1952). Welsh granges are also covered in Williams (1965 and 1990). For Roystone Grange see Hodges (1991) and Wildgoose (1991). The Yorkshire granges are discussed in Donkin (1978) and Waites (1961, 1962 and 1967). For village planning see Roberts (1987), for Somerset see Aston (1988) and Costen (1991).

For arable farming see Glasscock (1973), also Brandon and Short (1990). The Dorset quote is from Taylor (1970). Peterborough's clearances are discussed in King (1973) and Steane (1974). For the Cistercians see articles by Donkin (1978) and Waites (1961, 1962 and 1967); for Wales see Cowley (1977) and Williams (1984) from where the quotes are taken. Fens and marshes are covered in Darby (1940 and 1983) (for the Fens) and Williams (1970) (for Somerset). For the East Riding of Yorkshire see Sheppard (1958). For Sussex see Brandon (1974). For Furness see Rollinson (1967); for Newminster see Newton (1972). Sheep farming is discussed in Glasscock (1973), Donkin (1973 and 1978). The Pegolotti list of English monasteries is published in Cunningham (1927) and data from it are mapped in several places. For Winchcombe see Hilton (1957).

Fisheries are discussed in Bond (1988) and McDonnell (1981) and generally in Aston (ed. 1988); for fisheries and vineyards in Domesday Book see Darby (1977).

The sources for monastic industrial and quarrying activity are widely and thinly spread. Mills are discussed in Holt (1988), Luckhurst (n.d.) and Pelham (n.d.) and also Donkin (1978), as is other activity. For quarrying see Parsons (ed. 1990), Salzman (1952) and Harvey (1975). The quotes are from Hoskins (1976). Coal is also discussed in Owen (1984); lead in Gough (1967) for Somerset and Raistrick (1977) for Yorkshire; iron in Nicholls (1866). Other sources for industry include

Steane (1984), Blair and Ramsay (1991), Senior (1989), Beresford and St Joseph (1979) and chapters by Donkin, Glasscock and Baker in Darby (ed. 1973).

For towns and urban development see Beresford (1967) especially pp. 130–3 and 326–7 from which the quote is taken. See also Aston and Bond (1976) especially pp. 74–7. The George Hotel, Winchcombe is described in Shoesmith and Morriss (1989) and the George Inn, Norton St Philip in Williams *et al.* (1987). For the topography of monastic estates in Wales see Williams (1984 and 1990); for the Benedictine lands of Evesham Abbey, see Bond (1973), for Abingdon Abbey, Bond (1979).

Chapter 8 *The later Middle Ages and the Dissolution*

For the background to the later Middle Ages see Knowles (1955 and 1959) and Youings (1967). The figures for the number of monasteries and the staff in them in 1348–9 are from Woodward (1972) and Dickinson (1961). For Sheen see Cloake (1977 and 1990).

Many of the books already listed cover the Dissolution of the Monasteries; see in particular Knowles (1959 and 1976), Youings (1971) and Hoskins (1976). For a good county study (Leicestershire) of monastic estates on the eve of the Dissolution see Jack (1967). An extremely good regional study, with a good general background to the national context, is Bettey (1989).

For the gardens on monastic sites after the Dissolution see Brown (ed. 1991); the discussion on Lincolnshire gardens is in this by Wilson.

For Lacock see Burnett-Brown (1986), for Hailes see Winkless (1990). There seems to be no published comprehensive survey of those monastic churches which survived to be used in the post-Dissolution period, for whatever reason. There is much useful information in Morris (1979). For air photographs of ruined sites, cropmarks and parchmarks see Knowles and St Joseph (1952), Edwards and Wade-Martins (1987).

Chapter 9 *From the Dissolution to the present day*

For the use of ruins see Robinson (1990) on Tintern, for Fountains, Mauchline and Greeves (1988), for Roche see Coppack (1990), for Rievaulx see the National Trust leaflet on *The Rievaulx Terrace* (1989), for The Leasowes and Shenstone see Hadfield (1977) and for Furness see Dickinson (1965). The background is discussed in Ousby (1990).

There is no obvious source for the nineteenth-century monasteries although Green (n.d., *c.* 1981?) has a lot of useful material; the guide books available at a few monasteries give some information – see for example Lacey (1985) for Mount St Bernard, Stephan (1922) and later editions for Buckfast Abbey, and Flint (1987) for Prinknash Abbey.

For studies of modern monks and nuns, some of them not particularly sympathetic, see Moorhouse (1969), Boulding (1982), Lockhart (1985), North (1987) and Loudon (1992). It is difficult to get up to date information on modern monasteries. For the situation at the end of the war see Anson (1949); Farmer (1980) has a map of the situation in 1979; currently the *Benedictine and Cistercian Monastic Yearbooks*, being 'A guide to the abbeys, priories, parishes and schools of the monks and nuns following the Rule of St Benedict in Great Britain, Ireland and their foundations overseas', Ampleforth Abbey, York, is published annually and gives accounts of all existing communities. I am most grateful to Father Philip Jebb, prior of Downside Abbey, Somerset, for discussing the present situation of modern monasteries with me on a number of occasions.

For sites which can be visited see the annual guide books of English Heritage, Historic Scotland, Cadw (Welsh Historic Monuments) and the National Trust. Ellis Peters' books about the adventures of Brother Cadfael at the Benedictine abbey of Shrewsbury numbered at least sixteen by 1987. For Norton see Greene (1989 a and b), for Hulton, Wise (1985) and Klemperer (1991), and for Sandwell, Hodder (1991).

BIBLIOGRAPHY

L. Abrams and J.P. Carley (eds) 1991, *The Archaeology and History of Glastonbury Abbey: essays in honour of the ninetieth birthday of C.A. Ralegh Radford* The Boydell Press, Woodbridge.
P. Addyman and R. Morris (eds) 1976, *The Archaeological Study of Churches* Council for British Archaeology, Research Report 13.
T. Allen 1986, *Dean Court: A Medieval Settlement* Oxford Archaeological Unit.
P. Anson 1949, *The Religious Orders and Congregations of Great Britain and Ireland* Stanbrook Abbey Press, Worcester.
M. Aston 1972, 'The earthworks of Bordesley Abbey, Redditch, Worcestershire' *Medieval Archaeology* 16, pp. 55–9.
M. Aston 1985, *Interpreting the Landscape: Landscape Archaeology in Local Studies* Batsford, London.
M. Aston 1988, 'Settlement Patterns and Forms' in M. Aston (ed.) *Aspects of the Medieval Landscape of Somerset: Contributions to the landscape history of the county* Somerset County Council, Taunton, pp. 67–81.
M. Aston (ed.) 1988, *Medieval Fish, Fisheries and Fishponds in England* British Archaeological Reports, British Series 182, Oxford.
M. Aston 1993, 'The development of the Carthusian order in Europe and Britain: a preliminary survey' in Carver (ed.).
M. Aston and T. Rowley 1974, *Landscape Archaeology: An Introduction to Fieldwork Techniques on Post-Roman Landscapes* David and Charles, Newton Abbot.
M. Aston and J. Bond, 1976, *The Landscape of Towns* Dents, London.
M. Aston and A.P. Munton 1976, 'A survey of Bordesley Abbey and its water-control system' in P. Rahtz and S Hirst (eds) *Bordesley Abbey* British Archaeological Reports 23, Oxford, pp. 24–37.
M. Aston and R. Leech 1977, *Historic Towns in Somerset* Committee for Rescue Archaeology in Avon, Gloucestershire and Somerset, Bristol.
M. Aston and I. Burrow 1982, 'The Early Christian Centres 600–1000 AD' in M. Aston and I. Burrow (eds) *The Archaeology of Somerset: A Review to 1500 AD* Somerset County Council, Taunton, pp. 119–21.
M. Aston and J. Bettey 1990, 'Hinton Charterhouse' *Avon Past* 15 Autumn, pp. 8–20.
A.R.H. Baker 1973, ' Changes in the Later Middle Ages' in Darby (ed.) pp. 186–247.

K. Barker 1988, 'Aelfric the Mass-priest and the Anglo-Saxon Estates of Cerne Abbey' in K. Barker (ed.) *The Cerne Abbey Millennium Lectures* Cerne Abbas.
M.W. Barley and R.P.C. Hanson (eds) 1968, *Christianity in Britain 300–700: papers presented to the conference on Christianity in Roman and Sub-Roman Britain held at the University of Nottingham*, Leicester University Press.
G.D. Barnes 1984, *Kirkstall Abbey 1147–1539 an historical survey* Thorseby Society Vol. 108 No. 128, Leeds.
H.V. Le Bas and W.H. St John Hope 1905, 'Mount Grace Priory: the Founding of the Carthusian Order' and 'Architectural History of Mount Grace Charterhouse' *Yorkshire Archaeological Journal* Vol. 18, pp. 241–309.
G.C. Baugh and D.C. Cox 1988, *Monastic Shropshire* Shropshire Libraries, Shrewsbury.
T.J. Van Bavel 1984, *The Rule of Saint Augustine: masculine and feminine versions* Darton, Longman and Todd, London.
Bede, *A History of the English Church and People* Penguin Classics.
M. Beresford 1957, *History on the Ground: Six Studies in Maps and Landscapes* Lutterworth, London.
M. Beresford 1967, *New Towns of the Middle Ages: Town Plantation in England, Wales and Gascony* Lutterworth, London.
M.W. Beresford and J.K.S. St Joseph 1979, *Medieval England: an aerial survey* Cambridge University Press, Second Edition.
J.H. Bettey 1989, *Suppression of the Monasteries in the West Country* Alan Sutton, Gloucester.
M. Biddle 1965–1972, 'Excavations at Winchester' Interim Reports: third to ninth, 1964 to 1970 *The Antiquaries Journal* Vol. 45 Part 2, to Vol. 52 Part 1.
M. Biddle, H.T. Lambrick and J.N.L. Myres 1968, 'The Early History of Abingdon, Berkshire, and its Abbey' *Medieval Archaeology* 12, pp. 26–69.
M. Biddle and D.J. Keene 1976, 'Winchester in the Eleventh and Twelfth Centuries' in M. Biddle (ed.) *Winchester in the Early Middle Ages: An Edition and Discussion of the Winton Domesday* Clarendon Press, Oxford, especially p. 306 onwards.
M. Biddle and B. Kjolbye-Biddle 1992, 'Repton and the Vikings' *Antiquity* Vol. 66 No. 250 March, pp. 36–51.
J. Bird and D.G. Bird (eds) 1987, *The Archaeology of Surrey to 1540* Surrey Archaeological Society, Guildford.
J. Blair 1991, *Early Medieval Surrey: Landholding, Church and Settlement* Alan Sutton and Surrey Archaeological Society, Stroud.

J. Blair 1992, 'Anglo-Saxon Minsters: A Topographical Review' in J. Blair and R. Sharpe (eds) *Pastoral Care Before the Parish* Leicester University Press, pp. 226–66.
J. Blair and N. Ramsay (eds) 1991, *English Medieval Industries: Craftsmen, Techniques, Products* Hambledon Press, London.
P.H. Blair 1962, *An Introduction to Anglo-Saxon England* Cambridge University Press.
P.H. Blair 1976, *Northumbria in the Days of Bede* Victor Gollancz, London.
J.L. Bolton 1980, *The Medieval English Economy 1150–1500* Dent, London.
C.J. Bond 1973, 'The Estates of Evesham Abbey: a preliminary survey of their medieval topography' *Vale of Evesham Historical Society Research Papers* Vol. 4, pp. 1–61.
C.J. Bond 1979, 'The Reconstruction of the Medieval Landscape: the estates of Abingdon Abbey' *Landscape History* Vol. 1, pp. 59–75.
C.J. Bond 1988, 'Monastic Fisheries' in Aston (ed.), pp. 69–112.
C.J. Bond 1989, 'Water management in the rural monastery' in Gilchrist and Mytum (eds), pp. 83–111.
C.J. Bond 1991, 'Mittelalterliche Wasserversorgung in England und Wales' in Grewe (ed.), pp. 149–83.
C.J. Bond 1993, 'The Growth and distribution of the Premonstratensian order in medieval Europe: a preliminary survey' in Carver (ed.).
C.J. Bond and J.B. Weller 1991, 'The Somerset Barns of Glastonbury Abbey' in Abrams and Carley (eds), pp. 57–87.
M. Boulding (ed.) 1982, with an Introduction by P. Jebb *A Touch of God: Eight Monastic Journeys* S. Bede's Publications, Massachusetts.
E.G. Bowen 1954, *The Settlements of the Celtic Saints in Wales* University of Wales Press, Cardiff.
E.G. Bowen 1977, *Saints, Seaways and Settlements in the Celtic Lands* University of Wales Press, Cardiff.
H. Brakspear 1908, 'Stanley Abbey' *Wiltshire Archaeological and Natural History Magazine* 35, pp. 541–81.
P. Brandon 1974, *The Sussex Landscape* Hodder and Stoughton, London.
P. Brandon and B. Short 1990, *A Regional History of England: The South East from AD 1000* Longman, London.
W. Braunfels 1972, *Monasteries of Western Europe: the architecture of the orders* Princeton University Press/Thames and Hudson, London.
C.N.L. Brooke 1985, 'Monk and Canon: Some Patterns in the Religious Life of the Twelfth Century' in Sheils (ed.), pp. 109–29.

A.E. Brown (ed.) 1991, *Garden Archaeology* Council for British Archaeology, Research Report 78.
E. Burman 1986, *The Templars: Knights of God* Crucible.
J. Burnett-Brown 1986, *Lacock Abbey, Wiltshire* The National Trust.
I. and C. Burrow 1990, 'Witham Priory: the first English Carthusian monastery; Excavations 1965–69 by P. Barlow and R. Reid and their context' *Somerset Archaeology and Natural History* 134, pp. 141–85.
J. Burton 1986, 'The Foundation of the British Cistercian houses' in Norton and Park (eds) pp. 24–39.
A.J. Butler 1884, *Ancient Coptic Churches of Egypt* 2 Volumes Clarendon Press, Oxford.
L.A.S. Butler 1981, 'The Boundaries of the Abbey of Aberconway at Maenan, Gwynedd' *Archaeologia Cambrensis* 130, pp. 19–35.
L. Butler 1982, 'The Cistercians in England and Wales: a survey of recent archaeological work 1960–1980' in Meredith P. Lillich (ed.) *Studies in Cistercian Art and Architecture* Vol. 1, Cistercian Studies Series Vol. 66, Kalamazoo, Michigan.
L. Butler 1984, 'The Houses of the Mendicant Orders in Britain: Recent Archaeological Work' in P.V. Addyman and V.E. Black (eds) *Archaeological Papers from York presented to M.W. Barley* York Archaeological Trust, pp. 123–36.
L. Butler 1987, 'Medieval urban religious houses' in J.R. Schofield and R. Leech (eds) *Urban Archaeology in Britain* Council for British Archaeology, Research Report 61, pp. 167–76.
L.A.S. Butler and R.K. Morris (eds) 1986, *The Anglo-Saxon Church: Papers in History, Architecture and Archaeology in Honour of Dr H.M. Taylor* Council for British Archaeology, Research Report 60.
E. Cambridge 1988, *Lindisfarne Priory and Holy Island* English Heritage, London.
L. Cantor 1983, *The Medieval Parks of England: A Gazetteer* Department of Education, Loughborough University of Technology.
R.D.Carr, A. Tester and P. Murphy 1988, 'The Middle-Saxon settlement at Staunch Meadow, Brandon (Norfolk)' *Antiquity* Vol. 62, No. 235, pp. 371–7.
M. Carver (ed.) 1993, *In Search of Cult* Boydell and Brewer, Woodbridge.
H. Chadwick 1967, *The Early Church* Pelican History of the Church Vol. 1, Penguin.
D.J. Chitty 1966, *The Desert a City* Basil Blackwell, Oxford.

H. Clarke 1984, *The Archaeology of Medieval England* Colonnade Books, The British Museum, London.
H. Clarke and A. Carter 1977, *Excavations in King's Lynn 1963–1970* Society for Medieval Archaeology Monograph Series 7, London.
J. Cloake 1977, 'The Charterhouse of Sheen' *Surrey Archaeological Collections* Vol. 71, pp. 145–98.
J. Cloake 1990, *Richmond's Great Monastery: The Charterhouse of Jesus of Bethlehem of Shene* Richmond Local History Society Paper 6.
H.M. Colvin 1951, *The White Canons in England* The Clarendon Press, Oxford.
J. Cook and T. Rowley (eds) 1985, *Dorchester through the Ages* Oxford University Department for External Studies, Oxford.
G. Coppack 1986a, 'The Excavation of an Outer Court Building, perhaps the Woolhouse, at Fountains Abbey, North Yorkshire' *Medieval Archaeology* 30, pp. 46–87.
G. Coppack 1986b, 'Some Descriptions of Rievaulx Abbey in 1538–9: The Disposition of a Major Cistercian Precinct in the Early Sixteenth Century' *Journal of the British Archaeological Association* 139, pp. 100–33.
G. Coppack 1990, *English Heritage Book of Abbeys and Priories* Batsford, London.
G. Coppack 1991, *Mount Grace Priory* English Heritage, London.
G. Coppack 1993, *English Heritage Book of Fountains Abbey* Batsford, London.
M.D. Costen 1991, 'Some Evidence for New Settlements and Field Systems in Late Anglo-Saxon Somerset' in Abrams and Carley (eds), pp. 39–55.
M. Costen 1992, 'Dunstan, Glastonbury and the Economy of Somerset in the Tenth Century' in N.I. Ramsey, M. Sparks and T. Tatton-Brown (eds) *St Dunstan: His Life Times and Cult* The Boydell Press, Woodbridge, pp. 25–44.
P. Courtney 1980, 'The Monastic Granges of Leicestershire' *Transactions of the Leicestershire Archaeological and Historical Society* Vol. 56, 1980–1, pp. 33–45.
P. Courtney 1989, 'Excavations in the Outer Precinct of Tintern Abbey' *Medieval Archaeology* 33, pp. 99–143.
P. Courtney and M. Gray 1991, 'Tintern Abbey after the Dissolution' *Bulletin of the Board of Celtic Studies* 38, pp. 145–58.
I.B. Cowan and D.E. Easson 1976, *Medieval Religious Houses: Scotland* Longman, London.
F.G. Cowley 1977, *The Monastic Order in South Wales, 1066–1349* Studies in Welsh History, University of Wales

Press, Cardiff.
R. Cramp 1969, 'Excavations at the Saxon monastic sites of Wearmouth and Jarrow, Co. Durham: an interim report' *Medieval Archaeology* Vol. 13, pp. 21–66.
R. Cramp 1976a, 'Monastic Sites' in Wilson (ed.), pp. 201–52.
R. Cramp 1976b, 'St Paul's Church, Jarrow' in Addyman and Morris (eds), pp. 28–35.
D.H.S. Cranage 1926, *The Home of the Monk: an account of English monastic life and buildings in the Middle Ages* Cambridge University Press.
D. Crouch 1990, *William Marshall: Court, Career and Chivalry in the Angevin Empire 1147–1219* Longman, London.
W. Cunningham 1927, 'The Wool Trade in the Thirteenth and Fourteenth Centuries' in *The Growth of English Industry and Commerce during the Early and Middle Ages* Cambridge University Press, 5th edition, pp. 628–41.
D. Dales 1988, *Dunstan: Saint and Statesman* Lutterworth, Cambridge.
R. Daniels 1988, 'The Anglo-Saxon Monastery at Church Close, Hartlepool, Cleveland' *Archaeological Journal* 145, pp. 158–210.
H.C. Darby 1940, *The Medieval Fenland* Cambridge University Press.
H.C. Darby 1977, *Domesday England* Cambridge University Press.
H.C. Darby 1983, *The Changing Fenland* Cambridge University Press.
H.C. Darby (ed.) 1973, *A New Historical Geography of England before 1600* Cambridge University Press.
W. Davies 1982, *Wales in the Early Middle Ages* Leicester University Press.
W. Davies 1992, 'The myth of the Celtic Church' in Edwards and Lane (eds), pp. 12–21.
G.R.C. Davis 1958, *Medieval Cartularies of Great Britain: A Short Catalogue* Longman, London.
J.C. Dickinson 1950, *The Origins of the Austin Canons and their Introduction into England* SPCK, London
J.C. Dickinson 1961, *Monastic Life in Medieval England* Adam and Charles Black, London.
J.C. Dickinson 1965, *Furness Abbey* English Heritage, London.
R. Donkin 1973, 'Changes in the Early Middle Ages' in Darby (ed.), pp. 75–135.
R.A. Donkin 1978, *The Cistercians: studies in the geography of medieval England and Wales* Pontifical Institute of Medieval Studies, Toronto.
J.S. Donnelly 1954, 'Changes in the grange economy of English and Welsh Cistercian abbeys 1300–1540' *Traditio* Vol. 10, pp. 399–458.

A. Dornier (ed.) 1977a, *Mercian Studies* Leicester University Press.
A. Dornier 1977b, 'The Anglo-Saxon monastery at Breedon-on-the-Hill, Leicestershire' in Dornier (ed.), pp. 155–68.
F.R.H. DuBoulay 1966, *The Lordship of Canterbury: An Essay on Medieval Society* Nelson, London.
D.N. Dumville 1992, *Wessex and England from Alfred to Edgar* The Boydell Press, Woodbridge.
C. Dyer 1980, *Lords and Peasants in a Changing Society: The Estates of the Bishopric of Worcester 680–1540* Cambridge University Press.
C.C. Dyer 1988, 'The Consumption of Fresh-water Fish in Medieval England' in Aston (ed.), pp. 27–38.
D.A. Edwards and P. Wade-Martins 1987, *Norfolk from the Air* Norfolk Archaeological Unit, Norfolk Museums Service, Norwich.
N. Edwards and A. Lane 1992 (eds), *The Early Church in Wales and the West* Oxbow Monographs 16, Oxford.
D.H. Evans *et al.* 1983–4, 'Further Excavations and Fieldwork at Llanthony Priory, Gwent' *Monmouthshire Antiquary* Vol. 5 parts 1 and 2, pp. 1–61.
E. Evans 1966, *Prehistoric and Early Christian Ireland: a guide* Batsford, London.
J. Evans 1938, *The Romanesque Architecture of the Order of Cluny* Cambridge University Press.
J. Evans 1950, *Cluniac Art of the Romanesque Period* Cambridge University Press.
A. Everitt 1986, *Continuity and Colonization: the Evolution of Kentish Settlement* Leicester University Press.
D.H. Farmer 1985, *Saint Hugh of Lincoln* Darton, Longman and Todd, London.
D.H. Farmer (ed.) 1980, *Benedict's Disciples* Fowler Wright, Leominster.
D.H. Farmer (ed.) 1980, *The Benedictines in Britain* British Library Series No. 3, The British Library, London.
Lord Fletcher 1980, 'The Monastery at Lérins' *Journal of the British Archaeological Association* 133, pp. 17–29.
H. Flint 1987, *The Old House: St Peter's Grange, Prinknash* Prinknash Abbey.
A. Forey 1992, *The Military Orders: from the twelfth to the early fourteenth centuries* Macmillan, London.
I.Ll. Foster and G. Daniel (eds) 1965, *Prehistoric and Early Wales* Routledge and Kegan Paul, London.
P.S. Fry 1986, *Rievaulx Abbey* English Heritage, London.
G.N. Garmonsway (ed.) 1953, *The Anglo-Saxon Chronicle* Everymans Library, Dent, London.
M. Gelling 1992, *The West Midlands in the Early Middle Ages* Leicester University Press.
M. Gervers (ed.) 1982, *The Cartulary of the Knights of St John of Jerusalem in England: Secunda Camera, Essex* Records of Social and Economic History New Series 6, published for the British Academy by the Oxford University Press.
J.H.P. Gibb and R.D.H. Gem 1975, 'The Anglo-Saxon Cathedral at Sherborne' *Archaeological Journal* 132, pp. 71–110.
R. Gilchrist and H. Mytum (eds) 1989, *The Archaeology of Rural Monasteries* British Archaeological Reports, British Series 203, Oxford.
R. Gilyard-Beer 1990, *Cleeve Abbey* English Heritage, London.
R.E. Glasscock 1973, 'England circa 1334' in Darby (ed.), pp. 136–85.
W.H. Godfrey 1953, 'Recent discoveries at the Temple, London, and notes on the topography of the site' *Archaeologia* Vol. 95 Second Series 45, pp. 123–40.
J. Godfrey 1962, *The Church in Anglo-Saxon England* Cambridge University Press.
J.W. Gough 1967, *The Mines of Mendip* David and Charles, Newton Abbot.
R. Graham 1901, *St Gilbert of Sempringham and the Gilbertines: a history of the only English monastic order* Elliot Stock, London.
R. Graham 1929, *English Ecclesiastical Studies: Being some Essays in Research in Medieval History* SPCK, London.
R. Graham and A.W. Clapham 1926, 'The Order of Grandmont and its Houses in England' *Archaeologia* 75, pp. 159–210.
B. Green n.d., 1980?, *The English Benedictine Congregation: A Short History* Catholic Truth Society, London.
J.P. Greene 1989a, *Norton Priory: The Archaeology of a Medieval Religious House* Cambridge University Press.
J.P. Greene 1989b, 'Methods of interpretation of monastic sites' in Gilchrist and Mytum (eds), pp. 313–25.
J.P. Greene 1992, *Medieval Monasteries* Leicester University Press.
K. Grewe 1991, 'Mount Grace Priory (Yorkshire, GB)' in Grewe (ed.), pp. 264–7.
K. Grewe (ed.) 1991, *Die Wasserversorgung im Mittelalter* Verlag Philipp von Zabern, Mainz am Rhein.
A. Gwynn and R.N. Hadcock 1970, *Medieval Religious Houses Ireland* Longman, London.
M. Hadfield 1977, *The English Landscape Garden* Shire, Princes Risborough.
I. Hall 1982, 'Medieval Buildings' in Miller *et al.* pp. 46–54.
S.A. Harrison 1990, *Byland Abbey* English Heritage, London.
B. Harvey 1977, *Westminster Abbey and its Estates in the Middle Ages* Clarendon Press, Oxford.
J. Harvey 1975, *Medieval Craftsmen* Batsford, London.
J. Harvey 1981, *Medieval Gardens* Batsford, London.
T.G. Hassall, C.E. Helpin, M. Mellor *et al.* 1989, 'Excavations in St Ebbe's, Oxford 1967–76 Part 1' *Oxoniensia* Vol. 54, pp. 71–278.
C. Heighway and R. Bryant 1986, 'A Reconstruction of the Tenth Century Church of St Oswald, Gloucester' in Butler and Morris (eds), pp. 188–95.
C.G. Henderson and P.T. Bidwell 1982, 'The Saxon Minster at Exeter' in Pearce (ed.), pp. 145–75.
J. Herbert 1985, 'The Transformation of Hermitages into Augustinian Priories in Twelfth-Century England' in Sheils (ed.), pp. 131–45.
C. Hewitt 1985, *English Cathedral and Monastic Carpentry* Phillimore, Chichester.
A. Du Boulay Hill and H. Gill 1908, 'Beauvale Charterhouse, Notts' *Transactions of the Thoroton Society* Vol. 12, pp. 69–94.
B.D. Hill 1968, *English Cistercian Monasteries and their Patrons in the Twelfth Century* University of Illinois Press, Urbana.
D. Hill 1981, *An Atlas of Anglo-Saxon England* Basil Blackwell, Oxford.
P. Hill 1988 and 1991, *Whithorn 2 Excavations 1984–1987 Interim Report* and *Whithorn 3 Excavations 1988–1990 Interim Report*, The Whithorn Trust.
Hillaby, J. 1987, 'Early Christian and Pre-Conquest Leominster: An Exploration of the Sources' *Transactions of the Woolhope Naturalists Field Club* Vol. 45 Part 3, pp. 557–685.
R.H. Hilton 1957, 'Winchcombe Abbey and the Manor of Sherborne' in H.P.R. Finberg (ed.) *Gloucestershire Studies* Leicester University Press, pp. 89–113.
D.A. Hinton 1990, *Archaeology, Economy and Society: England from the fifth to the fifteenth century* Seaby, London.
S.F. Hockey 1970, *Quarr Abbey and its Lands 1132–1631* Leicester University Press.
M.A. Hodder 1991, 'Excavations at Sandwell Priory and Hall 1982–88' *South Staffordshire Archaeological and Historical Society Transactions* Vol. 31 1989–90, pp. 1–227.
R. Hodges 1991, *Wall to Wall History: The Story of Roystone Grange*

Duckworth, London.

R. Holt 1988, *The Mills of Medieval England* Blackwell, Oxford.

W.H. St John Hope 1890, 'On the Whitefriars or Carmelites of Hulne, Northumberland' *Archaeological Journal* 47, pp. 105–29.

W.H. St John Hope 1901, 'The Gilbertine Priory of Watton, in the East Riding of Yorkshire' *Archaeological Journal* 58, pp. 1–34.

W. Horn and E. Born 1979, *The Plan of St Gall: A study of the architecture and economy and life in a paradigmatic carolingian monastery* 3 Volumes University of California Press, Berkeley, Los Angeles and London.

W.G. Hoskins 1976, *The Age of Plunder – The England of Henry VIII 1500–1547* Longman, London.

W.G. Hoskins 1988, *The Making of the English Landscape* with an introduction and commentary by Christopher Taylor, Hodder and Stoughton, London.

P.J. Huggins 1972, 'Monastic Grange and Outer Close Excavations, Waltham Abbey, Essex, 1970–1972' *Transactions of the Essex Archaeological Society*, pp. 30–127.

P.J. Huggins 1973, 'Excavation of Monastic Forge and Saxo-Norman Enclosure, Waltham Abbey, Essex, 1972–73' *Essex Archaeology and History* 5, pp. 127–84.

P.J. Huggins 1978, 'Excavation of a Belgic and Romano-British farm with Middle Saxon cemetery and churches at Nazeingbury, Essex 1975–6' *Essex Archaeology and History* Vol. 19, third series, pp. 29–117.

K. Hughes 1966, *The Church in Early Irish Society* Methuen, London.

M. Hughes and P. Stamper 1981, 'The Alien Priory of St Andrew, Hamble, Hampshire' *Proceedings of the Hampshire Field Club Archaeological Society* 37, pp. 23–39.

P. Hunting 1981, *Royal Westminster* Royal Institute of Chartered Surveyors.

C.A. Hutchison 1989, *The Hermit Monks of Grandmont* Cistercian Studies Series 118, Cistercian Publications, Kalamazoo, Michigan.

C.R. and M. Irwin 1990, *The Gilbertines and Ravenstonedale* Kirkby Stephen, Cumbria.

S. Jack 1967, 'Monastic Lands in Leicestershire and their administration on the eve of the Dissolution' *Transactions of the Leicestershire Archaeological and Historical Society* Vol. 41 1965–6, pp. 9–40.

T. James 1978, 'A survey of the fishponds, watercourses and other earthworks at the site of Whitland

Abbey and Iron Forge' *The Carmarthenshire Antiquary* 14, pp. 71–8.

T. James 1992, 'Air photography of ecclesiastical sites in South Wales' in Edwards and Lane (eds), pp. 62–76.

H. James 1993, 'The Cult of St David in the Middle Ages' in Carver (ed.).

C.N. Johns 1960 and 1962, 'The celtic monasteries of North Wales' *Transactions of the Caernarvonshire Historical Society* 21, pp. 14–43 and 23, pp. 129–31.

I. Kershaw 1973, *Bolton Priory: the economy of a northern monastery 1286–1325* Oxford University Press, London.

S. Keynes and M. Lapidge (eds) 1983, *Alfred the Great: Asser's Life of King Alfred and other contemporary sources* Penguin Books.

C. Kightly 1988, *A Mirror of Medieval Wales: Gerald of Wales and his journey of 1188* Cadw: Welsh Historic Monuments, Cardiff.

E. King 1973, *Peterborough Abbey 1086–1310: A study in the land market* Cambridge University Press.

P. Klein and A. Roe 1987, *The Carmelite Friary, Corve Street, Ludlow: Its History and Excavation* Birmingham University Field Archaeology Unit.

W. Klemperer 1991, *Hulton Abbey: History and Archaeology* City Museum and Art Gallery, Stoke-on-Trent.

D. Knowles 1940, *The Monastic Order in England: A history of its development from the times of St Dunstan to the fourth Lateran Council 940–1216* Cambridge University Press, second edition 1963.

D. Knowles 1948, 1955 and 1959, *The Religious Orders in England* 3 Volumes Cambridge University Press with later editions.

D. Knowles 1969, *Christian Monasticism* World University Library, Weidenfeld and Nicolson, London.

D. Knowles 1976, *Bare Ruined Choirs: the Dissolution of the English monasteries* Cambridge University Press.

D. Knowles and J.K. St Joseph 1952, *Monastic Sites from the Air* Cambridge University Press.

D. Knowles and R.N. Hadcock 1953, *Medieval Religious Houses England and Wales* Longman, London, later edition 1971.

A.C. Lacey 1985, *The Second Spring in Charnwood Forest* The East Midlands Studies Unit of Loughborough University in association with Mount Saint Bernard Abbey.

B. Lackner 1972, *Eleventh-Century Background of Cîteaux* Cistercian Studies Series 8, Cistercian Publications, Washington.

G. Lambrick 1968, 'Buildings of the Monasteries at Abingdon from the late

Seventh Century to 1538' in Biddle *et al.*, pp. 42–59.

G. Lambrick and H. Woods 1976, 'Excavations on the second site of the Dominican Priory, Oxford' *Oxoniensia* Vol. 41, pp. 168–231.

G. Lambrick *et al.* 1985, 'Further excavations on the second site of the Dominican Priory, Oxford' *Oxoniensia* Vol. 50, pp. 131–208.

G. Lawless 1987, *Augustine of Hippo and His Monastic Rule* Clarendon Press, Oxford.

C.E. Lawrence 1984, *Medieval Monasticism: the forms of religious life in western Europe in the Middle Ages* Longman, London.

H. Leyser 1984, *Hermits and the New Monasticism: a study of religious communities in western Europe 1000–1150* Macmillan, London.

LGC – *La Grande Chartreuse* par un Chartreux Quatorzième Edition, 1984.

J. Loades (ed.) 1990, *Monastic Studies: the continuity of tradition* Headstart History, Bangor.

J. Loades (ed.) 1991, *Monastic Studies: the continuity of tradition* Headstart History, Bangor.

M.D. Lobel (ed.) 1969, *Historic Towns: Maps and Plans of Towns and Cities in the British Isles, with Historical Commentaries, from Earliest Times to 1800* Vol. 1, Lovell Johns-Cook, Hammond and Kell Organization. Includes Banbury, Caernarfon, Glasgow, Gloucester, Hereford, Nottingham, Reading and Salisbury.

M.D. Lobel (ed.) 1975, *Historic Towns* Vol. 2, The Scolar Press in conjunction with The Historic Towns Trust. Includes Bristol, Cambridge, Coventry and Norwich.

R.B. Lockhart 1985, *Halfway to Heaven: The Hidden Life of the Sublime Carthusians* Thames Methuen, London.

M. Loudon 1992, *Unveiled: Nuns Talking* Chatto and Windus, London.

D. Luckhurst n.d., *Monastic Watermills: a study of the Mills within English Monastic Precincts* SPAB, London.

J. McDonnell 1981, *Inland Fisheries in Medieval Yorkshire 1066–1300* University of York, Borthwick Institute of Historical Research, Borthwick Papers 60.

E.J. Martin 1929, 'The Templars in Yorkshire' *Yorkshire Archaeological Journal* Vol. 29, pp. 366–85.

D. Matthew 1962, *The Norman Monasteries and their English Possessions* Oxford University Press.

M. Mauchline and L. Greeves 1988, *Fountains Abbey and Studley Royal, North Yorkshire* The National Trust.

O.F.A. Meinardus 1961, *Monks and*

Monasteries of the Egyptian Deserts American University at Cairo Press, Cairo, Egypt.

R. Midmer 1979, *English Medieval Monasteries 1066–1540* Heinemann, London.

E. Miller 1951, *The Abbey and Bishopric of Ely: The Social History of an Ecclesiastical Estate from the tenth to the early fourteenth century* Cambridge University Press.

E. Miller and J. Hatcher 1978, *Medieval England: Rural Society and Economic Change 1086–1348* Longman, London.

K. Miller, J. Robinson, B. English and I. Hall 1982, *Beverley: An Archaeological and Architectural Study* Royal Commission on Historical Monuments England, Supplementary Series: 4, HMSO London.

M. Millett and S. James 1983, 'Excavations at Cowdery's Down, Basingstoke, Hampshire, 1978–81' *Archaeological Journal* 149, pp. 151–279.

G. Moorhouse 1969, *Against All Reason* Weidenfeld and Nicolson, London.

S. Moorhouse and S. Wrathmell 1987, *Kirkstall Abbey: volume 1 The 1950–64 excavations: a reassessment* West Yorkshire Archaeological Service, Wakefield.

S. Moorhouse 1989, 'Monastic Estates: their composition and development' in Gilchrist and Mytum (eds), pp. 29–81.

M. Morgan 1946, *The English Lands of the Abbey of Bec* Clarendon Press, Oxford.

R. Morris 1979, *Cathedrals and Abbeys of England and Wales: the building church, 600–1540* Dent, London.

R. Morris 1989, *Churches in the Landscape* Dent, London.

R. Muir 1981, *Shell Guide to Reading the Landscape* Michael Joseph, London.

V.E. Nash-Williams 1950, *The Early Christian Monuments of Wales* University of Wales Press, Cardiff.

V.E. Nash-Williams 1952, 'The Medieval Settlement at Llantwit Major, Glamorgan' *Bulletin of the Board of Celtic Studies* Vol. 14, pp. 313–33.

R. Newton 1972, *The Northumberland Landscape* Hodder and Stoughton, London.

H.G. Nicholls 1866, *Iron Making in the Olden Times: as instanced in the Ancient Mines, Forges and Furnaces of the Forest of Dean*, reprinted McLean, Coleford, 1981.

H.C. Nisbet and R.A. Gailey 1960, 'A survey of the antiquities of North Rona' *Archaeological Journal* Vol. 117, pp. 88–115.

E.R. Norman and J.K.S. St Joseph 1969, *The Early Development of Irish Society – the evidence of aerial photography*

Cambridge University Press.

R. North 1987, *Fools For God* Collins, London.

C. Norton and D. Park (eds) 1986, *Cistercian art and architecture in the British Isles* Cambridge University Press.

L. Olsen 1982, 'Crantock, Cornwall, as an Early Monastic Site' in Pearce (ed.).

L. Olson 1989, *Early Monasteries in Cornwall* Boydell Press, Woodbridge.

Ordnance Survey 1966, *Britain in the Dark Ages*.

Ordnance Survey 1973, *Britain before the Norman Conquest*.

Ordnance Survey 1978, *Monastic Britain* third edition.

I. Ousby 1990, *The Englishman's England: taste, travel and the rise of tourism* Cambridge University Press.

C. Owen 1984, *The Leicestershire and South Derbyshire Coalfield 1200–1900* Moorland Ashbourne for Leicestershire Museums.

F.M. Page 1934, *The Estates of Crowland Abbey: A Study in Manorial Organisation* Cambridge University Press.

D. Parry 1984, *The Rule of Saint Benedict* Darton, Longman and Todd, London.

D. Parsons (ed.) 1975, *Tenth-Century Studies: Essays in Commemoration of the Millenium of the Council of Winchester and 'Regularis Concordia'* Phillimore, London and Chichester.

D. Parsons 1977, 'Brixworth and its monastery church' in Dornier (ed.), pp. 173–90.

D. Parsons (ed.) 1990, *Stone: Quarrying and Building in England AD 43–1525* Phillimore, Chichester.

H.E.J. Le Patourel and B.K. Roberts 1978, 'The significance of moated sites' in F.A. Aberg (ed.) *Medieval Moated Sites* Council for British Archaeology, Research Report 17, pp. 36–45.

S.M. Pearce 1978, *The Kingdom of Dumnonia: studies in history and tradition in South Western Britain AD 350–1150* Lodenek Press, Padstow.

S.M. Pearce (ed.) 1982, *The Early Church in Western Britain and Ireland* British Archaeological Reports, British Series 102, Oxford.

C. Peers 1967, *Rievaulx Abbey* English Heritage, London.

R.A. Pelham n.d., *Fulling Mills: a Study of the Application of Water Power to the Woollen Industry* SPAB.

K.J. Penn 1980, *Historic Towns in Dorset* Dorset Archaeological Committee, Dorchester.

C. Platt 1969, *The Monastic Grange in Medieval England: A Reassessment* Macmillan, London.

C. Platt 1978, *Medieval England: a social history and archaeology from the Conquest to 1600 AD* Routledge and Kegan Paul,

London.

C. Platt 1984, *The Abbeys and Priories of Medieval England* Secker and Warburg, London.

M.W. Ponsford 1975, *Excavations at Greyfriars Bristol* Bristol Museum and Art Gallery.

R. Poulton 1988, *Archaeological Investigations on the site of Chertsey Abbey* Research Volume of the Surrey Archaeological Society 11, Guildford.

S. Raban 1977, *The Estates of Thorney and Crowland: A study in medieval monastic land tenure* Occasional Paper 7, Department of Land Economy, University of Cambridge.

O. Rackham 1980, *Ancient Woodland: its history, vegetation and uses in England* Edward Arnold, London.

C.A. Ralegh Radford 1962, 'The Celtic monastery in Britain' *Archaeologia Cambrensis* 111, pp. 1–24.

C.A. Ralegh Radford 1967, 'The Early Church in Strathclyde and Galloway' *Medieval Archaeology* Vol. 11, pp. 105–26.

C.A. Ralegh Radford 1981, 'Glastonbury Abbey before 1184: Interim Report on the Excavations, 1908–64' in *Medieval Art and Architecture at Wells and Glastonbury* British Archaeological Association, pp. 110–34.

J.A. Raftis 1957, *The Estates of Ramsey Abbey: A study in Economic Growth and Organisation* Pontifical Institute of Medieval Studies, Studies and Texts 3, Toronto.

P. Rahtz 1976, 'The building plan of the Anglo-Saxon monastery of Whitby Abbey' in Wilson (ed.), pp. 459–62.

P. Rahtz 1979, *The Saxon and Medieval Palaces at Cheddar* British Archaeological Reports, British Series 65, Oxford.

P. Rahtz 1991, 'Pagan and Christian by the Severn Sea' in Abrams and Carley (eds), pp. 3–37.

P. Rahtz 1993, *English Heritage Book of Glastonbury* Batsford, London.

P. Rahtz and S. Hirst 1974, *Beckery Chapel Glastonbury 1967–8* Glastonbury Antiquarian Society, Glastonbury.

A. Raistrick 1977, *Lead Mining in the Yorkshire Dales* Dalesman, North Yorkshire.

N. Ramsay and M. Sparks 1988, *The Image of Saint Dunstan* The Dunstan Millenium Committee, Canterbury.

J. Rhodes 1989, 'Lanthony Priory' *Glevensis* 23, pp. 16–30.

J.D. Richards 1991, *English Heritage Book of Viking Age England* Batsford, London.

S.E. Rigold 1977, 'Litus Romanum – the Shore forts as mission stations' in D.E. Johnston (ed.) *The Saxon Shore*

Council for British Archaeology, Research Report 18, pp. 70–5.

B.K. Roberts 1987, *The Making of the English Village* Longman, Harlow.

D.M. Robinson 1980, *The Geography of Augustinian Settlement* British Archaeological Reports, British Series 80.

D.M. Robinson 1990, *Tintern Abbey* Cadw: Welsh Historic Monuments, Cardiff.

W. Rodwell 1981, *The Archaeology of the English Church: The study of historic churches and churchyards* Batsford, London.

W. Rodwell 1982, 'From Mausoleum to Minster: The Early Development of Wells Cathedral' in Pearce (ed.) 1982.

W. Rollinson 1967, *A History of Man in the Lake District* Dent, London.

Royal Commission on the Ancient and Historical Monuments of Scotland (RCAHMS) *Argyll: An Inventory of the Monuments* Vol. 3 Mull, Tiree, Coll and North Argyll, 1980; Vol. 4 Iona, 1982; Vol. 5 Islay, Jura, Colonsay and Oronsay, 1984.

Royal Commission on Ancient and Historical Monuments in Wales and Monmouthshire *Anglesey* 1937.

Royal Commission on Ancient and Historical Monuments in Wales and Monmouthshire (RCAHMW) *Caernarvonshire* Vol. 2 Central, 1960; Vol. 3 West, 1964.

Royal Commission on Ancient and Historical Monuments in Wales *Glamorgan Volume 1 Part 3 The Early Christian Period* 1976.

Royal Commission on Ancient and Historical Monuments in Wales *Glamorgan Volume III: Medieval Secular Monuments Part II. Non-Defensive* 1982.

J. Ryan 1931, *Irish Monasticism Origins and Early Development* Longmans, London.

L.F. Salzman 1952, *Building in England down to 1540: a documentary history* Clarendon Press, Oxford.

P.H. Sawyer 1968, *Anglo-Saxon Charters: An Annotated List and Bibliography* Royal Historical Society, London.

P.H. Sawyer 1978, *From Roman Britain to Norman England* Methuen, London.

J. Schofield and T. Dyson 1980, *Archaeology of the City of London* City of London Archaeological Trust, Museum of London, London.

E. Searle 1974, *Lordship and Community: Battle Abbey and its Banlieu 1066–1538* Pontifical Institute of Medieval Studies, Studies and Texts 26, Toronto.

A. Selkirk 1968, 'South Witham' *Current Archaeology* 9, July, pp. 232–7.

J.R. Senior 1989, 'The selection of dimensional and ornamental stone types used in some Northern monasteries – the exploitation and distribution of a natural resource' in Gilchrist and Mytum (eds), pp. 223–50.

J.A. Sheppard 1958, *The Draining of the Hull Valley* East Yorkshire Local History Society.

W.J. Sheils (ed.) 1985, *Monks Hermits and the Ascetic Tradition* Ecclesiastical History Society Vol. 22 Studies in Church History, Blackwell, Oxford.

R. Shoesmith and R.K. Morriss 1989, *George Hotel, Winchcombe – an Interim Report* City of Hereford Archaeology Committee.

P. Sims-Williams 1990, *Religion and Literature in Western England 600–800* Cambridge University Press.

R.A.L. Smith 1943, *Canterbury Cathedral Priory: A Study in Monastic Administration* Cambridge University Press.

J.M. Snelling 1971, *St Benet's Abbey* Norfolk Norwich.

R.W. Southern 1970, *Western Society and the Church in the Middle Ages* Pelican History of the Church Vol. 2, Penguin.

P. Stafford 1985, *The East Midlands in the Early Middle Ages* Leicester University Press.

J.M. Steane 1974, *The Northamptonshire Landscape* Hodder and Stoughton, London.

J.M. Steane 1984, *The Archaeology of Medieval England and Wales* Croom Helm, London.

F.M. Stenton 1943, *Anglo-Saxon England* Clarendon Press, Oxford, and later editions.

J. Stephen 1922, *Buckfast Abbey: A History* Buckfast Abbey, and later editions.

D.S. Sutherland and D. Parsons 1984, 'The Petrological Contribution to the Survey of All Saints church, Brixworth, Northamptonshire: an Interim Account' *Journal of the British Archaeological Association* Vol. 137, pp. 45–64.

C. Taylor 1970, *Dorset* Hodder and Stoughton, London.

C. Taylor 1983, *Village and Farmstead: A History of Rural Settlement in England* George Philip, London.

C. Taylor 1989, 'Somersham Palace, Cambridgeshire: A Medieval Landscape for Pleasure?' in M. Bowden, D. Mackay and P. Topping (eds) *From Caithness to Cornwall: some aspects of British Field Archaeology – Papers presented to Norman V. Quinnell* British Archaeological Reports, British Series 209, pp. 211–24.

C. Taylor, P. Everson and R. Wilson-North 1990, 'Bodiam Castle, Sussex' *Medieval Archaeology* 34, pp. 155–7.

H.M. and J. Taylor 1965, *Anglo-Saxon Architecture* Vols 1 and 2 Cambridge University Press.

C. Thomas 1967, 'An Early Christian Cemetery and Chapel on Ardwall Isle, Kirkudbright' *Medieval Archaeology* Vol. 11, pp. 127–88.

C. Thomas 1971, *Britain and Ireland in early Christian times AD 400–800* Thames and Hudson, London.

C. Thomas 1971a, *The Early Christian Archaeology of North Britain* University of Glasgow, Oxford University Press, London.

C. Thomas 1981, *Christianity in Roman Britain to AD 500* Batsford, London.

C. Thomas 1985, *Exploration of a Drowned Landscape: Archaeology and History of the Isles of Scilly* Batsford, London.

C. Thomas 1988, 'Tintagel Castle' *Antiquity* Vol. 62 No. 236 September, pp. 421–34.

C. Thomas 1993, *English Heritage Book of Tintagel*, Batsford, London.

E.M. Thompson 1895, *A History of The Somerset Carthusians* John Hodges, London.

E.M. Thompson 1930, *The Carthusian Order In England* London.

M.W. Thompson 1986, 'Associated monasteries and castles in the Middle Ages: a tentative list' *Archaeological Journal* 143, pp. 305–21.

R. Thompson 1987, *William of Malmesbury* The Boydell Press, Woodbridge.

K. Tiller 1992, *English Local History: An Introduction* Alan Sutton, Stroud.

D. Tomlinson 1991, 'Flixborough: A Middle Saxon Settlement on Humberside' *Rescue News* 54, pp. 6–7.

H. Torp 1957, 'Some aspects of Early Coptic Monastic Architecture' *Byzantion* Vols 25–7, 1955–7, pp. 513–38 Brussels.

W. Urry 1967, *Canterbury under the Angevin Kings* University of London, The Athlone Press.

B. Waites 1961, 'The Monastic Settlement of North-East Yorkshire' *Yorkshire Archaeological Journal* Vol. 40, part 159, pp. 478–95.

B. Waites 1962, 'The Monastic Grange as a factor in the settlement of North-East Yorkshire' *Yorkshire Archaeological Journal* Vol. 40, part 160, pp. 627–56.

B. Waites 1967, *Moorland and Vale-Land Farming in North-East Yorkshire: the Monastic contribution in the thirteenth and fourteenth centuries* University of York, Borthwick Institute of Historical Research, Borthwick Papers 32.

C.C. Walters 1974, *Monastic Archaeology in Egypt* Aris and Philips, Warminster.

B. Watterson 1988, *Coptic Egypt*

Scottish Academic Press, Edinburgh.
J. Weatherhill 1954, 'Rievaulx Abbey: the stone used in its building with notes on the means of transport and a new study of the diversion of the River Rye in the twelfth century' *Yorkshire Archaeological Journal* Vol. 38, pp. 333–54.
K. Wessel 1965, *Coptic Art* Thames and Hudson, London.
H.G. Evelyn White (edited by Walter Hauser) 1932 and 1933, *The Monasteries of The Wadi 'N Natrun* Part 2 The History of the Monasteries of Nitria and Scetis and Part 3 The Architecture and Archaeology, Metropolitan Museum of Art, Egyptian Expedition, New York.
M. Wildgoose 1991, 'The Drystone Walls of Roystone Grange' *Archaeological Journal* 148, pp. 205–40.
D.H. Williams 1965, 'The Cistercians in Wales: Some Aspects of their Economy' *Archaeologia Cambrensis* Vol. 114, pp. 2–47.
D.H. Williams 1984, *The Welsh Cistercians* Vols 1 and 2, Caldey Island, Tenby.
D.H. Williams 1990, *Atlas of Cistercian Lands in Wales* University of Wales Press, Cardiff.
E.H.D. Williams, J. and J. Penoyre and B.H.C. Hale 1987, 'The George Inn, Norton St Philip, Somerset' *Archaeological Journal* 144, pp. 317–27.
M. Williams 1970, *The Draining of the Somerset Levels* Cambridge University Press.
D.M. Wilson (ed.) 1976, *The Archaeology of Anglo-Saxon England* Cambridge University Press.
D.R. Wilson 1991, 'Old gardens from the air' in Brown (ed.), pp. 20–35.
D. Winkless 1990, *Hailes Abbey Gloucestershire: The Story of a Medieval Abbey* The Spredden Press, Stocksfield, Northumberland.
P.J. Wise (ed.) 1985, *Hulton Abbey: A Century of Excavations* Staffordshire Archaeological Studies 2, City Museum and Art Gallery, Stoke on Trent.
S. Wood 1955, *English Monasteries and their patrons in the thirteenth century* Oxford University Press.
H. Woods 1987, 'Excavations at Wenlock Priory 1981–6' *Journal of the British Archaeological Association* Vol. 140, pp. 36–75.
G.W. O. Woodward 1972, *The Dissolution of the Monasteries* Pitkin Pictorials, London.
S. Wrathmell 1984, *Kirkstall Abbey – The Guest House – A Guide to the Medieval Buildings* West Yorkshire Archaeology Service, Wakefield.
B. Yorke (ed.) 1988, *Bishop Aethelwold: his career and influence* Boydell and Brewer, Woodbridge.
J. Youings 1967, 'The Church' in J. Thirsk (ed.) *The Agrarian History of England and Wales* Vol. 4 1500–1640, Cambridge University Press, pp. 306–95.
J. Youings 1971, *The Dissolution of the Monasteries* Allen and Unwin, London.
G. Zarnecki 1972, *The Monastic Achievement* Thames and Hudson, London.

Index

(Sites and information in the captions are indexed as if part of the text.)

Gall, St 54–5
gardens 19, 27, 38, 42–3, 50, 51, 54, 68,
 70, 89, 90, 92, 94, 101, 107, 108, 110,
 144–5, 149, 150, 152
Garendon Abbey 76, 115, 117, 131, 146
Garway 32
gatehouse 90, 92, 94, 97, 98, 99, 101,
 102, 104, 107, 108, 110, 115, 136
Gaul 25, 26, 50
Gerald of Wales 30, 119, 120
Gifford, William 68
Gilbert of Sempringham 83
Gilbertines 83–4, 107, 115, 116–17, 120,
 125, 127
Gildas 33
Glasscock, Robin 126
Glastonbury Abbey 26, 38, 48, 50, 51,
 54, 56–8, 61–3, 112–13, 117, 122–3,
 127, 129, 130, 134, 138, 147, 150, 156
Gloucester 41, 49, 57, 61, 85, 106–7,
 110, 113, 147, 148
Godley 49
Godney 48
Goswick family 144
Gough, J.W. 132
Govan 28
Gozbert 54
granary 89, 97
Grande Chartreuse, La 69–70
Grandmont 72
Grandmontines 72–3, 101–3
granges 22, 71, 78, 90, 97, 106, 108,
 111, 112–17, 119–22, 125–8, 138–40,
 146, 149–50
Great Coxwell 111–12
Great Easton 119
Great Malvern Priory 147
Greece 25
Green Ore 132
Greenhow 132
Gregory the Great 39, 40, 46
Grey Friars 85, 108–10
Griff Grange 115, 120
Grosmont Priory 72
guest-house 25, 34, 50, 54, 70, 89, 90,
 92, 97, 98, 101, 136
Guigues, Prior 70
Guisborough Priory 82, 116, 126, 127,
 131
Guthlac, St 48–9, 122
Guthrum 53
Gwent 30–1, 74
Gwynedd 34

Hackness Dale 127
Hadcock, R. Neville 15
Hadrian 48
Hailes Abbey 13, 76, 145–6, 148
Haito 54
Halesowen Abbey 14, 102, 151–2
Hampton 129
Hanbury 41
Handale 126
Harding, Stephen 72
Harold, King 64
Hartlake Rhyne 123

Hartland 83
Hartlepool 39, 44–5, 134
Hatherop 71
Haverholme 83
Hawkshead 126
Hawling 128
Hazelbury 130
Healaugh 75
Heane 46
Heathcote Grange 115
Heighway, Carolyn 61
Helens, St 34
Hemel Hempstead 154
Hempholme 125
Henry I 76, 83, 94
Henry II 19, 70, 71, 76
Henry III 76
Henry V 141–2
Henry VI 102
Henry VII 141
Henry VIII 12, 13, 143
Hereford 46, 48, 85
hermitages 25–30, 32–4, 38, 39, 40, 49,
 51, 75, 83
hermits 24–5, 28, 48–50, 51, 68–9, 72,
 75, 82, 87, 92, 140, 141, 154
Hertford 48
Hertfordshire 49, 119
Hexham 39, 41, 42
'high farming' 117–18
Highbridge 123
Hilda, St 39
Hill, David 15
Hill, Peter 27
Hinton Charterhouse 71, 101, 132, 136,
 145
Historic Scotland 13, 155
Hoddon 28
Hodnant 33
Holbeck 80–1
Holderness 122
Holloway 115
Hollytreeholme 125
Holmcultram 76
Holy Island 30, 36–8
Holy Sepulchre, canons of 83
holy wells 30, 35
Holywell Hall 115
Honoratus, St 25
Hood 78
Horncastle 47
Horne 141
Horner family 147
Horton 57, 60, 63
Hoskins, William 16, 129, 131
hospitals 25, 82, 92, 110, 145
Hugh of Avalon 71
Hugh of Grenoble 69
Hull 72, 123–5, 134
Hulne Priory 87, 110
Hulton Abbey 77, 100, 157
Huntingdon 82
Hurst 78
Hwicce 46, 48
Hywel Dda 28

Illauntannig 28
Illtud 32
industry 45, 50, 54, 70, 89, 98, 108,
 129–32, 139
infirmary 90, 92, 97
Inquisitions of the Ninth 127
investment 16, 17, 20, 64, 117, 129,
 139–40
Iona 28, 35, 36–7, 40
Ireland 15, 25, 26, 27, 28, 35, 46, 84
iron 89, 126, 131–2, 138, 139
islands 25, 26, 27, 28, 30, 32–4, 37–9,
 48–9, 51, 53, 122
Italy 25, 26, 68, 70, 85, 87, 141, 154
Ives, St 134

Jarrow 39, 42–3, 45, 50, 51, 61
Jerusalem 82
Jervaulx Abbey 78, 115, 128, 144
Jesuit Order 152, 155
John, King 76, 150
John Gualbert of Florence, St 68–9
Jura 28

Keevil, Graham 59
Kekmarsh 125
Kent 39–40, 64, 117, 122, 130
Keverne, St 34
Kew, St 34
Keyngham 125
Keynsham Abbey 82
Kidland 126
Kidwelly 66
kilns 22, 108
Kingarth 28
Kings Lynn 85, 87–8
Kingsbridge 134
Kingswood Abbey 78
Kintyre 28
Kinwarton 112
Kirby Misperton 125
Kirkby Malzeard 132
Kirkham Priory 76, 82, 104, 127
Kirkheaton 120
Kirkstall Abbey 74, 75, 77, 96, 98, 120,
 129
Kirkstead Abbey 75, 98, 99
kitchens 20, 50, 92, 108
Knights Hospitaller 81–2, 108
Knights Templar 81–2, 108, 129, 134
Knowles, David 15, 61, 63, 65, 67, 154
Kyneburgha, St 41
Kyneswitha 41

Lacock Abbey 145
landscape archaeology 16, 98, 115
Langewydd 77
Langstrath 132
Lanthony Priory 106–7
Lastingham 38
latrines 20, 61, 90, 92, 97, 98, 101, 102
Launceston 34
Lawson Park 126
lay brothers 20, 68–72, 74–5, 78, 84,
 115, 118, 119, 122, 141
lead 22, 89, 132, 138
Leasowes 152